THE MAGNETIC
MUSIC MINISTRY

EFFECTIVE CHURCH SERIES

BILL OWENS

Edited by HERB MILLER

THE MAGNETIC MUSIC MINISTRY

Ten Productive Goals

ABINGDON PRESS
Nashville

THE MAGNETIC MUSIC MINISTRY

Library of Congress Cataloging-in-Publication Data

Owens, Bill, 1950–
    The magnetic music ministry/Bill Owens: edited by Herb Miller.
        p.   cm.—(Effective church series)
    Includes bibliographical references.
    ISBN 0-687-00731-3 (alk. paper)
    1. Church music—Instruction and study.   2. Choirs (Music)
3. Church musicians.   I. Miller, Herb.   II. Title.   III. Series.
MT88.095   1996
264'.2—dc20
                                                        95-38534
                                                        CIP
                                                        MN

96 97 98 99 00 01 02 03 04 05 — 10 9 8 7 6 5 4 3 2 1

MANUFACTURED IN THE UNITED STATES OF AMERICA

CONTENTS

FOREWORD

Music, in addition to consuming 40 percent of the worship time, sets the tone for the rest of the service. When people say that they like the worship music, they are saying, "Music creates and re-creates in me a state of mind, being, and experience not otherwise possible."

The big problem: Church leaders often have difficulty obtaining the insights necessary to design a worship music program that meets the spiritual needs of all age ranges. Often, leaders unknowingly amputate their church's future by wall-to-wall reruns of effective church music from the 1950s. Young adults will not put up with what they define as poor music, in order to hear good preaching. If forced to choose between good music and good preaching, they will pick a church with music that spiritually re-creates them but has less effective preaching.

Owens addresses this complex situation with theological integrity and music methods that hold the old and the new in creative tension. He knows that what is familiar to people with pre–1946 birthdates can seem deadeningly dull to the new generation of worshipers. Yet he also knows that *too much of the new* can become distractingly destructive to pre–1946 birthdate worshipers. He knows how to bring the old and new together in a way that honors tradition without being buried by it. He also understands how music fits into the congregation's ministry of spiritual nurture for members, numerical membership growth, and active involvement of new attenders.

In a popular cartoon, a quartet of swamp animals burst forth in song. One of them asked the leader how he thought they sounded. The leader, Pogo, wisely and diplomatically observed, "Well, er y'know—it ain't so much how good it sounds—it's how good it feels on the way out."*

Some things must do more than *feel effective;* they must actually *be effective.* Owens's practical suggestions can help church music to be both.

*Early 1990, *Chicago Tribune,* "Pogo" comic strip.

Herb Miller
Lubbock, Texas

ACKNOWLEDGMENTS

To Pam, my incredible wife, for your love, devotion, and constant strength.

To Michael and Kevin, you are God's special blessing to me.

To my parents, Doc and Tommye Owens, for your unconditional love, for my education, and for introducing me to God.

To my sister, Lauren Newman, and nephew, Alex Newman, for always keeping joy in my life.

To my in-laws, Bert and Virginia Grimes, for loving me like a son.

To the staffs and members of Middletown Christian Church, Louisville, Kentucky; Beargrass Christian Church, Louisville, Kentucky; First Christian Church, Danville, Kentucky; and to all of my colleagues in the Christian Church (Disciples of Christ) for giving me the privilege of learning and working with dedicated Christians and for affirming my ministry.

To Donald Henrickson, Bruce Hoagland, Richard Hensel, and many other music professors at Eastern Kentucky University for developing my essential skills.

To Kay Roebuck, for your friendship and for opening so many doors for me in the recording industry.

To Percy Metcalf, for being a faithful brother in Christ, for helping me to break down cultural barriers, and for your inspirational singing.

ACKNOWLEDGMENTS

To Herb Miller, Margo Woodworth, and my other friends at the National Evangelistic Association and to Fred Craddock, Kennon Callahan, George Barna, Lyle Schaller, George Hunter, Carl George, Tony Campolo, Robert Bast, Roy Oswald, and John Guest for your "cutting edge" information and influence.

To Dave Aspy and Patti Killion for advice and encouragement that made this book possible.

To God the creator, to Jesus Christ my savior, and to the Holy Spirit for providing the source of all my strength and motives and for giving me the joy of abundant life!

I

WITNESS THE ROLE

A recently hired choir director was about to begin his first worship service. After the Sunday morning anthem rehearsal, one of the longtime choir members approached him. He expected her to offer words of welcome and encouragement.

"Someone is in my seat!" she said with great authority.

His expectations shattered, he quickly reviewed his training and realized that he had not been taught how to respond to such a situation. "So this is why they call the music department the war department," he thought. "Should I put this woman in her place? She could be an officer of the board or the wife of an important person. I could lose my job over something as ridiculous as someone sitting in her seat. I could make the other person move and still lose my job for the same reasons."

His idealistic first Sunday morning experience quickly became a realistic education about human behavior. His first thought was to say, "Madam, I'm sure there are no reserved seats in heaven, so don't expect one here!" Wisely, he mustered up the insight to respond, "I don't know what the policy has been in the past, but I'm sure you will be an effective singer no matter where you sit. The person in your usual seat will feel privileged because you have made him or her feel accepted and important by giving up your regular seat." The woman left for the choir loft with a smile on her face, and the choir director sighed with great relief. He had weathered his first storm in the music ministry.

Accept Truths About Ministry

One of the world's greatest truths: Regardless of how much education we receive or how positive an attitude we project, situations will always arise that surprise us and make us feel unprepared. We leave our institutions of higher learning with hopes and dreams of making a difference and earning a living. We later realize that neither God nor people measure our success or effectiveness by how much we know or earn, but by what and how we share.

Reality leads us to another truth about ministry: Churches and their programs must always be open to change in order to meet the needs of those they serve. The difficulty lies in effecting necessary change in a nonthreatening manner. Many of us are like the woman who was reluctant to give up her usual seat. Familiarity produces comfort. Change often means we must give up something. Yet each of us has a different comfort zone. Meeting the needs of a few forces others to conform or go elsewhere. Providing something for everyone promotes variety, interest, and acceptance.

Finally, persons gravitate to churches that relate to their life experiences. Today's church visitors (especially baby boomers) form quick opinions and make many decisions based on perception. Quality worship music is not only paramount to them but frequently serves as the reason for their return. Churches that offer the visitor's favorite music styles in quality presentations magnetically attract them by accepting their music.

Characteristics of Magnetic Music Programs

More than ever before, the music ministry is a changing, vital part of the total ministry of the church. In order to understand what this ministry has to share, we must first identify its importance within the mission of the church. In most growing churches, effective music ministries have five essential characteristics or goals.

1. Enhance Worship. The principal role of the music ministry is to enhance the corporate worship experience and thereby move persons into a closer relationship with God. In vocal music this occurs when effective Christian texts are delivered through motivating musical interpretations. The most effective instrumental music causes us to reflect upon our relationship with God through familiar or unfamiliar melodies.

In order to witness the gospel through music, successful music ministers choose music and texts that motivate people into life-changing Christian experiences. Too often, leaders select music based on personal preferences rather than how the music affects others. Churches that allow this to happen usually present only one style of music and meet the needs of only a few.

One of the most difficult tasks a choir director or soloist faces is to offer music that both challenges and motivates, while offering a quality presentation. When we begin to learn a song or anthem, it becomes ours. When we share it with the choir or our family, it becomes theirs. When we offer it in the church, it belongs to the corporate body of the congregation. An effective musical offering is selected and presented on the basis of how it will call the congregation to a greater witness and relationship to God—as well as on the ability of the musical group or individual to present the music.

In many churches, choirs and soloists force their voices to fit the music rather than fit the music to their voices. This is especially true when music ministries become focused in-

13

ward—trying to meet the needs of the music leaders—rather than outward. For example, some choir directors only use soloists from within the choir and force their soloists to sing music that is beyond their present ability. Some also choose not to sing a selection if no one is able to sing it. This option is a good compromise if the choir is only presenting anthems. But in musical dramas, oratorios, or masses, each selection is critical to the story. To leave a portion out would be like leaving part of a wall unpainted. An occasional outside soloist or ensemble can be motivating and educational. Most churches do not hesitate to utilize a guest speaker. Using a guest soloist or musical group is no different.

Choir directors should develop and encourage soloists from within the choir. However, because music is also dominant in the entertainment industry, congregations often inaccurately perceive some soloists as egotists. This danger is always present, regardless of the commitment of the soloist and the sincerity of the presentation. It is extremely difficult for talented persons to appear humble.

Effective presentations are based on both reasonable musical ability and motivating theology in order to move people into a closer relationship with God. When soloists, ensembles, or choirs attempt music beyond their present ability or give poor presentations, the congregation is placed in "forced worship." Instead of focusing upon the message and musical interpretation, the listener focuses upon the "not too soon arrival" of the end of the song or anthem. Poorly presented music is ineffective and counterproductive. Musical excellence becomes an offering to God. Poor presentations become a barrier.

In the book *The Frog in the Kettle*, George Barna says:

> Local churches must take a hard look at their performance and dedicate themselves to excellence in all they do. In today's marketplace, people are critical and unforgiving. They have high expectations, and they give an organization only one chance to impress. In this type of environment, a church

would be better off doing a few things with excellence than many things merely adequately.[1]

Successful music ministries offer praise not pain. They focus upon "presenting" rather than performing. Christian music is an offering of one's spiritual gift, not an opportunity to showcase talent. Soloists, ensembles, and choirs are first and foremost accountable to God, then the congregation, and finally to themselves. Church music programs grow by sharing strengths and accepting limitations; not by limiting their strengths through forced presentations.

Effective worship music that provides reasonable opportunities for spiritual and musical growth is multidimensional in style, complexity, tempo, and dynamics. It is even more effective when it is thematic with sermons, scriptures, and prayers. According to Kennon Callahan in *Twelve Keys to an Effective Church*, "music is 40 percent of the worship service." He states:

> Music is extraordinarily important in the course of the worship service, and a solid music program is vital to achieve corporate, dynamic worship. A strong music program generally has three ingredients: planning and spontaneity, balance and variety, and quality and depth.[2]

2. Witness and Develop. A second role of the music ministry is to witness the theology of the church while developing musical excellence. Many choir leaders and soloists are first attracted to a song or anthem because of how it feels, or how impressive the arrangement is, rather than what message it delivers. This observation does not imply that energetic or complex vocal music is ineffective. Melody, harmony, and arrangements are meant to support, interpret, and enhance what the text is saying.

The church music department communicates God's love through the context of the church's worship and mission.

Growing churches send a well-defined message of "who we are" and "what God has called us to be." Writing a mission statement clarifies this message.

A mission statement defines the purpose of the church. One church developed the following mission statement.

"The purpose of this church shall be as revealed in the New Testament, to win people to faith in Jesus Christ and commit them actively to the church, to help them grow in the grace and the knowledge of Christ, that increasingly they may know and do his will, and to work for the unity of all Christians and with them engage in the common task of building the Kingdom of God."

Once the mission statement is defined, departments, committees, and staff can write corresponding goals and objectives that support the mission statement. Church members are effectively assimilated into the life of the church when they feel a sense of purpose, direction, and value.

Develop at least a five-year strategic plan that shows the present operating status of the church and what the church hopes to accomplish at the end of five years. Include information such as:

- Mission Statement
- Values
- Vision
- Who We Serve
- Long-range Goals
- Assumptions
- Strengths
- Weaknesses
- Challenges
- Opportunities
- Critical Issues
- Strategies
- Future View

The apostle Paul said, "Therefore, my beloved, be steadfast, immovable, always excelling in the work of the Lord, because you know that in the Lord your labor is not in vain" (1 Cor. 15:58). If our goal is to excel in the work of the Lord, then our music in witness and worship will honor God through superior presentations.

In one southern church, an older choir member was having difficulty adapting from a small choir ministry into a program with numerous choirs and many new faces. The previous choir director served part-time, and the new music minister was a skilled, full-time, motivated person. The choir member accused the music minister of turning the music program into a music conservatory. His complaint (on the surface) was about the music program. In reality, the underlying issue was about his difficulty accepting change.

The objective of the church is to develop many conservatories. Christ challenged us to teach others as he taught us. "Go therefore and make disciples of all nations, baptizing them in the name of the Father and of the Son and of the Holy Spirit, and teaching them to obey everything that I have commanded you. And remember, I am with you always, to the end of the age" (Matt. 28:19-20). The effective and faithful church is a conservatory of evangelism, worship, prayer, pastoral care, outreach, music, and preaching, to name a few.

Prior to the 1970s, it was not uncommon for children in elementary grades to receive music instruction at least twice a week or more. In many school districts today, music classes have become merely once a week or biweekly sing-a-long experiences. Some music teachers travel to several schools, and children who cannot afford private lessons have limited musical education. This crisis is due to the enormous financial cutbacks in the arts. In metropolitan areas, many large churches are filling the void in the school music programs. They offer lessons in hand chimes, handbells, Orff rhythm instruments, and music theory—along with vocal and instrumental choirs. Children's ministries such as Kids Club and LOGOS also include theme meals, Bible study, and gym time, which are scheduled around choir rehearsals. This total menu approach creates the most effective programming for balancing theology with musical development.

3. Offer Spiritual Growth and Community. Another goal of the music ministry is to offer spiritual growth, fellowship, and a sense of community. The visible choir is a good indicator of church life. Growing choirs reflect commitment, enthusiasm, and the sense of feeling needed. They provide opportunities for service, small group assimilation, and spiritual experiences. Even in small churches, no other program crosses generational lines and is as accepting as the choir. In many churches, the choir is the only group where singles of all ages feel accepted, needed, and comfortable. It also serves as the entry point toward their active participation.[3]

The most fortunate churches develop youth choirs that offer teenagers self-esteem, acceptance, a sense of contribution, and worship experience. Without a youth choir, teenagers often feel like visitors or part of the decor. The choir gives them visibility and provides a strong nuclear group in which to build a growing youth ministry.

Though the anthem conveys the spiritual message of the text, it also provides the needed emotional expression of faith that is sometimes suppressed in a worship service that has less music. This element actually relates more to the introvert versus extrovert spiritual experience. The introvert often feels God's presence through a reverent *a cappella* anthem; whereas the extrovert is more likely to experience the glory of God through an upbeat powerful anthem accompanied by an instrumental ensemble. This is not to infer that all introverts and extroverts experience God in these ways, but each of us draws our energy and expresses our faith differently. The most effective formula to meet the needs of many is to offer a multidimensional music ministry.

4. Reach. The fourth essential role of the music ministry is to effectively reach the churched and unchurched. Like a magnet that draws metal objects, an effective music ministry is one of the main entry points for new church members.

In the foundational stages of music ministry development, the music minister/choir director must serve many roles, for example, principal evangelist, teacher, conductor, coordinator. But once established, a productive music ministry can literally recruit, nurture, and motivate itself.

Talented persons who present excellence as an offering to God are "magnet people." They tend to draw others of similar quality, regardless of the program or area of ministry they represent. The college blue-chip basketball recruit will go to a school where there are other outstanding players because he or she wants to be on a winning team. Quality music programs are like colleges that traditionally produce winning programs in all areas of athletics or academics. They consistently draw the most talented people. This principle is especially true in growing music ministries.

To build a reputation that a church is good at everything is difficult. When a church focuses on a few programs or ministries, develops them, and shares them with the community, they become tremendous "bragging opportunities" for evangelism.

The most effective evangelism is by word of mouth. Someone new to the community often asks, "Where is First Church?" or "What do you know about First Church?" Imagine their thoughts if the response is, "Oh, that's the church with the great music program." Building a tradition of excellence will plant many positive seeds that germinate into new members.

Expressive music—music that touches the heart—is the number one most effective tool to attract baby boomers, according to the 1994 findings of the Louisville Institute Conference on "baby boomers and the Changing Shape of American Religion." Number two was preaching and "What kind of role model is the pastor?" Number three was the "experiential dimension." Boomers want the church to touch on life as they know it. This is even more important than belief or denominational heritage.

In *The Contagious Congregation*, George Hunter suggests that we must use "indigenous methods for receptive people."[4] He refers to this illustration from *Ten Steps for Church Growth* by Donald McGavran and Winfield Arn. "The good fisherman continues to seek responsiveness until he discovers the right bait for a particular fish during a particular season. He knows when he has the right bait—he's catching fish. As fish respond to one approach and not to another, so do people."[5] The music ministry has become one of the successful "baits" for evangelism. "And Jesus said to them, 'Follow me and I will make you fish for people'" (Mark 1:17).

Offering music that represents the local community musical diet is smart fishing. Sometimes, however, fish swim against the current and a different bait of music every now and then will land the unexpected. For example, .when new families move into a community, their musical taste may be different from that of their neighbors.

Many of the megachurches with several thousand members have successfully developed a definitive context by confining their music, preaching, outreach, and other ministries to contemporary styles. Most of these churches have architecture and landscaping similar to contemporary homes. Since almost 75 percent of the United States population was born after 1945, this strategy will continue to be effective. However, churches offering both contemporary and traditional music will reach an additional group that carries a high percentage of established church attenders. Many of these people are highly educated and become dependable church leaders and contributors.

5. Effect Positive Social Change. The fifth important role of the music ministry is to effect positive social change among all cultures in order that we may truly be one in Christ. "There is no longer Jew or Greek, there is no longer slave or free, there is no longer male and female; for all of you are one in Christ Jesus" (Gal. 3:28).

The two most significant influences that have transcended or broken down cultural barriers throughout the world are sports and music. Each has had both positive and negative results. On the positive side, nothing else has come close to these two bonding experiences. Success in most sports and music requires each participant to share and to depend on one another. Both also have common goals with recognition for success and a cohesion that provides a sense of family and importance.[6]

Christian music, however, goes further by providing an opportunity to express our innermost feelings and our spirituality through the love of God and one another. A magnetic music ministry is a powerful influence for developing a harmonious multicultural society. In order to effect positive social changes for the future in a secular world, we must model Christian behavior today not only to our children and youth but also to adults.

One of the great challenges of the church today is to develop inclusive language without destroying our heritage of great hymns. We should acknowledge the dominance of masculine lyrics in many traditional hymns. Theologians are continually struggling with these questions, such as what lyrics can be altered, how they are to be altered, and what lyrics should be left intact.

Composers, their families, and their publishing companies are making many of those decisions. In most instances, contemporary composers prefer not to have their lyrics changed and they will bring suit against anyone who does. A famous example of unauthorized lyric altering and illegal photocopying is the song "Edelweiss" by Rogers and Hammerstein II from *The Sound of Music*. Some churches used and circulated a completely changed version of the lyrics with the original tune. This "new" song with Christian lyrics was sung frequently as a benediction. The families of the composers emphatically did not want such a change.

If permission is granted, nothing is wrong with setting a hymn tune to a new set of lyrics. This is common practice. Jane Parker Huber offers inclusive language with new lyrics set to familiar hymns in the book *A Singing Faith*. Conflict develops when familiar lyrics are partially altered. This can be just as offensive as not offering inclusive language.

Rather than alter meaningful Christian lyrics that are embedded in our minds, our focus should be on writing new lyrics. Most women are not offended by a few hymns with masculine references if they are balanced by hymns that offer feminine references or are gender neutral (i.e., "The Church's One Foundation"). God is not only our heavenly Father, but also an "everlasting rock" (Isa. 26:4), "Creator" (Isa. 40:28), "redeemer" (Ps. 19:14), and "spirit" (John 4:24) to name a few.

The way Christian music is taught to children is equally as important as the music, according to Rhonda J. Edge and Barbara Sanders. In the book *How to Lead Preschoolers in Musical Activities*, they write:

> Children are children, whatever their language—cultural backgrounds, they need to be understood, accepted, and loved. Be aware of the cultural backgrounds of the children in your music activity group or choir. Avoid singing songs, planning activities, or making remarks that could possibly be offensive to them.[7]

Youth choirs today appear to be making great strides toward multicultural acceptance. Unfortunately, in some churches indigenous youth music or anything with a beat has been limited to activities outside worship services. Communicative worship methods allow young people to feel accepted and important.

Successful church leaders know that youth are some of the most effective evangelists. Teenagers have little inhibition about inviting their friends to the youth choir or youth group.

In the book *50 Ways You Can Share Your Faith*, Tony Campolo and Gordon Aeschliman gave insight on the impact of youth music upon culture.

> One of the key elements of any culture is its music. It is criminal that many churches have tried to cut youth off from this aspect of their culture. Clearly, there are songs with despicable lyrics. That's not the issue. Rather than forbidding teenagers to listen to the bad stuff, you can help them by allowing some honest listening and discussion, as a knowledgeable youth pastor or other adult guides them into wisely evaluating what is harmful and what isn't.
>
> Tremendous poetry and inspiring music are being written by today's youth—songs that deserve the praise of any honest critic. The church has the opportunity to make a bridge back to young people through music.[8]

We do not have to wait for our children and youth to mature to effect positive social change. Several adult church choirs are achieving great results by offering multicultural music concerts and recordings that attract multiethnic groups. Some of the most popular are the Brooklyn Tabernacle Choir, the Alexandria Sanctuary Choir, and the Christ Church Choir. These large choirs have several talented composers who write effective evangelistic music. The Middletown Disciple Choir, which also specializes in multicultural music, is consistently booked over a year in advance.

There are several effective ways within the music ministry to develop an inclusive church with diverse ethnic and cultural groups. (1) Have some minorities serve as soloists or visible leaders—this sends a message of acceptance to all visitors; (2) hire minority persons to serve as choir directors or accompanists; (3) have worship service choir exchanges with minority congregations and invite their choirs to give concerts at your church; (4) schedule minority Christian artist concerts at your church; (5) offer combined or mass choir events where a variety of music from diverse ethnic groups is sung; and (6) always include hymns, songs, and anthems from several ethnic traditions within most worship services.

Social change becomes difficult if ministry remains within church walls. Offering outside concerts and tours inspires a church to be outward or mission focused. Concerts that help raise money for needy causes are a great way to share spiritual gifts for the benefit of humankind. Many churches are seeking outside groups to bridge the cultural gap. It has been said, "The most segregated moment in America is 11:00 A.M. on Sunday." Some churches are still using the "our way is the only way" method of worship. Magnetic music ministries are indigenous to numerous cultures. The mission of a music ministry is not to convert persons to the music leader's favorite music style. Humankind is diverse. When that diversity is unconditionally loved and lifted up, Christ's mission is glorified. The more inclusive a music ministry becomes, the more persons experience the Lord. *If we are to truly be one in Christ, it must happen from within the church.*

II

HIRE THE MOST GIFTED LEADERS

Once the church has established a mission statement, effective church departments and committees develop corresponding goals and objectives. These guidelines give direction for ministry style, staff hiring, and program development.

Without a clear mission statement, church leaders and laypersons become polarized and divided. Many attempt to implement their own desires rather than serve the needs of others. Since music preferences vary, this issue is especially relevant when acquiring church music staff.

Prioritize Salaries of Essential Employees

When hiring or compensating music staff, the church must understand the value of skilled music leaders. According to Kennon Callahan, after a pastor is employed the part-time or full-time director of music should be the second staff person hired, regardless of church size.[1] This opinion correlates to the principal music ministry role of enhancing corporate worship and thereby moving persons into a closer relationship with

God. Callahan states: "If only one thing can go well in a given local church, it is important that worship go extraordinarily well."[2]

Music staff employment should be based upon education, experience, a variety of skills, and, most important, leadership. Since music is extremely influential in reaching baby boomers, salary priorities and long-term employment should be given to highly skilled music leaders. Whether hiring a choir director, an organist, a pianist, or a paid soloist, successful music ministries require talented leaders, not prima donnas. Musical aptitude and talent will not transfer from the church musician to the layperson. Leadership, theology, knowledge, and skill development do.

It actually costs less to compensate a gifted music person competitively than to hire several part-time or full-time persons with inadequate salaries over a period of years.[3] Higher turnover requires additional training and negatively affects church growth and other staff. Also, other churches always consider underpaid gifted music leaders "fair game." Talented staff positively affect church growth and justify their own salaries through their effectiveness.

Magnetic music leaders offer laypersons a sense of need, value, and mission, which consequently develop stewardship. George Barna says: "Local churches that provide compelling reasons for giving, that offer Boomers tangible personal benefits from giving, and that illustrate the impact of the donated funds will have the greatest success at fund-raising."[4]

Seek Versatile Church Musicians Who Lead

Multiskilled church musicians are the most successful music program developers. One who can conduct, sing, play instruments, and provide other program leadership is far more valuable than a person with only one musical skill. Effective music leaders have a vision or game plan (goals and objectives) that laypersons can easily follow.

The task of school music teachers is to provide a well-rounded music education. Church musicians are called to offer a "divine encounter." Music reading, choosing quality music, and conducting are basic skills. In addition, most churches no matter what the size, expect the music leader to be an evangelist, a caretaker, a counselor, a motivator, and an assimilator who empowers laypersons. In his book, *Ministry and Music*, Robert H. Mitchell states: "The highest concern of the professional church musician must be to identify and participate in the mission of the church. 'Mission' is not a musical concept; it is a Biblical/theological one."[5] For example, the mission statement of one music department is "to offer a divine encounter through the spiritual gift of music whereby lives are changed."

Baby boomers attend churches that relate to their journeys. Successful choir directors first offer a substantial diet of indigenous music that is communicative to the majority of the congregation. In order to meet additional congregational needs for diverse musical preferences, they offer a variety of additional music styles. One-dimensional or one-style music programs meet few needs. The object of worship is God—not the music.

Prior to the 1970s, many anthems were accompanied by the organ. Today, the church organist must also function as a skilled pianist, a harpsichord player, and a synthesizer wizard. Many effective contemporary anthems require the organist or pianist to be part of an ensemble with several other instrumentalists. Unless additional music staff is available, the traditional organist must essentially evolve into a versatile keyboard player.

Churches utilizing worship teams require pianists and synthesizer players with improvisational skills. In many of these vocal and instrumental ensembles, musicians play from chord charts rather than printed music. They frequently must improvise modulations and new keys within the same song while remembering the original chord patterns.

Demand Excellence as an Offering

Church music programs usually decline when the choir director settles for mediocre presentations. Underpaid, under-educated, and overextended choir directors are frequent contributing factors to church choir apathy. When the music ministry becomes just a job, churches need to establish a search committee quickly.

The effective church musician constantly challenges his or her group by demanding excellence. Whether offering a two-part or eight-part anthem, God is revealed through quality music presentations. Poor quality musical offerings create a worship barrier that even the greatest sermon cannot overcome.

An important task is selecting the appropriate music for the voices and the talent level of the music groups. Experienced music staff select challenging music that is within the capability of the ensemble or soloist. The sensitive moments occur when music leaders must tell soloists they are not suited for a particular music selection. A better way to salvage their self-esteem is to inform them that the music does not fit their voice.

Many small church choirs are afraid of attempting music that is challenging, new, or of a different style. In these situations, several choir members may complain and want to sing a familiar anthem. (See "Offer Effective Rehearsals and Presentations" in chapter 7.) Once the choir director gives up leadership to the choir, it becomes difficult to regain control and develop growth.

This does not imply that the music leader should use the "it's my way or the highway" approach. The effective choir director balances his or her presentations by alternating complexity, style, tempo, and dynamics within a series of selections. Too much sameness creates boredom, apathy, or inadequacy. To faithful choir members, qualitative variety music is the spice of life. Laypersons are more receptive to new challenges when they have achieved recent success. Regardless of the musical presentation, excellence is always a motivating factor and an offering.

Develop, Recruit, and Nurture with Enthusiasm

Enthusiasm is an essential leadership characteristic for a choir director. Nothing rivals this infectious feeling that can mask weaknesses and motivate a choir.

Choir members appreciate choir directors who are exemplary at loving God, their family, their job, and life enthusiastically. No one who works all day wants to spend an evening with a drill sergeant church choir director who complains more than encourages.

Criticism should always be constructive and balanced by positive reinforcement. If a tenor is singing flat, never correct him individually in front of the entire group. They probably know who is singing flat anyway. A better approach is to direct criticism to the entire section by indicating that the tenors are under pitch. Then be sure to give them a pat on the back when excellent intonation occurs.

Effective music leaders continually give vision to their musical groups. As each new group is added, the group's goals and objectives should be made as clear as a road map to the choir members.

If the group is a new concert choir offering multicultural music, a goal would be to reach baby boomers with a variety of highly evangelistic music. Another goal could be to raise funds at concerts through love offerings for needy causes in the community. A third goal might be to create visibility and a positive image for the church and Jesus Christ. A fourth goal might be to break down culture barriers that segregate society.

Objectives need to be specific and tangible with accountability built into each one. For instance, specific objectives for the same choir might be:

- We will offer six community concerts during the year.

- We will raise two thousand dollars for needy causes.
- We will add ten new choir members this year.
- We will distribute five thousand promotional fliers for each concert.
- We will contact five free media sources to promote each concert.
- We will offer effective music from different ethnic traditions in each concert.

Set objectives to meet goals, and set goals that point toward the church and choir mission statements.

Successful music leaders utilize an organized "community process" for evangelism, such as the following seven-step program:

1. The minister or minister of evangelism informs the choir director of a prospective alto choir member who recently visited the church.
2. The choir director makes a home visit or an invitational phone call and a choir information pamphlet is left or mailed.
3. The choir director informs the alto section captain of a prospective alto and she follows up with an invitational call.
4. The new choir prospect has her name on her folder with an assigned number and an assigned robe as she arrives at the rehearsal. The section captain and choir director individually greet her and show her to her seat.
5. She is welcomed and introduced to the entire choir by the director at the end of the rehearsal.
6. Every choir member welcomes her following the closing prayer.
7. If she does not return the following week, a "we missed you" phone call is made by the director and/or the alto section captain.

This process assimilates the church visitor into the life of the church even before a decision to join the church is made. If she returns for another rehearsal, she will probably join the church as well as the choir.

A frequently neglected vital responsibility of choir directors and other church leaders is to *nurture* their flock. The most important guidelines are: (1) know your flock, and (2) let them hear your voice. It has been said that people don't care how much you know until they know how much you care. Jesus said: "I am the good shepherd. I know my own and my own know me, just as the Father knows me and I know the Father. And I lay down my life for the sheep. I have other sheep that do not belong to this fold. I must bring them also, and they will listen to my voice. So there will be one flock, one shepherd" (John 10:14-16).

Several important actions are required in order to successfully nurture any church music group.

- Absent choir or church members must be contacted within four weeks or they often will not return. Regardless of the circumstances, everyone wants to feel needed and important in any group.
- Each choir practice should include time for prayer, prayer concerns, and joys. Celebration acknowledgments, such as birthdays, births, or new jobs build community and self-esteem.
- Ill or hospitalized choir members need at least a phone call or a visit from the choir director. Other church staff should be notified of the illness.
- Get well or sympathy cards should be sent to choir members and their families. Food and flowers should be sent from the choir when an immediate family member dies.
- Birthday cards or celebrative phone calls from the choir director are an extra touch of church family.

Choir members are enthusiastic, faithful, caring, and loving persons when their choir director is also.

III

ESTABLISH A GROWTH BUDGET

When budgeting for programs, churches tend to think in short terms or immediate needs. Certainly, if the roof is leaking, there is no choice but to fix it. However, in most cases, the return on dollars spent is greater when a church budgets proactively rather than reactively. Regardless of church size, good stewardship requires that every dollar is growth accountable and achieves maximum results. Music leaders have many opportunities to utilize this type of budgeting.

Budget for New Music, Supplies, and Equipment

After acquiring an effective music staff, the music program priorities are: (1) music, (2) supplies, and (3) equipment. Every item should be viewed as a tool for ministry. Like many tools, these necessary program needs eventually become worn or obsolete. When they do, get rid of them!

Churches are notorious for being pack rats. The worst choir scenario is when the new prospective church member opens an octavo music copy and it crumbles onto the floor. No matter how useful or important these items have been, they must be either continually repaired or replaced. A few out-of-print music copies are not sufficient for a large choir. However, they become a blessing to a small church choir. Efficient music departments regularly donate unused music and equipment to churches that need them rather than allow them to deteriorate. The frugal church musician looks for every opportunity to stretch dollars. One church music minister approached the manager of a Christian bookstore and offered to give that store his exclusive business. In return, he wanted an increase in the retail discount for the music and supplies he purchased. The manager agreed to increase most items from a 20 percent discount to 30 percent. Eventually, their relationship spread to other church staff members and all of the church's programs began receiving greater discounts. Everyone wins when these types of opportunities are explored.

When searching for new anthems, economical choir directors save considerable dollars on music that is purchased in a collection form. When sold individually, expensive octavos will decrease or limit the budget for new anthems. Usually, collections of about ten or more anthems cost around five times the price of single octavos. If all or most collection anthems are used, a significant savings is realized. The rule to remember is do not buy collections for only one or two anthems.

Necessary music supplies include a wide range of needs. Association dues, bulletin boards, handbell gloves, handbell covers and tables, soundtrack tapes, music stands, music folders, handbell polish, folder cabinets, stereo supplies, and subscription fees are examples. For a small fee, many music distributors offer subscriptions with demonstration tapes for all new music copies they recently have published. If the choir director is a frequent buyer from that distributor, significant research time and money are saved by these subscriptions.[1]

Music instruments and equipment such as pianos, synthesizers, and sound systems are always needed. The acoustic piano is still an indigenous instrument for all ages and cultures. Even with other electronic instruments, the acoustic piano fits well. However, if the church has several pianos, it is wise to purchase a synthesizer or a clavinova. These versatile electronic instruments can duplicate numerous instrumental sounds, they never need tuning, and many are less expensive than an average acoustic piano.

Quality sound equipment is one of the most important ministry tools. After all, the congregation attends worship to hear God's word revealed through the various worship elements. A sound system can be either an effective worship *tool* or a *turn off.*

Most church leaders and laypersons are ignorant about sound equipment. Their lack of knowledge often leads them to purchase the least expensive equipment. This usually backfires and additional expenses exceed the original cost of a quality system. Before purchasing sound equipment have a committee attend other church services where they can hear the minister and music well, regardless of seating location. Church leaders usually will share information about the company that installed their sound system. It is wise to acquire at least three bids from reputable dealers before purchasing sound equipment.[2]

For portable sound equipment, the same research process is appropriate. In addition, a good portable system should disassemble easily and have rack-mounted units for efficiency and protection. The following is a list of the components in a quality portable sound system and the purpose of each:

1. A *mixer* serves as the control board for the entire system.
2. A *power conditioner* maintains 120 AC voltage when a power source fluctuates.
3. A *processor* offers multiple effects, including reverberation and delayed sound.
4. An *equalizer* allows desired balance of settings for low, middle, and high frequencies.

5. Two *power amplifiers* control the main and monitor systems.
6. A *crossover* separates and sends all frequencies to the appropriate speakers.
7. Two *full directional speakers* project all high and most middle range sounds.
8. One or two *bass cabinets* project all low and some middle range sounds.
9. A *CD player* plays sound tracks.
10. *DAT* (Digital Audio Tape) and/or *cassette players* play sound tracks or can record sound.
11. One or more *monitor speakers* provide vocal and instrumental playback to the musical group.
12. A *multipaired cable*, also known as a *snake*, allows efficient microphone and amplifier connections to the mixer.
13. *Patch, speaker,* and *microphone cables* connect all system components.
14. Quality *microphones* and *stands* offer maximum group and solo pickup and sound projection.
15. *Rack cases* for components enable easy breakdown, portability, and protection of the system.
16. Two *tripods* mount and raise the full directional speakers for sound efficiency and acoustical adjustment.[3]

A sound system of this quality additionally serves as an evangelism tool, especially for youth and young adult choir members.

Budget for Equipment, Instrument, and Robe Maintenance

An efficient music department observes the following guidelines for servicing the music program's equipment:

- Maintain all equipment, from pianos to sound systems.

- Clean and demagnetize the record and playback heads on cassette recorders.
- Tune acoustic pianos and pipe organs at least twice a year. If instruments are located in rooms where the temperature fluctuates, more tunings are necessary. Instrument age also affects the number of necessary tunings.
- Polish handbells frequently. The more handbell choirs a church has, the more maintenance is necessary. Purchase handbell cloths and polish often.
- Reinforce, replace, or donate music copies as necessary.
- Clean and repair choir robes regularly. The average life of a choir robe should be about ten to twelve years. Many churches wait twenty or more years before purchasing new robes. Worn-out choir robes are growth barriers. Successful choirs do not wear robes that are in poor condition.

Budget for Banquets, Picnics, Retreats, and Tours

Churches often nickel-and-dime their members with too many potlucks and fund-raising events. Banquets, picnics, retreats, and tours require budgetary support dollars that indicate the importance of these events and the choirs that are involved. Beyond their obvious objectives, these community-building events are essential for growth. Growing churches offer occasions where child care, food, and transportation are provided.

A church with an effective music program underwrites at least one-third of total choir tour expenses. This keeps tour fees and fund-raising at attainable levels and elevates the important contributions of the choir members.

Budget for Necessary Musicians and Soloists

Church choirs that accompany most presentations with the organ meet only the needs of a few. Additional instrumentalists, ensembles, and soloists not only satisfy many musical preferences, but they are also uniquely effective for evangelism.

Imagine someone looking for a church home during the Advent season. One church is presenting a cantata accompanied by organ. Down the street another church offers a Christmas pageant that includes a drama with several choirs, guest soloists, and an orchestra. Many visitors would choose to attend the second church.

Small churches cannot afford orchestras. Yet, a guest brass choir or string ensemble and several graded choirs can offer an enticing presentation for church visitors. Also, guest soloists and groups provide variety, education, excellence, and evangelism for any church.

Christian artist concerts, revivals with guest soloists, and supplemental soloists for services and choir concerts return far more than the dollars spent. They also attract visitors that otherwise would not have attended.

Budget for Recordings

The most fortunate churches offer recordings of their choirs or small ensembles. Though usually produced by large churches, recordings offer any church tremendous visibility and evangelism opportunities. Regardless of size, a growing church with a professionally sounding music group should budget for a recording project. For example, some churches utilize memorial gifts, fund-raisers, and concert donations to raise recording funds, or private contributors may underwrite most of these expenses.

First and foremost, the object of the recording should not be to raise church funds, but to glorify God. The by-products of effective recordings are church visibility, evangelism, mission, self-esteem, and then whatever financial blessings that come. Budgeting for recordings includes:

- Studio recording and mastering time
- Two-inch master reel-to-reel and DAT (digital audio tape) or 1/4-inch reel-to-reel tape
- Necessary musicians, vocalists, and rented equipment
- Cassette and CD jackets, including graphics
- The number of cassettes or compact discs ordered
- License fees to the copyright holders of any published songs

The most expensive part of these projects is usually studio time. Multitrack recordings require several days. Most recording studios will discount their studio time for large projects. Someone must serve as the project leader or producer. Otherwise, the recording will reflect the old proverb "too many cooks in the kitchen spoil the broth." If no one is experienced, hiring a skilled producer will save dollars and elevate the quality of the recording. To get the best price bid out recording projects to several studios. One studio may offer a package price with unlimited time to a choir, ensemble, or leader that has recording experience.[4]

The most important financial consideration is to have the musical group rehearsed and prepared before the project. Do not plan to rehearse while paying for expensive studio time!

For information regarding license fees, contact The Harry Fox Agency, Inc., 711 Third Ave., 8th Floor, New York, NY 10017. They distribute royalties to the publishers who are the copyright holders for the music. Do not distribute your recordings until licenses are received, signed, and returned to HFA. Any lyric changes must be approved by the publishers directly.

Without promotion, the sales of your recording will dwindle. Scheduling outside concerts and events provides opportunities to sell the recordings. Some Christian bookstores sell recordings on consignment; however, they often expect as much as a 40 percent commission.

Churches of any size can benefit from a quality recorded music group: (1) Persons will be reached outside the church walls that had not visited the church; (2) the music program will add an effective recruiting tool that is easily passed on to others; and (3) the recorded ensemble or choir will gain self-esteem, confidence, and valuable experience that is inspiring to others.

IV

DEVELOP OTHER LEADERS AND SUPPORT GROUPS

One of the most important leadership skills necessary for music ministers is the ability to develop other leaders and support groups. Growing music ministries utilize lay leadership for new choirs, choir officers, departments, and committees. Staff leadership should be reserved for groups that require highly skilled direction. In the book *Prepare Your Church for the Future*, Carl George says:

> Every local fellowship consists of many specific roles that not even Reverend Multi-Gift can fill single-handedly. A minister who wants to experience a championship season must come to view every group leader as a team coach and every parishioner as a potential player. Otherwise, the pastor will become so wrapped up in all the other tasks that the most important one slips: the developing of lay cell-group leaders.[1]

Burned-out choir directors become counterproductive to the church, their families, and themselves. Church music staff are often focused upon the immediate task or crisis. They frequently lose sight of the potential direction other staff and lay music department leaders can provide.

Expanding the leadership circle is like enjoying all of your favorite food without gaining extra weight. Effective music ministers consider two essential factors when developing additional leaders or support groups: leadership training and turnover.

A frequent mistake committed by many churches is to place laypersons in leadership positions without offering them training or guidelines. These unfortunate individuals usually start out enthusiastically and end up discouraged. When this occurs, it is very difficult to recruit them as leaders again. Someone wisely said, "Give a man a fish and you feed him for a day; teach him how to fish and you feed him for a lifetime."

Develop New Directors and Accompanists

Once the staff music leader has established at least four graded vocal and several instrumental choirs, it is necessary to either hire or develop other lay leadership. These choirs may consist of one hundred or more active choir members. Yet the music leader functions as a shepherd not only to these choir members, but also to their families. The size of that group could be equivalent to a church with three hundred or more active members. New groups and leaders meet additional needs and provide continued growth and assimilation. Trios, quartets, and some small ensembles usually do not require highly skilled leadership, but larger groups do.[2]

A set of guidelines or a job description empowers a new leader to begin immediately. Short and simple written expectations will also make leadership recruiting easier. Lengthy, scholarly explanations tend to end up in a drawer or in "file thirteen" (the garbage can).

THE MAGNETIC MUSIC MINISTRY

One large church uses the following guidelines for additional music staff and volunteer directors of their youth and children's choirs:

1. Develop, teach, and promote vocal and instrumental choirs with a spiritual and educational emphasis.
2. Report to the minister of music and music department.
3. Schedule all presentation dates with the minister of music prior to the beginning of the fall season.
   a. Choose music selections to present; however, changes may be made before the newsletter deadline, which is every other Monday. Notify the minister of music and the church secretary of any changes.
   b. Schedule music selections in advance to enable all choir members and their parents to plan their schedules around those dates. This also provides flexibility when it is necessary to switch a presentation date with another choir due to a scheduling conflict.
   c. Use the minister of music as a resource for music selections and scheduling.
4. Order all music, equipment, and supplies through the minister of music. Give receipts and invoices to him or her.
5. Utilize your choir representative as an assistant leader and communicator. Keep your choir representative informed of any choir members needing transportation. Notify your choir representative and the minister of music of frequently absent choir members. In cases of emergency or if you need to contact a parent or another individual, use your choir representative. Do not leave your choir unattended.
6. Inform your choir members and parents that choir rehearsals will always follow the county school schedule. If schools are canceled, all rehearsals are canceled that day. If schools are canceled in the middle of the school day prior to choir rehearsals, all choir rehearsals will be can-

celed. Rehearsals will not be canceled on school in-service days.

7. Maintain accurate information on all choir members. Notify the minister of music, the church secretary, and your choir representative of any new additions, deletions, or changes of address.

8. Turn out all lights and secure the rehearsal room if your choir is the last group meeting in the church that day. Store all equipment and leave the room prepared for the next rehearsal.

Skilled and versatile volunteer accompanists are scarce. Most pianists and organists have been trained in reading music. A few are improvisationalists and are able to play by ear. These unique individuals usually are the most effective and versatile keyboard players of indigenous music. A quality volunteer accompanist actually increases the music budget and serves as a capable substitute for paid music staff.

Utilize Department Officers and Choir Representatives

A music department should include at least the department chairperson, a secretary, choir representatives, and all directors.

The leadership role of the department chairperson is vital. He or she:

- Implements goals and objectives
- Establishes support committees
- Oversees expenditures
- Assists music leaders
- Leads departmental meetings
- Reports to the church board

A departmental secretary usually takes minutes at all meetings and delivers copies to all necessary church leaders and departments.

Most choir representatives consist of adults and youth who participate in the choir they represent. Elected adult and youth choir presidents should serve as choir representatives. An appointed parent serves as a children's choir representative.

A list of choir representative responsibilities may include:

- Serve as a representative for your assigned choir at all music department meetings.
- Assist those choir members needing transportation. Recruit parents by zip codes to serve as volunteer car pool drivers.
- Assist the choir director by contacting parents and/or choir members with extended absences. Inform your choir director of any reason choir members are absent.
- Be present at all rehearsals and presentations to assist the choir director in whatever capacity is necessary.
- In case of emergency, call 911, choir parents, and other adults for immediate assistance. This allows the choir director to remain with the choir.

Elect Choir Officers

Effective adult and youth choirs hold annual elections for officers to facilitate efficiency, pastoral care, and evangelism. Without choir officers, the director becomes a gofer (one who goes for everything). The larger the choir, the more important officers are. Every church is different, but leadership structure and coordination are foundational success factors.

One church uses the following job descriptions for adult and youth vocal choir officers. Note that the title "section captain" is used instead of "section leader." The office of section leader traditionally refers to the person who is the best singer in the section. A section captain serves multiple functions and is not required to sound like Beverly Sills, the opera singer.

President

- Oversees the pastoral care and attendance of the entire choir.
- Serves as the choir representative at music department meetings.
- Assists other officers in their roles.
- Welcomes all new choir members.
- Assists the choir director and section captains in the recruiting and assimilation of new choir members.
- Serves as the telephone tree coordinator when necessary.

Vice President

- Serves as a substitute for the president in his or her absence.
- Assists the choir director by helping to coordinate all choir social functions.
- Serves as banquet committee chairperson.

Treasurer and Christian Concern Coordinator

- Collects donations for flowers and cards for those experiencing a crisis.
- Sends flowers, a planter and/or coordinates meal donations from the choir for those members who have lost a loved one.
- Sends cards from the choir to members who are in crisis or are ill.

Section Captain

- Oversees the pastoral care and attendance of all persons in his or her section.

- Takes attendance of the section at all rehearsals and presentations and returns that information to the choir director.
- Serves as the robe assistant and folder assigner for all new choir members in the section.
- Acquires needed music from the librarian for those in the section who are missing a copy.
- Contacts prospective choir members for the section and invites their participation.
- Serves as the telephone tree coordinator for the section when necessary.
- Acquires a substitute to cover these responsibilities when he or she is absent.

Choir Librarian

- Assists the choir director by filling choir folders with all scheduled music.
- Collects and files used music from all section captains and from any remaining folders.
- Provides music to the section captains at rehearsals for all choir members.
- Recruits volunteer assistants when necessary.

Choir officer responsibilities are different in every church. However, the important contribution each officer makes is vital to the group. The choir is more than a group of singers or instrumentalists. It is a cell-group flock that serves the mission of the church and provides community, care, evangelism, assimilation, and service opportunities.[3]

In the words of the apostle Paul,

The gifts he gave were that some would be apostles, some prophets, some evangelists, some pastors and teachers, to equip the saints for the work of ministry, for building up the body of Christ, until all of us come to the unity of the faith and of the knowledge of the Son of God, to maturity, to the measure of the full stature of Christ. (Eph. 4:11-13)

V

PRESENT A VARIETY OF MUSICAL STYLES

The first step toward spirit-filled singing in worship is for the church to specify its main evangelistic context. Later, it can select songleaders, styles, and texts of music.

Inspiring and well-planned hymns, praise choruses, and anthems facilitate the flow of the worship service. These should provide a balance of praise, reverence, style, tempo, and complexity of text and music. The selection process is enhanced by matching the texts of the music to the theme of the sermon and scripture(s).

Enhance Worship with Thematic Coordination

Thematic worship coordination between music staff and those who preach is essential if the congregation is to experience the gospel. Although the normal demands of any minister make this a difficult pattern to develop, it is well worth the effort.

Most music leaders require at least a month's advance notice of sermons and scriptures to prepare worship teams, choirs, and organists. Fortunately, some pastors prepare their sermons six months in advance. However, in most cases this is an unrealistic expectation.

Increase Attendance with Multiple Styles

A total thematic worship service is the most effective method for empowering the congregation with the gospel. However, the music style, execution, and quality of music determine the age of the persons who will attend the church and influence their reception of the text.

In his book *How to Reach Secular People,* George Hunter quotes Rick Warren, the minister of the fast-growing Saddle-back Valley Community Church, which uses only contemporary music. He states:

> In my opinion, music is the most important factor in determining your evangelistic target, even more than preaching style. . . .
>
> But when you choose your music, you are determining exactly who you are going to reach, and who you are not going to reach. More than any other factor, tell me what the music is in a church, and I will tell you who that church will be able to reach and who they will never be able to reach.[1]

Churches located in the South, Midwest, and most rural communities should offer some southern gospel music. This style of music is similar to country music and a large percentage of the local population will find it appealing.

If the congregation is multicultural, contemporary black gospel hymns and spiritual anthems are imperative. Even at suburban churches, baby boomer Caucasians love black gospel music. They grew up listening to the Motown sound of the Temptations, the Four Tops, the Supremes, and other talented groups.

In the book *Jubilate! Church Music in the Evangelical Tradition*, Donald Hustad gives insight into how God uses the effectiveness of indigenous music:

> We should expect that new musical styles will appear in periods of renewal and evangelism. This both demonstrates the creativity of the Holy Spirit at these times, and offers a fresh message for communicating the gospel. . . . Musical sounds common to the secular world are effective in pre-evangelizing the uncommitted. Furthermore, this illustrates the incarnational character of the gospel, which uses ordinary human speech and music to communicate the divine message to human beings; in turn, the music and speech may be used by the Holy Spirit to transform ordinary, sinful people into members of the family of God![2]

The apostle Paul said, "I have become all things to all people, that I might by all means save some" (1 Cor. 9:22*b*).

If the musical direction is limited to traditional or "classical" hymns and anthems, then the church will attract two groups: persons fifty-five and older, and those who are highly educated. This is independent of the leader. Only 2 to 4 percent of all annual record sales in the United States are classical music. However, a complete avoidance of classical music is a mistake because it is such an important part of our heritage, and is inspirational to many.

Meet Needs Through Balance

Effective churches offer a balance of complexity, style, tempo, and dynamics to meet various congregational needs. For example, one growing church has a woodwind choir, handbell choirs, and a classical vocal ensemble, which balance, but do not displace, their gospel and contemporary music approach. Periodically, the church uses harpsichord with Baroque anthems and organ to accompany congregational hymns and the choir. Acoustic piano, synthesizers, and sound tracks are used more frequently. Instead of a traditional organ prelude, they use a synthesizer to accompany the opening worship music called "Singspiration." This alternative segment emphasizes praise choruses and gospel hymns. The hymns of praise, communion, and invitation usually are balanced with one traditional hymn, one contemporary hymn, and one gospel hymn. This variety maintains an emphasis toward the target group of baby boomers, yet still provides something for all ages and various cultural groups.

How a song or anthem is presented is just as important as its content. Music is an expressive art form. Effective presentations are interpreted according to music period and style. A successful Baroque anthem with a fugal exposition utilizes "terraced dynamics" (without crescendos and decrescendos). Also, the subject melody (*cantus firmus*—"fixed song" in Latin) must be audible as it appears within several voice parts and interacts around a musical maze of harmony. However, an effective black gospel anthem with a soloist offers total freedom for improvisation. Unlimited interaction between choir and soloist with expressive nuances is characteristic.

A wise rule to follow is to present each song or anthem the way the composer intended it to be offered. Over a period of time, the congregation will develop an appreciation for many styles and the church will attract more visitors.

In some churches, only one musical style and one choice of instrumental accompaniment is presented. When this occurs, the church evangelism ministry is handicapped in its ability to reach people who prefer different styles and alternative instruments.

Offer a Variety of Accompaniments

In the traditional service, the success or failure of the hymn singing depends mostly on the competency of the organist. No matter how skilled the songleader(s) or the size of the choir, "the organist has the power," second only to God. Churches blessed with a talented organist can achieve a flowing worship service. Regardless of other effective worship elements, those organists who struggle to play even a hymn can destroy the worship experience.

Gifted organists inspire hymn singing by utilizing free accompaniments, modulations, and multiple registrations. They also understand that their role is to accompany hymn singing—not to play louder so the congregation will sing louder. Utilizing additional instrumentalists to play with the organ also adds variety and enhances congregational singing and anthems.

In large churches such as the Saddleback Community Church or Willow Creek Community Church, orchestras and bands often accompany congregational singing. Many churches use an orchestra only twice a year with Lenten and Advent concerts. Unfortunately, most facilities do not have adequate space for large ensembles.

Several synthesizers can be used to limit the size of an orchestra or ensemble. For example, one synthesizer can play many percussion parts: bells, chimes, conga drums, a gong, the sound of wind, and other special effects. Using MIDI (Musical Instrumental Digital Interface), several electronic instruments connected together offer record and playback capabilities.

One church uses MIDI for sequencing a pipe organ. The organist prerecords the service music on a single disc. While he or she moves to the piano or directs the choir, someone pushes a sequencer button and the organ plays. This sequencing procedure eliminates "dead time" and allows even small church music leaders great flexibility.[3]

These versatile components are wonderful tools that engage people in creative worship. Space problems can only be solved through expensive alterations. On the other hand, the synthesizer, which has become "sanctified," allows churches of any size an inexpensive way to add creative options into their worship services.

Begin Change with Leadership

How would a worship or music department introduce contemporary, black gospel, or southern gospel music to a church that has consistently offered only traditional or classical hymns and anthems? Changes in worship start with the leadership of the church. Christ called the church to be a community of faith, and each of us is called to effectively witness to that faith by making disciples. Altering theology is not necessary to explore techniques and styles of ministry that have proved to be evangelistic.

A Disciples of Christ church introduced praise choruses with a few gospel hymns at one of their elder and deacon retreats. This music was presented as having been effective in growing churches. The music minister informed them that this Singspiration music would be used as an addition to the service to effectively reach unchurched baby boomers. The elders and deacons loved it. They also were amazed at how quickly they learned both the melodies and the words.

The following Sunday the service began with Singspiration instead of the organ prelude. The same praise and gospel choruses were used that were sung at the retreat, with the elders and deacons seated throughout the congregation and singing confidently. People began to enter the sanctuary from an overcrowded foyer, and fewer persons continued talking. Most were singing. Preparation guarantees touchdowns!

Surprisingly, more positive comments about the Singspiration music were heard from senior citizens than from any other age group. One of the older Sunday school teachers exclaimed, "How wonderful it is for us to learn the scriptures through singing" (e.g., "How Majestic Is Your Name," "Thy Word," "Seek Ye First"). Later a synthesizer was added to accompany the praise and gospel choruses along with a worship team, which included four people singing the music in parts.

Many large churches include a band with their worship team. Often these ensembles include singers, a bass guitarist, an acoustic pianist, a jazz organist and/or synthesizer player, and a drummer. They literally celebrate an hour of Christian music before the sermon begins.

Offer Praise Choruses

The content formula for an effective Singspiration or praise chorus worship segment is to present a variety of tempos, dynamic contrast, and complexity. Many churches offer about six songs with usually no more than two stanzas or verses. The first song is inspirational, praise oriented, and invitational. Two examples would be, "Come Let Us Worship and Bow Down" or "O Come Let Us Adore Him." The songs that follow have contrasting tempos, dynamics, and complexity of text and music.

Three worthwhile rules to follow are:

- Sing no more than two up-tempo or two slower songs consecutively.
- Offer balance by not using more than two complex choruses or two simple choruses in sequence.
- Provide at least one or two southern gospel choruses within each Singspiration segment.

The final song could be a reverent intercession or petition to God that leads into an invocation. During the prayer, the synthesizer might be played softly in the background, presenting a reverent and meditative atmosphere.

The popular praise chorus produces trends. A more "spiritual feeling" occurs when these conditions are met:

- The songs are presented consecutively with little musical introduction.
- No one announces the songs or choruses.
- The texts of the choruses are presented on a giant screen or in a worship bulletin.

- Many chorus texts speak "to" God rather than "about" God.
- The melodies are easy to sing.

Some churches that use screens also include biblical pictures or scenes that have the chorus texts superimposed over them. This method provides congregations an opportunity to vicariously experience the text through visual images.

Before printing texts in a bulletin or copying text to project on a screen, a church copyright license must be obtained. Several umbrella organizations offer licensing from many publishing companies. One of the largest is:

CCLI (Christian Copyright Licensing, Inc.)
17201 N.E. Sacramento St.
Portland, OR 97230
(800)234-2446

The cost per church is based on the average worship attendance. The 1995 annual fee for a church with six hundred attenders is $265. If a song is not listed under CCLI, but the publishing company is, a church may print or project that song once the license fee is paid. However, the song may not be used if it is not on the song list or if the copyright owner is not included within the publisher list. In this case, permission to use the song must be obtained directly from the publisher or copyright owner.

Develop Effective Songleading

Once the evangelistic target or "context" has been determined, the selection of a songleader or songleaders becomes important. Congregational singing can be led effectively in one of two ways:

1. *The minister of music or an outstanding singer in the church serves as the songleader.* An individual songleader must be a quality singer preferably with musical training and a versatile,

projecting voice. Quality leadership requires that he or she be skilled in singing different musical styles, improvising, and maintaining constant eye contact with the congregation. In his book *Twelve Keys to an Effective Church*, Kennon Callahan suggests: "It is important that music be played and sung competently and that the people who sing it be committed Christians. Their commitment as Christians will not compensate for a lack of competence."[4]

Using a songleader who is a college voice major graduate is a tremendous advantage. He or she will have not only a projecting voice but also adequate breath support for long phrases and extensive range. However, many trained singers cannot make the transition from singing classical music to contemporary or gospel music.

In one church, an opera singer is the songleader. She has a magnificent voice, but no one can understand her. Her diction and vibrato make the hymns sound like Italian arias. This discourages congregational singing.

Offering indigenous music includes selecting, singing, and/or instrumentally presenting some of the local music styles of that particular culture. Before selecting a songleader, effective music departments require an audition and demonstration tape.

In many growing churches today, songleaders and small ensembles use hand-held microphones instead of standing behind a pulpit or lectern microphone. Often the praise choruses are memorized so that eye contact is maintained. Some songleaders prefer to direct the congregation as they would the choir. However, if the songleader has developed the following leadership skills, then direction by waving one's arms usually is unnecessary. They are:

- Maintaining eye contact with the congregation.
- Projecting his or her voice.
- Interpreting different musical styles with improvisational techniques.

• Singing with enthusiasm or reverence when required.

Churches utilizing orchestral accompaniment with hymns usually require a conductor. Poor visibility and acoustics also make conducting necessary. If the sound system is inadequate, even the most effective sermons, anthems, and songs can become ineffective.

2. *Use an ensemble such as a trio or quartet to lead congregational singing.* The same important leadership requirements apply to both the ensemble and the single songleader; however, using an ensemble to lead singing involves several other factors:

• Individual ensemble leaders do not require phenomenal voices.
• In the ensemble, more emphasis is placed upon blending.
• With an adequate sound system, a quartet can fill a large sanctuary with powerful praise.

Unfortunately, in many churches, no one leads the singing. The organist simply plays loud or soft and everyone is expected to "join in" the hymn singing with the one-hundred-rank organ leading the way. This is one of the methods that baby boomers are rejecting in mainline churches. When the expert musician is a combined organist/choir director, this problem occurs more frequently. In this dual position, even the most qualified person cannot maintain eye contact with the congregation. A choir director in such a position cannot be heard vocally and must rely on the choir to interpret eye, head, and shoulder direction. Although the choir should enhance congregational singing, effective leadership is not possible from such a large group that must constantly look at the organist.

In another church, both the individual songleader and worship team quartet lead congregational singing. The Singspiration begins the worship with a quartet singing in parts for eight to nine minutes. The music is presented without any pause so that a spiritual atmosphere may occur. The melody is doubled with one male and one female voice combined with alto and tenor vocalists. (A bass part is not necessary but could be added. When the melody is doubled by a male and female voice, the harmonies become closer. Sometimes an additional bass part would conflict with the male melody singer. A standard SATB quartet works fine, but it is much easier for the congregation to hear the melody when it is doubled at the sounding octaves.) Following Singspiration, the single songleader leads the more traditional order of worship. The hymns of praise, communion, and invitation vary in styles.

Some general worship team rules are:

- Set aside regular practice time for those who lead worship music. Most worship teams practice once a week.
- Introduce only one new praise or gospel chorus per Sunday and then sing it two or three additional Sundays before it rotates off the song list.
- Select reasonable keys for congregational singing. Any melody that ascends higher than E-flat (fourth space of the treble clef) discourages some persons from singing.
- Attend other growing churches and workshops to gain new ideas that are applicable to your own services.
- Listen to Christian radio stations and cassette samples for new praise chorus material.

The choir plays an important leadership role because it contains the best singers in a congregation. When the choir sings, so does the congregation. After all, congregational singing is a participatory event.

Offer Indigenous Presentations

When an effective individual or ensemble leads the congregation, the singing and instrumental style is adapted to the indigenous culture of the music presented. "Peace Like a River" should not be presented in the same style as "All Glory, Laud, and Honor" and vice versa. Amazingly, some church musicians and vocalists eradicate the spiritual feeling developed by "Let Us Break Bread Together." Some churches make it sound like a march. Effective church musicians and vocalists believe that great music exists in many styles. If they do not, the congregation will never be flexible or accept change.

One outstanding church organist said her college teacher often emphasized that classical music was the only music worthy for God. She later realized the absurdity of that presumption. A church she visited using contemporary music gained over one thousand new members in one year. In a *Net Results* article entitled "Singing the Wondrous Story," by the editor Herb Miller, we are encouraged to be "worship focused" with our music. Miller wrote:

> Hymn singing is not for the benefit of musicians but for the edification of believers. Choir directors in growing churches do not try to make worship services into music appreciation courses. The most important question about church music is not "Who wrote it?" or "What style is it?" The most important question about church music is "Does it move people closer to or further away from God?"[5]

Although music in worship is very important, winning persons to Jesus Christ is more important. Skillful presentations of indigenous music honor that culture and create an atmosphere where effective worship can take place.

A magnetic music ministry offers music styles in three ways: (1) focuses on indigenous music, (2) incorporates inspiring songleading, anthems, solos, and ensembles that are thematically planned, and (3) balances contemporary, gospel, and classical presentations.

VI

PROVIDE ASSIMILATION

Would you invite friends to dinner and not feed them? Many declining churches are inadvertently setting a similar poor example for their new members and their families. Clergy often hear the saying, "Central Church is pretty good at adding new members, but then they walk right out the back door!" .

Worship, theology, and mission are the most important elements of our faith. However, church leaders must not rely on these three fundamental ingredients to carry the load of evangelism and assimilation. Growing churches do not operate on the premise cited in the movie *Field of Dreams*: "If you build it they will come." Small and mid-sized churches with limited music programs frequently must learn this lesson.

In his book *Prepare Your Church for the Future*, Carl George says that many persons leave smaller churches and begin to attend large metropolitan churches even when they do not emphasize evangelism. He states:

Some develop a gravitational pull on the unhappy, the disillusioned, and the underutilized from other churches. . . . Finally, people with a high level of musical talent or cultivated taste may decide that their small church lacks opportunities for using their gifts or for providing the level of musical refinement that their culture requires. Musicians and artists frequently join others with similar interests. Their search often leads them to the larger church.[1]

Developing a musical context of "who we are" and "what God has called us to be" enhances the potential to draw talented music people. However, a magnetic music ministry assimilates them into a group positioned for growth by providing a sense of value, need, and community. Creating multiple opportunities or "musical menus" builds a solid foundation similar to a tree as it spreads its roots and limbs. Jesus said, "I am the vine, you are the branches. Those who abide in me and I in them bear much fruit, because apart from me you can do nothing" (John 15:5).

A magnetic music ministry employs four effective ways to assimilate new church members and prospective church members. These methods may also reactivate some nonparticipating members.

Develop a Feeder Program

The best way to grow a music department is to develop a feeder program with graded multiple choirs. Churches that focus on creating children's choirs ultimately develop a core group for growing youth choirs. Some churches begin the choral experience with a beginner choir for ages three, four, and five. Others choose to begin at first through third grade. Most of these little people will alter the melody line frequently and touch our hearts. However, the important reasons for their participation are not only for musical instruction and appreciation.

An excellent method to recruit these new singers is to convince their parents that the beginner choir will enhance their child's development. Children's choirs offer Christian lyrics with Christian values, new friends, self-esteem, and the confidence to be in front of a large group. As a result of their participation, these children may become excellent speakers, musicians, or vocalists. (Parents usually fantasize their child as a future CEO or successful musical artist at this point.)

The key to their participation is to provide transportation. An increasingly large segment of the population consists of single and dual working parents. Alternative transportation with a neighbor, a car pool, or an assigned church van driver is necessary and effective. This is also true for older children and for youth under driving age. Regardless of the music quality or interest of the individual, young people cannot participate in a choir if they lack transportation.

Once children or youth establish a pattern of attendance, their parents, extended family, and friends will come to hear their presentations. When this occurs the magnetic music ministry:

- Increases worship attendance
- Creates an entry point for prospective members
- Opens a reentry point for inactive members

Concurrent programming is also a successful tool for recruitment and assimilation. While Mom or Dad is attending Bible study, adult choir, or an evening worship service, their children can be at their choir rehearsals and other programs. However, most churches do not have sufficient staff or church space for concurrent programming. Developing lay leadership and having access to alternative space becomes essential in this case.

Another concurrent scheduling method recruits children for the choir but offers little assimilation for their parents. While their child is at choir practice, Kids Club, or LOGOS, the parent goes to the grocery store, runs errands, or shops for Christmas presents. Although this self-serving decision should not be a primary motive for choir participation, church leaders know it happens frequently—especially at vacation Bible schools.

Entry points open in many ways. Convenience is always a motivating factor to parents. In the book *The Frog in the Kettle,* George Barna says: "While money will continue to play a major role in our decisions and actions, by 2,000 we will have shifted to using time as our dominate indicator of value."[2]

A growing church offers answers to the spiritual and physical needs of the culture(s). Future church growth will reflect the old 1960s slogan: "If you're not part of the solution, you're part of the problem."

Most experts agree on two productive ways to develop a youth choir. One method is to hire a skilled, charismatic director and build the program around this magnetic personality. Though young people will rally behind this unique individual, a great drop in participation will occur when he or she leaves. People should join the church (the Body of Christ), not the pastor or another staff person.

A better method is to offer a quality Christian musical and take it on a tour. Youth love to travel, and the tour eliminates the usual school and other scheduling conflicts. The director will have a "captive audience" with an opportunity to develop a bonded and committed group. These lasting tour experiences withstand the loss or change of a choir director.

Youth choirs that offer both a gifted, charismatic leader and tours will experience rapid growth. Whether or not the youth minister is also the choir director, he or she should be with the choir tour. The tour is prime time for youth group development. Youth choir members are often the nucleus of a youth group.

One of the most difficult dilemmas large church music leaders must face is whether or not to divide youth into two choirs. Curriculum in schools and churches is now separately geared for middle school and high school youth. Music directors in growing programs are often forced to make decisions based on curriculum rather than physical maturation, programming, and available leadership. Consider the following five factors:

1. *The church expects quality music with many youth participants to fill the choir loft.* Even with large numbers and sound reinforcement, few middle school choirs project their voices to fill a large sanctuary. Most visiting families with youth are seeking a church where their child can be one of many participants. A large youth choir gives visitors a positive perception of the church. Youth participation is always centered first around relationships and the number within the group. "If everybody is in the choir, it must be cool." To young people, large choir numbers reflect success with potential friendships and acceptance with the "in crowd."

2. *The development of middle schools has altered the traditional fourth through sixth grade choir.* "What do we do with the sixth graders?" Since the inception of middle schools, sixth graders generally no longer desire to interact with elementary children. Their maturity level is too young for high school youth and the boys' voices have not changed.

3. *A middle school choir requires music leaders to adjust staff time and programming for all choir rehearsals and presentations.* Most large church music programs offer about eight to ten music groups. Though youth choirs enjoy singing beyond worship service presentations, the worship service offers visibility for youth choir evangelism and self-esteem. Worship time restraints offer limited church presentation opportunities. Adult and youth choirs require consistent worship and rehearsal experiences for growth. Generally, without multiple services, alternative presentation opportunities, and additional music staff, a middle school choir becomes counterproductive to music ministry growth.

4. *More than ever before, once teenagers begin driving, they desire jobs to pay for gas, dates, entertainment, and future college expenses.* With most baby boomer families financially handicapped, teenagers leave youth programs for jobs that provide their only

source of spending money. These limited part-time jobs usually conflict with church programming. In many churches, older youth choir leadership is diminishing.

5. *Church youth programs are now forced to compete for the youth's time with an increasing number of after-school activities.* In addition to traditional athletic programs, dance and drill teams, other nontraditional athletic teams, and community youth groups compete for time. The worst threat is when these activities and fund-raising events are scheduled on Sunday mornings and evenings.

As a result of these and other conflicts, youth choir leadership today comes mostly from tenth graders and a few older youth. The answer to the complex issue of "to divide or not to divide" must be realistic not idealistic.

Small and large church music programs have no choice. The small music ministry should not divide the youth music program and the large program must divide it. The difficulty lies in medium-sized "on the bubble" programs that include between forty to eighty active youth.[3] Effective church leaders build in success factors when starting new programs. Criteria for developing a middle school and high school choir are:

- **Size of the active choir pool.** One hundred youth in grades seven through twelve generate an average worship participation of fifty to sixty singers. Dividing that group and including incoming sixth graders should be a successful starting point.
- **Size of the music budget.** Funds must be available to purchase music for the unchanged male voices. Fit the music to the voice(s).
- **Number of worship services.** Several choirs often require multiple services. Each additional choir decreases worship service presentation opportunities for all other choirs, ensembles, and soloists. A minimum of two to three worship services or a concurrent youth church serv-

ice in a separate location and an additional middle school mini-tour are imperative.

- **Rehearsal convenience.** Concurrent rehearsal programming with separate music staff for both youth choirs is preferable. Parents with children of different ages will make only one trip to church instead of two.
- **Availability of transportation.** Alternative transportation for many youth must be offered and supervised.
- **Adult support.** Youth parents, church leaders, and staff must be part of the decision-making process. Their support maximizes the success factors.

Many adult choirs are experiencing a continual drop in participation. These choirs (more often in mainline churches) tend to have an average age of fifty-five or older. Adults of all ages are successfully assimilated into music groups by three methods that counter these declining trends.

1. Use many different styles of music. *Symptom:* Some church choirs only offer one style of music usually accompanied by the organ. (Their creed is "the only great composers are the dead composers.") As the choir decreases in size, the director is forced to do less challenging music. Then the gifted singers become bored or leave.

Action possibilities: Perform a variety of music with a heavy emphasis on contemporary and gospel styles to develop interest. Using additional alternative instruments or quality sound tracks draws younger music persons. Develop small ensembles singing with hand-held microphones. Add a band with synthesizers, guitars, and drums, as well as a quality sound system.

2. Encourage fellowship. *Symptom:* The adult choir sings or meets only at worship services and rehearsals. New choir members leave as fast as they come. The group becomes an uninviting clique.

Action possibilities: Schedule concerts for needy causes at other churches and include the choir in combined or ecumenical choir events. These outside experiences develop an inviting, mission focused choir. Choir retreats (with food) for preparing Christmas or Easter concerts are motivating and successful. They also eliminate the last-minute pressure of preparing for the concert. Most important, the choir director will avoid a nervous breakdown before the concert! Picnics, recognition banquets, and mini-tours are great opportunities for growth and building relationships.

3. Provide child care. *Symptom:* Younger adult choir members with children leave the choir or miss rehearsals and presentations because they cannot afford or find a sitter.

Action possibilities: Families with young children today are overmortgaged, financially overextended, and overcommitted. The greatest service the church can provide for these folks is a sitter service for any church function. Choir rehearsals then become a "parents' night out" and a great tool for choir and church growth.

Offer Service Opportunities

A second way to provide music assimilation is to offer opportunities for service. This includes both visible service in the choir or as a soloist, and less visible service as a music department assistant. A magnetic music ministry assimilates persons of all generations, genders, and cultures. Effective music leaders create opportunities for sharing the various spiritual gifts represented in his or her music department. The apostle Paul tells us:

> Now there are varieties of gifts, but the same Spirit; and there are varieties of services, but the same Lord; and there are varieties of activities, but it is the same God who activates all

of them in everyone. To each is given the manifestation of the Spirit for the common good. (1 Cor. 12:4-7)

In addition to choirs and soloists, successful music leaders offer less visible service opportunities that expand the effectiveness of their music programs. Choir directors that delegate responsibilities free themselves for those tasks that only a music expert can perform. Examples of delegated responsibilities are:

1. Transportation. Volunteer drivers are needed to transport children and youth to rehearsals and some presentations. A neighborhood children's car pool program is also effective and essential for single working parents.

2. Return of items to the general lost-and-found. The choir room often functions as the lost-and-found location for the entire church. Someone could be responsible to take all unidentified items to the general lost-and-found, where the items will have a better chance of returning to their owners.

3. Music library. Someone is needed to perform the three basic functions of a music librarian. More individuals are needed to staff the music library as the number of choirs and their size grow. The librarian's duties are:

a. Stamp the church's address and assigned catalog identification number on music copies. Identification on music copies minimizes the potential for music to be lost or misplaced and makes storage easy.

b. Assign choir folders and robes, fill choir folders and their cabinets, and collect used music copies. An efficient way to simplify the folder and robe assignments is to give each choir member the same folder number as his or her robe.

c. Maintain a current computer database of the contents of the music library. (In many churches, a staff secretary does this.) Most efficient music leaders want to track the following information:

- Type of music, such as "octavo"
- Title

- Composer
- Arranger
- Voicing
- Accompaniment
- Date of last use
- Catalog identification number
- Number of copies
- Publisher
- Distributor
- Theme
- Bible reference, if any
- Reorder reference for lost or additional copies
- Brief comment section about the selection

This information saves the music leader valuable time and less trips to the choir room and music stores. Several music software programs are available for church computer libraries. Also, generic database programs, such as Paradox, allow users to set up their own headings, and therefore, create their own music library.

4. Handbell maintenance and setup. Persons are needed to maintain and setup handbells, handbell tables, and table covers. This includes polishing, tightening, and repairing bells and tables and also cleaning their covers. Many small and large churches have one set of handbells that includes several octaves. However, if there are multiple handbell and/or hand chime choirs, these sets will need maintenance frequently. Handbell gloves require washing according to their usage. For one handbell choir, every two months should be adequate. Multiple choirs require more washings. If possible, each handbell choir should have its own gloves to lengthen the life of the gloves and avoid misplacement. In one church, some senior citizens choose to serve as glove washers. In most churches, choir members wash their own gloves.

5. Instrument tuning and care. Pianos, harpsichords, and pipe organs must be tuned regularly. Some churches may have persons capable of tuning a piano or a harpsichord, but tuning a pipe organ usually requires highly skilled persons. If the congregation has many meetings in the sanctuary and often adjusts the thermostat, the instruments in the sanctuary will require frequent tunings, which becomes expensive. The temperature in the sanctuary should be kept at 72 degrees Fahrenheit to minimize the need for tunings. Church meetings are more effective when held in rooms based on group size.

6. Robe maintenance. Choir officers usually oversee robe maintenance and assignment. Choir robes must be cleaned and straightened on a regular basis. Most cleaners will negotiate a reasonable price for exclusive business.

7. Sound equipment use and maintenance. Persons with sound engineering experience are needed to run sound equipment. Individuals skilled with a soldering iron are needed to repair items such as speaker and microphone cables. With many churches using soundtracks today, the trained sound engineer is one of the most important laypersons. When worship services and musical presentations go well, the sound engineer usually hears few comments, if any (no news is good news). However, when microphones are not on or when weird crackling noises occur in the speakers, the sound person is blamed. Church members and visitors have high expectations of quality sound persons and sound equipment. The persons who volunteer for this duty must be prepared for this attitude and accept it.

Most music leaders can fill each of these and many other necessary roles. Some churches inappropriately require them to do so, using the most highly skilled music person to fill responsibilities laypersons can do well. This denies laity the opportunity for service and feeling needed, and is poor stewardship on the part of the church.

Growing churches hire skilled music staff to be worship leaders, evangelists, teachers, caretakers, counselors, motivators, conductors, opportunity developers, and those who empower God's people.

Create Multiple Groups

Another method of assimilation is to create multiple vocal and instrumental choirs and ensembles. These musical menus offer a smorgasbord approach that also positions the music ministry and the church for immediate growth.

One evangelism method that several mainline denominations use is to continually start new satellite churches. In some cases, rather than becoming a large church, these churches seed new churches with their financial support and some of their own members. Their preference is for their church to remain a pastoral model church (less than 150 worshipers) in order to offer efficiency and better pastoral care. This approach allows the pastor to extend one-on-one ministry with each church member.

The expanding music ministry operates in a similar fashion. The choir or ensemble leader (paid staffer or layperson) serves as the pastor of his or her musical group. These satellite groups offer variety and uniqueness for churches of any size.

However, as the music ministry grows, so does the church. Statistics indicate that every choir member represents two to three additional persons in the congregation. If a church chooses to remain small, multiple choirs are counterproductive.

Most churches allow God to determine their size. In one growing church, a church leader said, "I am not going to stand at our front door and tell people they cannot worship with us because there is no room." The church that offers multiple music groups must be willing to accept church growth and change. Carl George says:

> Some churches function as music centers, wielding a powerful attraction on a segment of people who want certain musical experiences and opportunities. There may be a huge choir, a pipe organ, or a contemporary band with guitars and synthesizers. Whatever the variety of taste, these churches are places people enjoy attending for the music. . . . Church size, predictably, will relate to the size of the population segment that's drawn to the musical taste represented in that particular church.[1]

Many traditional music programs offer vocal and handbell choirs for children, youth, and adults. In small churches where vocal talent is scarce, a good handbell choir can be a core group for developing a vocal choir. However, some of these churches use the handbell choir as a crutch and never attempt to cultivate a vocal choir. A quality handbell choir is an asset, but it should never function as the primary church choir. Handbell choirs are specialized groups. They provide excellent musical training, coordination, a sense of family, and spiritual gift opportunities, but limit assimilation.

Larger church music programs also offer other instrumental and vocal groups. Woodwind and brass choirs, string ensembles, contemporary vocal groups, and full orchestras assimilate many persons. Though large churches offer several vocal choirs, they continue to increase the number of small vocal ensembles. These groups also function well in small churches as a nucleus for building larger choirs. They include a women's or men's ensemble, trios, quartets, and other small groups. Those choirs and ensembles using contemporary music are more effective with baby boomers, but a quality classical group every now and then meets additional needs.

Boomers grew up either watching or dancing to bands in nightclubs and on television. Like it or not, a quality Christian band with great vocalists places the baby boomer on home turf. Author and researcher Robert L. Bast indicates: "To put it positively, nearly all congregations in the United States experiencing significant membership growth make extensive use of contemporary music and see this music as integral to their growth."[5]

Provide Opportunities for the Talented and Less Talented

The fourth method of music assimilation is to provide developmental and meaningful opportunities for talented and less talented persons. Expectations of musical presentations are different between small and large churches according to Lyle Schaller. He states:

> The members of smaller congregations often are more toler-ant and more accepting of ad hoc "off-the-cuff" presentations and usually are willing to tolerate poorly planned programs. As the size of the congregation increases, however, that tol-eration begins to erode. The larger the congregation, the lower the tolerance level for sloppy performances.[6]

Choir leaders usually discover the talented soloists before they enter a choir. Their spies (faithful church members seated in the congregation) are fairly quick to inform them. The tal-ented soloist should have frequent opportunities to share his or her spiritual gift. If not, he or she will go elsewhere.

The music director then must somehow regularly schedule the talented soloist without allowing him or her to develop "the prima donna syndrome." Most talented persons are humble, grateful, committed, and sincere people. They often overcom-pensate to play down their exceptional skills.

Some churches have paid soloists or section leaders in their choirs. This can help produce quality presentations, but it often hurts recruitment. In these cases, less talented persons some-times feel inadequate or jealous.

Other churches pay the entire choir, especially in older inner city churches. Though they may attain quality music presenta-tions, these choirs almost eliminate evangelism for the choir.

A better way to utilize gifted soloists is to intersperse them within smaller groups of less talented persons. As they become teammates, peers will encourage their solo presentations and celebrate having such gifted individuals at their church. In these musical groups, gifted vocalists and musicians also teach less talented persons and raise the quality of their presenta-tions.

Above all, do not build a music program around a few gifted soloists. One or more may become ill, have a crisis, or leave. Continually seek out and develop other soloists.

If quality presentations are essential for church growth, how does the less talented person fit in? Not everyone is a quality soloist, but they might blend in a choir or in an ensemble. Those persons who do not blend well vocally could play instruments such as handbells. Some individuals who do not read music might sing in an alternative group that offers less difficult music. If they sit next to someone who does read music, they may develop an ear for hearing pitch and for learning music intervals. Some people have little musical talent, but they can serve as the music librarian or as a van driver to pick up children or youth.

Regardless of musical expertise, anyone can serve in the music ministry. The challenge for music leaders is to identify those opportunities and elevate their importance so that they become desirable.

Provide Opportunities for the Educated and Uneducated

George Barna's research indicates an increasingly large portion of the population will be in dire need of the church due to poverty. He states:

> In addition to the homeless, we will have to contend with those who are functionally illiterate; . . . culturally illiterate (in American customs); and people who work steadily, but are unable to make ends meet. These problems will be especially prevalent in our cities.[7]

Churches of all sizes must address this issue by providing multicultural music groups for the educated and uneducated. Regardless of culture or socioeconomic status, these ensembles or choirs are magnet groups that worship harmoniously. They draw boomers like bees to honey. Churches that continually offer one style of music (gospel, contemporary, or classical) inadvertently polarize or segregate cultures. This does not imply that the educated should give up Bach or Beethoven. But in addition, multiple menus of contemporary ensembles, gospel groups, and choirs should offer multicultural music. Barna goes on to say: "Bulletins, newsletters, and reports should have fewer words, and more pictures and symbols. Bible translations and hymnals must reflect the language skills of those using the materials."[8]

The more communicative worship becomes, the more persons experience God. An effective music ministry offers some music within each worship service that is not complex. Simple or less complex music may become a vehicle for the Holy Spirit, not only for the uneducated, but also for children. Many easy-to-sing praise choruses are very spiritual. When choosing worship music, sometimes *less is more.*

VII

OFFER EFFECTIVE REHEARSALS AND PRESENTATIONS

Effective planning produces growth. "The plans of the diligent lead surely to abundance, but everyone who is hasty comes only to want" (Prov. 21:5).

The productive music leader schedules his or her program like a finely tuned machine. As the number of ensembles and soloists increases, well-coordinated presentations and rehearsals become essential.

In a growing music ministry, many vocal choir members filter into additional groups such as handbell or woodwind choirs. These experienced individuals raise the quality of those groups. However, many choir members also serve as deacons, nursery workers, and so on. Preventing burnout is difficult when people are overutilized and overscheduled. George Barna says, "When we strive to incorporate people into the life and ministry of the church, we also need to be extremely sensitive to the value of the time we are asking people to surrender."[1]

Churches must acknowledge and meet the scheduling needs of their community. That mission field includes an increasing number of both dual working parents and divorced single parents. According to Barna, there is also "a growing trend toward partners having children without being married."[2] The strategically planned music ministry may become the entry point to Christian growth and community for many of these persons and their children.

Provide a Master Schedule

Careful planning achieves maximum participation and provides an opportunity for quality presentations. The choir offers its greatest witness and musical development when everyone is present.

Music leaders are often frustrated by after-school activities, vacations, and other conflicts that decrease church music group participation. Some of these situations are unavoidable. However, experienced choir directors plan their programs several months in advance. Regardless of church size, they make a master choir schedule for at least the busiest part of the year, working around as many school and other secular conflicts as possible. This schedule includes dates for picnics, banquets, retreats, and outside concerts, as well as worship presentations. Then, choir members can plan their optional activities around the master choir schedule.

Provide Convenient Scheduling

Effective scheduling is the "mother of all success factors." When making a schedule, remember these four key words: convenience, competition, consecutive, and concurrent.

Limited free time forces the choir member to make choices. Most successful music ministries plan according to convenience and age. For example, children's groups might rehearse on Wednesday afternoons and adults on Wednesday evenings; all youth groups could meet on Sundays.

Ineffective scheduling can decrease total church participation. For example, a church may discourage involvement by having one age group meet three or more times a week. Possibly, many of these persons also may serve on committees or have other school and recreational activities. Such scheduling may require people to choose between church and school or other recreational activities. Unfortunately, church activities will not be chosen all the time.

Avoid Schedule Conflicts

Be aware of church, school, and community programs and events that compete for the choir member's time. Fewer quality musical presentations and rehearsals are better than many mediocre ones. Cancel choir rehearsals on important family days such as Mother's Day, Father's Day, and Easter Sunday. Otherwise, choir members become burned out and resentful. Every person needs a break—even the choir director.

Use consecutive and concurrent programming to enhance participation. Also, convenient schedules help prevent sacred and secular conflicts. A consecutive adult schedule might include the following:

5:30 P.M. Family night dinner
6:00 P.M. Adult Bible study
6:45 P.M. Adult handbell choir
7:30 P.M. Adult vocal choir

Since everyone is not in an instrumental choir, a multiple menu of concurrent programming is also successful. A concurrent adult schedule in separate rooms could be:

5:30 P.M. Family night dinner
6:00 P.M. Adult Bible study and adult woodwind
           choir
6:45 P.M. Adult handbell choir and adult vocal
           ensemble
7:30 P.M. Adult vocal choir

In concurrent programming, the important factor to remember is that not everyone participates in every activity. Schedule preference should be given to those groups that offer unlimited assimilation, such as children, youth, and adult vocal choirs.

When scheduling music groups for worship, remember youth and especially adult choirs require regular presentations. They serve as "anchor" choirs that effectively support and motivate worship. Consistent quality presentations encourage growth and musical development. Growing vocal choirs significantly increase total worship attendance.

Maintain a Predictable Schedule

Music groups with high attendance usually offer quality music, convenient rehearsals and presentations, and predictable schedules. Adding new music and events creates variety and excitement to any group. However, participation dramatically increases by developing group relationships and consistent scheduling. Choir members look forward to rehearsals and presentations if they are well planned or become annual traditions. Off-the-cuff leadership motivates no one. Organized and scheduled music programs should not be canceled for other church programs. Canceling rehearsals or presentations sends the message that the group is not important. Every church participant needs to feel that his or her spiritual gift and service is vital.

Offer Flowing and Total Theme Worship

Motivating worship in growing churches may appear spontaneous at times, but usually effective church staff coordinate that spontaneity. In many instances, music presentations carry worship services when sermons and other elements are weak. baby boomers have little tolerance for "sedative worship." These overextended and overcommitted individuals expect worship to be an inspiring and motivating experience that leaves them with a sense of hope. In these quality moments, the boomer experiences a relationship with God.

In small churches with limited budgets, some choir directors are content to select easy-to-sing anthems, which often contain general Christian themes. However, even a small ensemble or soloist can plan thematic presentations if the pastor, music leader, and worship department work together. If thematic hymns enhance the sermon, then adding a thematic anthem and/or solo within the service will generate lasting effects. Staff and leadership planning retreats offer the opportunity for thematic and creative worship development.

Utilize Flexible Rehearsal Techniques

Each music director has unique skills and a distinctive personality. Also, every choir is different. However, the effectiveness of the teaching and conducting methods, the atmosphere of the rehearsal, and the sharing of the gospel are paramount for all choirs.

The following four-step teaching process is successful for both youth and adult vocal choirs and ensembles.

1. When teaching a new song, attempt to sing the song in its entirety. This gives the musical group the total concept and develops sight-reading. If the choir lacks music readers, use a demonstration tape or allow the piano to play the entire melody with the sopranos.

2. Teach the melody and/or parts by having each section sing the individual parts with the piano.

3. Then have the entire group sing phrases of the selection *a cappella*, concentrating on listening to one another for balance and pitch.

4. After the choir learns the melody and parts, add the piano or soundtrack accompaniment. Work on nuances and dynamics, and continue to develop interpretation according to music period and style.

NOTE: Children's choirs can be taught with the same process with one exception. In step one, the director must sing or demonstrate the entire song, since small children may not read well. Having them repeat portions of the piece sung by the director (the rote process) reinforces their confidence and learning.

This four-step approach allows the director to maintain group concentration while minimizing dead time for talking and other disruptions. Any choir can sing a selection with accompaniment if they can first sing it *a cappella*. Unaccompanied singing quickly develops intonation and blending.

Sometimes beginning with some historical background or stylistic explanation about the selection offers helpful direction. However, too much talking or explanation by the director creates boredom. The vocal choir comes to the rehearsals to sing, not to listen to a lecture.

When teaching musicals, especially to children and youth, an effective choir director schedules separate times to meet with those who have speaking parts. Otherwise, the rest of the group becomes bored or disruptive. After cast members learn their lines, the director can put them with the choir. In children's choirs, slower readers require extra attention, especially for facial expression and vocal projection.

With instrumental choirs such as handbells, an effective director chooses a teaching technique that matches the choir's experience. When introducing a new hand chime or handbell selection, especially to a beginner choir, attempt to play the entire piece. If necessary, the director may need to count every beat for them. Then have the choir members count the measure numbers out loud as they play the beginning of each measure. This allows those who are lost to catch up. If needed, the treble clef bells might work in one portion of the piece, and the bass clef bells could practice separately. The director will reinforce their confidence by having all ringers play only that portion of the piece. Following this, another section is practiced until the group can play the entire selection. Once the group is able to ring the complete song, dynamics and interpretation can be developed. Then, counting should be eliminated by only mentioning a measure number sporadically until it becomes unnecessary.

When selecting hand chime or handbell music for children, choose pieces that keep everyone busy and challenged. Many handbell choirs add additional notes by doubling the highest and lowest notes at the octaves.

Some churches utilize a partner method when they have too many children for available hand chimes or handbells. While one child is playing, his or her partner claps the rhythm and then alternates with the one playing. Then both learn the piece, and no one is left with nothing to do. Other churches have additional children play Orff rhythm instruments along with the handbell choir.

When scheduling vocal or instrumental music, the experienced director alternates slow and faster selections. If there are too many fast pieces, children and youth become overexcited. Too many slow songs produce boredom. A good rule to follow is: Use no more than two songs of similar tempo in sequence. Using a variety of accompaniment and styles holds interest.

The successful choir director makes choir rehearsals enjoyable experiences. Tired, working adult choir members or children and youth who have been at school all day have no desire for a boot camp rehearsal. Challenging rehearsals can also allow time for prayer, fun, concerns, and interaction.

VIII

OFFER SPECIAL PRESENTATIONS AND EVENTS

Growing churches consistently offer regular concerts and other musical events that produce visibility, evangelism, outreach, community, self-esteem, and sometimes ecumenism. However, the success of these events depends upon the promotion and quality of the presentation as well as the depth of the content.

A church choir may offer an excellent presentation, but if the event is not promoted, only a few regular attenders benefit. Promotion of any event creates program and church visibility.

The choir could offer Handel's *Messiah*, yet this work is beyond the ability of most small church choirs. Flat or off-key singing evangelizes no one. In many cases, several small and medium-size churches successfully combine to offer challenging music. The potential talent pool of gifted singers usually is increased by uniting choirs. Having several gifted singers in each voice part elevates the performance of less talented persons. In many communities these joint church experiences often are successful foundations toward developing ecumenical ministries.

Effective church choirs are mission focused. The most successful churches win people to Jesus Christ, help them grow spiritually, and teach them how to serve others. Special concerts and events should not be limited to home presentations. Staying behind church walls only services church attenders and promotes self-centeredness. Entry points for unchurched persons often occur at outside concerts and other community events.

Boomer visitors who attend special Christmas and Easter presentations are like TV "channel surfers." They often visit several churches until one instantly grabs their attention. Like the aroma of fresh-baked bread, a quality music event draws visitors back for more.

In his book *User Friendly Churches*, George Barna indicates that successful church programs are not measured by the number of leaders and participants. He states: "At growing churches, a program was deemed successful according to how many changed lives resulted from the outreach."[1]

Community concerts for needy causes raise our consciousness of Christ's mission. "For the Son of Man came to seek out and to save the lost" (Luke 19:10). A magnetic music ministry develops a sense of family through its common goals, care system, fellowship, and outreach. Participation in concerts and special events enhances those benefits.

Every church vocalist and instrumentalist enjoys successful presentations. Sharing that success with choir teammates builds enthusiasm and church family. Barna further says:

> The prospect of being associated with an activity—especially a spiritual activity—that is having a positive influence on people, or otherwise resulting in victory, will in itself, motivate enthusiasm, excitement and interest. Like it or not, success breeds success.[2]

Effective music presentations and events influence and change lives. Stagnant churches frequently offer only what they perceive to be as dignified music that maintains tradition or image. Christ came not to save our dignity, but our souls. Tradition and heritage play theological, educational, developmental, and cultural roles, which develop spiritual growth and musical excellence. However, the quality and content of any Christian music presentation or event should not be evaluated only on form, style, or tradition.

These special presentations offer music that uniquely inspires participants and attenders beyond Sunday morning experiences.

If a church offers Mozart's *Requiem* during Lent, it must have realistic expectations. Though this wonderful work is labeled as quality music in any circle, it offers limited appeal. The concert will draw those who are highly educated, age fifty-five and older, and some choir family members. Boomers do not communicate in Latin or listen regularly to requiems. The apostle Paul tells us,

> And if the bugle gives an indistinct sound, who will get ready for battle? So with yourselves; if in a tongue you utter speech that is not intelligible, how will anyone know what is being said? For you will be speaking into the air. (1 Cor. 14:8-9)

Churches that offer large classical presentations do so for the purposes of glorifying God, music appreciation, skill development, and sometimes for balancing musical styles. Declining churches cannot afford to offer such works. Any church that offers only classical music has set a course for "doom and gloom" evangelism. Magnetic music ministries offer a variety of special presentations and events with multiple music styles that meet the needs of many.

Offer Musical Dramas and Pageants

Effective musical dramas (also referred to as musicals) and pageants can be presented by choirs of all ages. Their increasing popularity has sold untold music copies, challenging composers to write more of them. Several factors make these presentations successful:

- They usually offer upbeat indigenous music that connects with all ages.
- They generally last forty-five to fifty minutes. This time frame fits adequately in most church services. These presentations also serve well as the sermon and give the pastor a break.
- Dramas offer fellowship, spiritual growth, self-esteem, and a sense of feeling needed. Also, they are one of the most effective evangelism tools. Boomers grew up watching sitcoms and movies.
- They usually offer multiple solos and cast parts. An average singer may not be adequate for a solo, but could play a character role. Even persons who are not in the choir participate as set builders, costume designers, stagehands, or makeup artists.
- They frequently offer spiritual experiences. Many musicals or pageants have a biblical theme and effectively relate the Bible to today's world. They are great tools for teaching the Bible, especially to children.

Large churches offering singing Christmas trees (choirs positioned on decorated layered platforms in a tree shape) accompanied by orchestras or several instrumentalists often utilize musical dramas with pageants. While the choir is confined to the tree surrounded by an orchestra, a drama takes place at the nearby manger scene. These multidimensional music and drama events usually "wow" church visitors into returning.

Offer Community Concerts and Choir Tours

Community concerts and choir tours are the essential "dangling carrots" that motivate any youth and adult choir. These highly effective events offer a common goal that develops excellence, generates community, creates visibility, focuses mission, and explodes evangelism.

Tired, overcommitted youth and adults are very difficult to motivate on a weekly basis. Special challenging concerts and tour music require them to concentrate. Improved weekly anthems and a sense of accomplishment and service are the by-products of this demanding material. Over a period of years, choir tours generate a few visitors from some of the toured locations.

When special events are offered, the choir members must depend on one another for success. These unique common goals build lasting relationships and family or team enthusiasm.

Performing concerts at other churches for needy causes can help a church develop a caring community image. If these presentations occur regularly, free newspaper promotions and fliers offer outstanding visibility.

Any group that achieves success on a common mission becomes motivated. Those choir leaders that clearly define the choir goals and objectives are more likely to be successful. A sense of purpose also justifies expenses for concerts and tours.

Quality concerts and tours are the most effective music ministry evangelism tools. Prospective church members may not realize the Holy Spirit is working through these events. They may be aware only that they want the fulfillment and joy the outstanding choir is experiencing. But, special presentations such as unique and exceptional music events and Christmas Eve and Easter Sunday services usually generate the most visitors.

Offer a "Mission" Tour

Choir tours are effective for adults and especially youth. It is difficult to commit adults with children to a lengthy choir tour, yet some churches do. The key to any successful tour is advance notice, planning, and mission.

One experienced minister of music realized every year he was asked the same questions at each preliminary youth tour meeting. As a result, he developed a choir tour handbook. Each year he simply hands out or mails this material to the youth and their parents, reducing the length of these meetings. Additionally, the book saves him valuable time, energy, and many phone calls.

Though every church offers tours differently, the following handbook information is how one director successfully develops a youth choir tour.

Youth Tour Handbook

1. What are the goals of the tours?

- To invite, welcome, and develop new choir members to be accepted persons in the choir and to give them a firm foundation in the expectations of them as youth choir members.
- To witness the gospel of Jesus Christ through musical dramas or other effective traditional and nontraditional methods.
- To promote youth choirs and youth groups within other churches as a part of an outreach ministry.
- To develop a community of faith within the youth choir and offer alternative Christian experiences.
- To bond the youth choir to the highest standard of excellence as an offering to God.

- To offer the youth an opportunity to see, experience, and appreciate the blessings of natural resources and historical places that perhaps many would otherwise never see.

2. Who should go on the choir tour and why?

Two major issues that young people face are self-esteem and acceptance. To effectively develop these areas, the tour establishes a common ground in which each person, regardless of age, feels important. The youth choir is a special group in which everyone and every voice part depends on one another for excellence. The younger singers (ninth and tenth graders) learn and develop musical techniques, friendships, and expectations at a quick pace because they are experiencing an effective workshop setting. The older senior high choir members have "been through the ropes" and provide a "big brother/sister" leadership with a sense of pride. This is not only a group that has accepted them, but also a church family that has become special to them.

One of the greatest challenges each church faces is effective programming that reaches busy people. On the tour, fewer distractions and less competition with secular activities occur.

In youth group meetings, the younger and older groups should be separated because different issues are important to each age group. However, it is also equally important to spend time as an inclusive Christian family where everyone feels important and accepted. The youth choir is not only a group where this happens, but it is also a building block toward Christian maturity. As youth choir members mature, they learn that, to God, time and talent offerings are just as important as financial contributions.

3. Why would churches want the choir to visit?

Churches are always looking for ways to develop their youth group, and according to most experts, a musical drama and/or tour are the most effective methods. Most churches do not have a youth choir, and they appreciate opportunities that help motivate their congregation to develop one. Many churches in mainline denominations are declining in membership, and they are continually looking for special events, especially in the summertime, to draw unchurched persons or prospective members to their church.

Music directors are constantly looking for new and effective material for motivating their choirs. These special musical events often serve as music reviews for other music leaders.

4. How are the tours selected?

Each year it is wise to cover a different geographical area, so that choir members joining the choir in ninth grade can experience many areas of the country before they graduate from high school.

Some churches call and request visits from quality youth choirs who are planning a tour for their part of the country. On each trip, the tour offers many historical and natural resource stops, especially for those choir members who would otherwise not experience these places. Beaches and/or theme parks are included when possible because everyone needs a break after several concerts, and these stops add variety to the trip.

Tour suggestions and input from parents, choir members, chaperones, and church staff are welcomed. When the tour stops have been scheduled tentatively, the music department is consulted, and if no objections are voiced, the plans proceed.

5. How are the chaperones selected?

The first chaperones are selected by special need. For example, an experienced sound person can double as a chaperone. Youth ministers can be chaperones as well as lead the other additional youth activities. They also will have an opportunity to develop relationships with the choir members and be able to recruit additional youth for the youth group. All youth should be encouraged to participate in all youth programs and/or activities.

Several choir parents may be selected because of obvious relationships and interest, however, all chaperones should be chosen because they relate well to youth.

Additional chaperones are selected according to the size of the group. Enough chaperones are enlisted so that each one supervises no more than five choir members. An equal balance of men and women chaperones is desirable to meet the needs of all youth and minimize the need for extra motel rooms.

6. What determines the cost of the tour?

The church members' offerings underwrite about one-third of the tour cost within the music department budget. This helps to keep the tour fee at an affordable price so that every choir member has an opportunity to go. Tour scholarships are provided when necessary. These funds are usually given by private individuals who recognize the importance of these tours. Ministry to youth and their families is a church priority, which is reflected by providing a youth choir tour.

The cost of each tour is based on two major components: (1) the number of people going; and (2) the number of miles and days to be traveled. Other factors also apply. Motel accommodations for some evenings are necessary on travel to beaches, theme parks, or long distance tours. Bus drivers are required to have separate motel rooms. This includes those nights in which choir members stay in church homes. Tour guides from major cities, natural resources, and sometimes historical locations are hired by the hour. The cost of lunches each day and all the meals during motel residence is not covered. Each person needs to bring extra money for T-shirts, souvenirs, snacks, and any additional expenses such as guided tours.

Amusement or theme park admission is included in the tour fee for all choir members and chaperones. A group rate usually is available for twenty-five or more persons. Complimentary passes are given for large groups and their chaperones. Breakfast, a potluck supper, and overnight housing in church member homes are provided when concerts or musical dramas are given. Most historical locations do not have an admission charge. Side tours usually do.

7. What should each choir member bring?

Watch: Each choir member should wear a watch at all times and be responsible for being on time. Choir members or chaperones should not depend on their roommates or hosts for wake-up calls. *Bring an alarm clock.*

Clothing: Shorts and short-sleeve tops are appropriate; however, nothing offensive to others will be allowed. Unless there is an assigned outfit for concerts, normal school clothes are appropriate for each event.

Money: An amount of $125 should be more than sufficient for the entire tour. However, if the choir members wish to purchase souvenirs, clothing, or any other items, they should bring additional money. It is wise to bring travelers checks instead of cash, if choir members have proper identification available. Many parents include an envelope of budgeted money for each day. This assists in developing a sense of responsibility as well as keeping choir members from running out of money.

Miscellaneous: Thank-you notes are needed for overnight church hosts. Each choir member and chaperone must keep his or her itinerary accessible at all times. Itineraries are also provided to parents.

8. What are the rules of the tours?

Each choir member is an ambassador for Christ and the church, and behavior must reflect this privilege. Group needs supersede individual needs or wishes. Any future tours depend on the group's witness and example during the entire trip.

All choir members are responsible to all chaperones. However, each chaperone is the immediate supervisor of no more than five choir members. All choir members report first to their assigned chaperone for any need or problem. Regardless of activity or location, the tour participants must model a Christian image.

Any behavior by a choir member that reflects poorly on the church or the choir will result in disciplinary action: (1) a prompt phone call will be made to the choir member's parents; and (2) parents will be required to pay for a choir member's bus trip home or be responsible for coming to retrieve that individual at the tour location. Disciplinary measures will result from the following offenses:

- smoking
- drinking
- absorbing any illegal substance
- continual tardiness
- foul language
- property damage (to churches, homes, motels, or buses)
- breaking curfew
- being in the room of someone of the opposite sex at any time except for authorized group meetings
- being a continual nuisance to others

Any choir member with knowledge of such behavior must immediately notify a chaperone or be subject to the same consequences. Any necessary discipline is decided and administered by the minister of music in cooperation with all chaperones.

Additional rules are:

- R-rated or offensive movies or music are prohibited during the tour.
- During side tours, at beaches, or at theme parks, no choir member may leave the group alone. Each choir member must have at least one other person with him or her at all times.
- Renting of any motorized vehicles is prohibited.
- Each choir member must have one parent sign a medical power of attorney form that allows the minister of music

or the minister of youth to acquire medical treatment for that individual should it be necessary. The insurance company and group number must be given on this form along with home and work phone numbers of parents.

- Choir members are expected to write a thank-you note to every overnight host when they stay in church member homes.
- Every choir member and chaperone is assigned job responsibilities on each tour. This teaches everyone to depend on one another and minimizes the burdens.
- Each choir member is responsible for his or her own luggage and additional personal items, regardless of who is assigned for loading and unloading luggage and equipment.
- All long distance phone calls from any location are to be either collect calls or charged to parents' phone credit cards.
- If the choir member must bring medication of any kind, the assigned chaperone and the minister of music must be notified in advance. Write the name of this medication on the back of the medical power of attorney form.
- Each choir member, a parent or guardian, and assigned chaperone must sign a covenant document that states they have read the rules of the tour and agree to abide by them.[3]

An important consideration is to double-cast character and soloist parts if the choir offers a tour musical drama. This gives the group a prepared substitute for an ill or disciplined choir member and offers more youth opportunities for experience. Create blue and red teams that alternate presentations and offer two home concepts (save the best for last!).

Schedule a youth choir party after the tour and invite all choir prospects to attend. Youth choir members who experience a successful tour are effective recruiters.

Offer Christian Artist Concerts

Quality contemporary Christian artist concerts offer variety, excellence, church visibility, and evangelism for any church. Many of these talented persons appear for love offerings, but some fortunate churches budget for them. Regardless of church size, these presentations create motivating spiritual experiences that may not occur during other services and events.

Choirs with gifted soloists are fortunate. Yet, if one or two persons are the only gifted soloists, over a period of time their presentation effectiveness may dwindle. Sameness creates boredom even with talented persons. Christian artist concerts offer new and exciting quality experiences.

The exceptional skills of Christian artists teach and motivate other singers and instrumentalists. Often their presentations provide new ideas and techniques for church vocalists and instrumentalists.

These concerts also offer excellent church visibility and evangelism. Growing churches frequently announce concerts and other programs in newspapers or fliers. Some effective churches print brochures that contain a series of scheduled Christian artist events. Regardless of church size, these concerts attract church visitors that otherwise would not have entered the church door. Indeed, a full church music calendar sends an impressive message to church visitors.

IX

CREATE
VISIBILITY

No matter how successful a church music program is, its effectiveness is always measured by its degree of visibility. Jesus said, "Let your light shine before others, so that they may see your good works and give glory to your Father in heaven" (Matt. 5:16). Even capable music leaders are sometimes so consumed with developing a quality presentation they often neglect the significance of this scripture. Nevertheless, every church growth expert extols its meaning.

Include Media Advertising

Many churches avoid media advertising because they are afraid of developing a marketing mentality. Invariably, some laypersons caution clergy not to market the church like a business. Yet, ironically, these members are quick to rely on their personal business skills and methods when serving as church leaders.

The key to any effective church advertising is to develop integrity and quality.[1] Music ministries that develop a positive reputation of mission and excellence glorify God by example.

Every possible advertising source should be explored when a church program becomes such an asset to the community.

One church developed a media list that consisted of free newspaper, radio, and TV sources. All sister denominational and ecumenical churches within a twenty-mile radius are included. They utilize at least seventy free news sources for every promoted event.

Even in large metropolitan areas, some newspapers publish a list of community religious events. Several TV and radio stations offer free local announcements as well. In rural communities, free media sources are more likely to offer greater church event coverage than do metropolitan areas.[2]

Successful church leaders continually seek out these sources and mail their event announcements at least two weeks in advance. Sometimes newspaper reporters follow up the news release and write a feature article about the event. When this occurs, visibility is greatly enhanced, regardless of church location.

Paid musical event promotions are more successful around Christmas and Easter. They also receive more coverage in rural communities since competition for newspaper advertising space or radio spots is limited.

Develop a Flier Ministry

Middletown Christian Church (Disciples of Christ) developed an inexpensive yet highly effective Neighborhood Flier Ministry. The following information from an article in *Net Results* magazine explains how it works.

> Promote special events at least once a month and no less than every other month. The exceptions are Advent and Lent, when we promote no more than two special events with fliers. (This also conforms to the dependable principle that says if a ministry is to be effective, it needs to meet on a regular basis but not overcommit its laypersons.)

For special events held on Sunday, distribute the fliers no sooner than the preceding Sunday afternoon and no later than Tuesday. People need sufficient time to schedule their activities. However, if the event is promoted too early, they forget about it.

Once a special event date is set, send a letter of notification from the minister of evangelism or department chairperson to all persons involved in the Neighborhood Flier Ministry. Do not depend on your church newsletter as your only source to inform volunteers. The letter should include the date of the special event, when the fliers will be ready, who is responsible for picking them up, and when they need to be distributed.

The Neighborhood Flier Ministry functions primarily through the leadership of laypersons. The minister of evangelism, department chairperson, or perhaps a layperson in advertising serves as the designer of the master copy. A coordinator oversees the distribution of the fliers and the follow-up phone calls to those captains who have not picked up their fliers. A captain is assigned to each neighborhood within a four to five mile radius of the church. The captain's responsibilities are to pick up the fliers at the church, assign streets to the church members participating in the flier ministry, and deliver the fliers to these neighborhood volunteers. They then stuff each flier in door handles, newspaper slots, etc., as it is against the law to stuff mailboxes. If one of the volunteers is unavailable to participate at the assigned time, the captain assigns someone else his/her streets, or the captain covers them.[3]

Regardless of church size, a Neighborhood Flier Ministry creates high visibility with minimal effort and cost.

Use Posters, Action Photos, Pamphlets, and Newsletters

Numerous inexpensive print methods can raise music ministry visibility. Posters and fliers attached to well-located bulletin boards and business locations are effective. Some printing companies print inexpensive choir photos on posters and fliers with plenty of available announcement space. On promotional posters and fliers, choir action photos are more interesting than still shots. Too many "zombie" (still) photos create sameness and lack interest.

Many successful churches develop pamphlets that contain information about church staff, programs, and how to become a church member. Each pamphlet contains more information than a general clergy home visit can provide. Once prospects receive them, these pamphlets also become highly effective assimilation guides. Pamphlets can be read at a convenient time and help the church get information into the homes of prospects.

One large music ministry pamphlet lists every choir and ensemble from age three to adult on the music insert card. The information includes names of the choirs, their age groups, directors' names, rehearsal times, and meeting places.

The church newsletter is a valuable connection to both the congregation and church prospects. Amazingly, some churches mail their newsletters only to church members. Yet one of the first things a visitor wants to obtain is information about current activities. Incidentally, bulk mail is a bargain compared to any other paid advertising method.

Effective music ministries focus their newsletter articles primarily on future presentations. Otherwise, these articles become boring reports on past performances instead of interesting notices of coming attractions.

Develop a Choir Tour Handbook

Although a tour handbook primarily functions as an information guide with expectations, it also provides music program visibility. Every youth choir member who has a positive tour experience shares that excitement with churched and unchurched friends. The handbook (see chapter 8) offers complete information that is easily passed among friends and parents.

Utilize Audio and Video Recordings

Magnetic music ministries offer quality audio and video recordings of special events, and these unique opportunities create self-esteem, enthusiasm, and significant visibility. One music minister bartered a video recording agreement with a local company. The company was to record every youth and adult choir concert or special presentation. In return, the company could sell all dubbed copies from the original master tape. Thus, the minister of music freed himself from making videotape copies and the video company received exclusive dubbing business. In addition, both the video company and the church music program gained visibility.

Quality recordings of exceptional music groups are extremely effective at creating visibility and evangelism. Persons who may not have attended a worship service become motivated prospective church visitors through exposure to quality audiocassette, CD, or video recordings.

Before making any form of recordings, permission must be granted by the copyright owners. Write the publishing companies and ask permission to duplicate presentations for non-profit purposes. Most publishing companies will allow a few amateur copies to be made. A convenient source is the Church Music Publishers Association, P.O. Box 158992, Nashville, TN 37215. For a fee of $2.00, CMPA will supply a current list of many sacred music publishers. For further information call (615) 791-0273.

Share the Joy

Word of mouth is the most effective church advertising. Successful music leaders train their choir and other church members to utilize their circle of influence for new choir and church prospects. When choir members share positive ministry news, they are as effective as any advertising medium. Verbal invitations to coworkers, neighbors, family, and friends aid visibility and evangelism. When a prospective choir member first experiences an exceptional concert, he or she probably will attend a worship service.

X

OFFER CONTINUING EDUCATION

Change is the greatest challenge church music programs face today. Many declining churches choose to avoid it, while growing churches seem to embrace it.

Continuing education provides the knowledge and skills to overcome the fear of change. Effective churches offer educational opportunities to help the music staff develop as music leaders who can continually challenge their musical groups and themselves.

Learn New Techniques and Trends

Because appropriate leadership techniques vary according to the size of the group, successful music leaders are skilled in both small and large group dynamics.

Usually, small group leadership is shared democratically with choir members, whereas large group leadership requires the director to take the initiative and lead. Large churches may have several large choirs. These groups require not only skilled direction but also intricate scheduling and additional lay leadership development (choir officers and assistants).

Choir evangelism also varies with church size. Lyle Schaller has asserted:

> Everyone knows it is far easier to enlist ten members to form a choir in a 100-member church than it is to recruit even 60, much less one hundred choir members, in the 1,000-member congregation. . . .
> The democratic choir director builds small choirs. The big choirs are developed by initiating and directive leaders.[1]

Since the 1980s, scheduling trends have changed. In the past rehearsals usually were scheduled around available staff time. Today, overcommitted boomers require concurrent and consecutive programming that meets their scheduling needs (see chapter 6). Also, choir rehearsal transportation is a major problem for both dual working parents and single parents. Because of these and other current social trends, churches must offer their music leaders educational opportunities that teach them how to address these needs.

Sharpen Essential Skills

Overcommitted choir directors often have difficulty finding the time to develop leadership, conducting, vocal, and instrumental skills among the choir members. Educational events allow them "focus time" to set priorities and a reprieve from the usual routine.

Certainly, a few voice lessons do not develop the next Sandi Patti any more than several conducting classes produce another John Williams. Yet, attendance at quality education events increases the confidence and self-esteem of most music leaders.

Educational events also sharpen skills and increase applicable information that benefits the choir. These events allow choir directors to review music and learn new leadership techniques.

The interaction with other colleagues often provides information as valuable as that offered by the workshop leaders.

Continuing educational courses often are available in metropolitan areas. Though workshops are easier for busy music leaders to fit into their schedule, periodic attendance at a quality higher education class is always beneficial. Fortunately, some churches offer sabbaticals to their clergy.

Learn About New Instruments

Effective continuing music education offers information and training for newly developed instruments. Each instrument serves as a valuable tool for worship and evangelism.

The most versatile instrument used today is the synthesizer. Its continual evolution has cost countless musicians job opportunities and scared traditional musicians into hyperventilation. However, workshops and most music equipment stores will provide adequate training on the synthesizer and other electronic instruments to church musicians upon request.

The synthesizer is an incredible electronic device that instantly connects with boomers. Their ears are accustomed to the synthesizer's wide range of mimicking capabilities as well as its numerous unique and combination sounds. With MIDI (Musical Instrumental Digital Interface), several electronic instruments can record or play together at the same time. Some synthesizers actually "sample" real instrument sounds and reproduce them like a CD recording. A quality synthesizer easily functions within any musical style.

Many churches use electronic drum machines instead of live percussion instruments. The drum tracks are prerecorded by a MIDI sequencer that sets the rhythm of the music while one or more musicians play additional instruments. Drum machines allow total volume control and rhythmic perfection, regardless of the church's acoustics.

A MIDI sequencer allows several electronic instruments to "talk to each other." Quality sequencers are actually musical computers. They serve as multitrack recorders with capabilities for editing; sound, tempo, and key altering; transposing; and music printing. With the push of a few sequencer and synthesizer buttons, one person can create an entire orchestral accompaniment. These versatile components allow even small churches to develop a unique musical attraction for visitors.

Learn About Audio, Video, and Lighting Systems

Effective clergy follow technological advances and educate themselves about new communicative worship tools. Quality audio, video, and lighting systems instantly "connect" with church visitors.

Sound equipment, an effective worship tool, is an ever-changing phenomenon. Power amplifiers that once weighed as much as fifty pounds now weigh less than ten pounds and have twice the power. Digital audiotape (DAT) machines record and play back with incredible clarity and without "generation loss" (diminishing sound presence). These and other efficient sound equipment components allow choirs and soloists to offer presentations that sound like professional recordings. Music equipment stores generally offer some sound equipment training when a purchase is made. Seminars on the use of sound equipment more often are held in metropolitan areas.

Though the church musicians may not know how to operate video equipment, they should be aware of its tremendous capabilities and impact. Baby boomers are visually trained. Not only do most of their homes have multiple televisions, but many also have VCRs and big screen TVs with "Dolby Pro-Logic" surround sound. These cultural changes are altering the way many churches worship.

Using a large video screen during worship serves several purposes.

- Hymns and praise chorus songs can be projected for congregational singing. Persons with poor eyesight can easily read the words.
- Congregational singing is improved because people are looking up rather than singing down into their hymnals. Also, they do not have to fumble through the bulletin to find page numbers or to follow the order of worship.
- Biblical pictures can be superimposed as a background to the specific hymn or song. These pictures can increase the effectiveness of dramas and concerts.
- During announcements, showing a few video slides of the youth choir tour or other program experiences generates visibility and evangelism for those groups.
- Once a video screen becomes "sanctified" (accepted), it helps limit bulletin size. Many churches have turned their Sunday morning bulletins into bulky information booklets.

Video screens allow worship to flow and appear spontaneous. Attenders become "extra-dependent" rather than "inner-dependent." *Effective worship removes barriers to God.*

With the increasing popularity of musical dramas and pageants, music leaders need to learn about theatrical lighting. The most efficient systems are controlled from one location, usually adjacent to the sound control panel or mixer (see chapter 4).

Many new lighting systems are computer operated and allow tremendous flexibility for worship services, concerts, dramas, and weddings. Less expensive systems should provide at least dimming capabilities for several chancel locations. For example, a quality lighting system allows the flexibility to change from one chancel drama scene to another without requiring a curtain. While lighting is dimmed over a soloist in one location, it can gradually become brighter over an ensemble twenty feet away. Regardless of the lighting system, centralize all controls.

Seek and Review Effective Music Sources

Workshops, seminars, and choral reading sessions usually are excellent short-term music education events. For maximum information and results, successful music ministers attend those events and higher education classes that are geared to the size of their church.

Experienced music ministers attend services or events of growing churches with effective music programs. Also, they may make an appointment with the minister of music of these churches to pick his or her brain for information and effective music.

Effective music ministers subscribe to several music publishers or distributors that offer new, "cutting edge" music and follow the sales statistics of the most popular selections. They also establish relationships with the music department persons at Christian bookstores, asking to be notified about any outstanding music reviewed.

Experienced choir leaders continually seek out music that is motivating and inspiring. This dynamic has nothing to do with who the composer is, the musical content and style, or when it was written. The criteria for inspirational Christian music is based on a missional directive. Effective music leaders offer "divine encounters" through quality music selections and excellent presentations. If the selection is not spiritually motivating or is presented poorly, the entire congregation may remain untouched by God's presence.

Growing churches are indigenous. They successfully communicate the gospel to the cultures they serve. Music leaders must be knowledgeable about the quality sacred music that exists in each musical style in order to meet the needs of today's congregations. *Christian music that touches hearts, changes lives!*

Notes

I. Witness the Role

1. George Barna, *The Frog in the Kettle: What Christians Need to Know About Life in the Year 2000*, ed. Ron Durham (Ventura, Calif.: Regal Books, 1990), p. 44.
2. Kennon L. Callahan, *Twelve Keys to an Effective Church* (San Francisco: Harper, 1987), p. 27.
3. Lyle E. Schaller, "Music in the Large Church," *Choristers Guild Letters* 31, no. 7 (March 1980): 51.
4. George G. Hunter III, *The Contagious Congregation: Frontiers in Evangelism and Church Growth* (Nashville: Abingdon Press, 1979), p. 108.
5. Donald A. McGavran and Winfield C. Arn, *Ten Steps for Church Growth* (New York: Harper & Row, 1977), p. 76.
6. Lyle E. Schaller, "The Ministry of Music and Church Growth," *Choristers Guild Letters* 36, no. 2 (October 1985): 25.
7. Rhonda J. Edge and Barbara Sanders, *How to Lead Preschoolers in Muscial Activities* (Nashville: Convention Press, 1991), p. 21.
8. Tony Campolo and Gordon Aeschliman, *50 Ways You Can Share Your Faith* (Downers Grove, Ill.: InterVarsity Press, 1992), p. 114.

II. Hire the Most Gifted Leaders

1. Kennon L. Callahan, *Twelve Keys to an Effective Church* (San Francisco: Harper, 1987), p. 48.
2. Ibid.
3. Ibid., p. 51.
4. George Barna, *The Frog in the Kettle: What Christians Need to Know About Life in the Year 2000* (Ventura, Calif.: Regal Books, 1990), p. 144.
5. Robert H. Mitchell, *Ministry and Music* (Louisville: Westminster John Knox, 1978), p. 16.

III. Establish a Growth Budget

1. Marvin D. Maxwell, Mom's Musician's General Store, 2920 Frankfort Avenue, Louisville, KY 40206.

2. Kenny Deweese, Far-Out Music, 2008 Coopers Lane, Jeffersonville, IN 47130.
3. Fred Helm, Music Warehouse, Inc., 3204 Bardstown Road, Louisville, KY 40205.
4. Hardy Martin, Allen-Martin Video Productions, 9701 Taylorsville Road, Louisville, KY 40299.

IV. Develop Other Leaders and Support Groups

1. Carl F. George, *Prepare Your Church for the Future* (Grand Rapids: Baker Books, 1991), p. 120.
2. Lyle E. Schaller, "Music in the Large Church," *Choristers Guild Letters* 31, no. 7 (March 1980): 49.
3. George, *Prepare Your Church for the Future*, p. 99.

V. Present a Variety of Musical Styles

1. George G. Hunter III, *How to Reach Secular People* (Nashville: Abingdon Press, 1992), p. 151.
2. Donald P. Hustad, *Jubilate! Church Music in the Evangelical Tradition* (Carol Stream, Ill.: Hope Publishing, 1981), p. 202.
3. J. Howard Griffith, "Wedding Bells Ring for Pipe Organ and Computer," *Net Results* 15, no. 8 (August 1994): 6.
4. Kennon L. Callahan, *Twelve Keys to an Effective Church* (San Francisco: Harper, 1987), pp. 27-28.
5. Herb Miller, "Singing the Wondrous Story," *Net Results* 12, no. 11 (November 1991): 12.

VI. Provide Assimilation

1. Carl F. George, *Prepare Your Church for the Future* (Grand Rapids: Baker Books, 1991), pp. 31-33.
2. George Barna, *The Frog in the Kettle: What Christians Need to Know About Life in the Year 2000* (Ventura, Calif.: Regal Books, 1990), p. 39.
3. Joel Mikell, et al., *Leading Youth Choirs* (Nashville: Convention Press, 1988), p. 29.
4. George, *Prepare Your Church for the Future*, p. 35.
5. Robert L. Bast, "Church Music and Church Growth," *Net Results* 12, no. 6 (June 1991): 21.
6. Lyle E. Schaller, "Music in the Large Church," *Choristers Guild Letters* 31, no. 7 (March 1980): 50.
7. Barna, *The Frog in the Kettle*, p. 218.
8. Ibid., p. 219.

VII. Offer Effective Rehearsals and Presentations

1. George Barna, *The Frog in the Kettle: What Christians Need to Know About Life in the Year 2000* (Ventura, Calif.: Regal Books, 1990), p. 44.
2. Ibid.

VIII. Offer Special Presentations and Events

1. George Barna, *User Friendly Churches: What Successful Churches Have in Common and Why Their Ideas Work*, ed. Ron Durham (Ventura, Calif.: Regal Books, 1991), p. 46.
2. Ibid., p. 34.
3. Bill Owens, *The Revelations Choir Tour Information Booklet*, author manuscript, pp. 1-8.

IX. Create Visibility

1. Kennon L. Callahan, *Twelve Keys to an Effective Church* (San Francisco: Harper, 1987), p. 81.
2. Ibid.
3. Bill Owens, "The Neighborhood Flier Ministry: An Effective, Inexpensive Evangelism Tool," *Net Results* 13, no. 12 (December 1992): 2. Reprinted by permission.

X. Offer Continuing Education

1. Lyle E. Schaller, "Music in the Large Church," *Choristers Guild Letters* 31, no. 7 (March 1980): 49-50.

Endorsements

Playing on the imagery of light and shadows, Dr. Effler brings clarity to the arena of pastoral counseling by examining God's interaction with the created world described in Genesis. Effler lays out eight principles, which he refers to as the Genesis Model for Christian counseling. Clarifying the differences between clinical counseling/therapy and pastoral counseling, he utilizes the fields of academic psychology and counseling and encourages Christian counselors to draw from these disciplines while addressing the complex, broken world in which we all live. *Shadows* engages readers with its personal tone while providing pertinent information about the field of pastoral counseling. An unexpected, but pleasant, surprise is the focused attention Effler gives to Christian counselors themselves, especially sagacious concerning their own "blind spots." This is a "how-to" book in one sense, yet it is also a valuable resource for examining one's own spirituality and relationship with Christ, especially within the context of pastoral counseling.

Terry Cross, PhD, Dean of the School of Religion and Professor of Systematic Theology, Lee University

Get ready for a journey into God's rest. *Out from the Shadows* is a unique combination of prophetic insight and spirit-led psychology that will bring healing to your soul. Rich with biblical foundation, real-life examples, and practical tools, both the novice and spiritual veterans will gain fresh insight from this sensitively written book. Doug Addison, Prophetic life coach, author of *Understand Your Dreams Now* and *Personal Development God's Way,* Dougaddison.com

Out from the Shadows is intelligently written, is true to the academic nature of a career in psychology, and presents a strong foundation for biblical and spiritual counselors. As a student of psychology with a calling to counsel, I am deeply indebted to the wisdom and information presented here. I know I will use this text's insights for years to come.

Alexis, Senior psychology major, Lee University

Dr. Effler illustrates a clear and understandable psychological and spiritual picture of where families are living today. As an In-Home Counselor and Case Manager, coming face-to-face with children and families living in their own "shadows", I have been helped by the practical, sound and effective interventions that have come from years of study, personal experience, and deep dependence on the guidance from the Holy Spirit. *Out From the Shadows* is an invaluable tool for those in the business of helping people through everyday decision making and, through more complex tragedies that people often encounter.

Stephen Kawakami: In-Home Counselor and Case Manager
at Camelot Care Centers South East Tennessee Region

While in Dr. Effler's Pastoral Counseling class in my senior year, I got up the courage to break off a destructive relationship that was killing me on the inside. The material presented, found in this text, is not about the material; it is about learning and choosing to live life differently.

Carmen, former Pastoral Counseling student, Lee University

As has been said, "If you don't know what to do, you do what you know." Bill's book helps us know just "what to do" in the "shadow times" of our life. This is a great resource for any of us on this journey of life.

Dr. Mark Brewer
President, The Ministry Lab Network, ministrylabmission.com

Out From the Shadows is a manual that clearly directs people onto pathways for increased Biblical discernment and empathetic caregiving. Dr. Effler applies the Creation story to the counseling setting in fresh new ways that in fact becomes a searchlight for persons wishing to pursue previously unexplored pain.

Lynne B. Grady, Ph.D.
Director of Counseling and Psychological Services
Young Harris College

Any counselor, educator, or pastor who calls themselves a growing and maturing Christian will discover *Out from the Shadows* to be a challenge to focus on healing their own emotional wounds as they continue to improve their ability to help others form an ever-deepening relationship with Christ.

Mike Speakman, LISAC, Licensed Substance Abuse Counselor, and author of *The Four Seasons of Recovery for Parents of Alcoholics and Addicts*. Mr. Speakman can be reached at mike@speakmancoaching.com.

Out from the Shadows is an indispensable resource for all those engaged in pastoral and professional counseling as well as anyone who longs to heal a hurting heart. Dr. Bill Effler combines scholarly precision, clinical experience, and spiritual insight that results in a practical road map for pastors and counselors seeking a holistic model of counseling.

Kevin Wallace, Senior Pastor, Redemption Point Church

Out From the Shadows

Biblical Counseling Revealed
in the Story of Creation

Dr. Bill Effler

WESTBOW®
PRESS
A DIVISION OF THOMAS NELSON
& ZONDERVAN

WestBow Press books may be ordered through booksellers or by contacting:

WestBow Press
A Division of Thomas Nelson & Zondervan
1663 Liberty Drive
Bloomington, IN 47403
www.westbowpress.com
1 (866) 928-1240

ISBN: 978-1-4908-6074-9 (sc)
ISBN: 978-1-4908-6076-3 (hc)
ISBN: 978-1-4908-6075-6 (e)

Library of Congress Control Number: 2014920780

Printed in the United States of America.

WestBow Press rev. date: 01/13/2015

Dedication

To all those who have helped me emerge
from my own shadows,
and to those committed to helping
others emerge from theirs,
I dedicate this book.

Give me power, dear Lord,
to speak the truth straightforwardly,
so that others may be built up in faith,
hope and love....
Teach me therefore, sweet Lord,
how to restrain the restless,
comfort the discouraged,
and support the weak.
Teach me how
to suit myself to
everyone according to
their nature, character and disposition;
give me,
an ability to understand
and willingness to receive....

Aelred, abbot of Rievaulx, England, 1109–1167

I am the LORD your God,
who rescued you from the land of Egypt,
the place of your slavery.

Exodus 20:2 NLT

The world breaks
everyone and afterwards
many are strong
at the broken places.
Ernest Hemingway

There is little danger that
we will take
this [ministry]
to fanatical extremes.
Our far greater danger
is that
we will
remain
content
to work and minister
on an almost totally human level.
Wesley L. Duewel

Contents

Part I
To Know:
A Biblical Foundation for Counseling

Part II
To Do:
The Genesis Model for Counseling

PART I

To Know:
A Biblical Foundation
for Counseling

Preface

I share a beloved quote from Margaret Thatcher: "As God once said, and I think rightly ..." Jesus is just a straight shooter. In each and every life, there will be pressures, trials, wounds, and baggage. But we were never meant to walk in the shadows *alone.*

In my family's possession is an antique double-oxen yoke, fashioned for two to work together. Jesus asks us to take His yoke, to transfer our heavy burdens onto His strong shoulders. He has also asked us to be yoked with others in order to set fellow prisoners free.

This, I believe, is deep in Bill's heart. He wants to share the light that dispels the shadows. Bill has personally experienced the cords of the grave coiled around him. It takes "Jesus with skin on" to remove the rags of death. Although our God may make darkness His covering, He speaks forth light and life, binding up the brokenhearted and setting captives free.

Bill's intent is to encourage and guide more of us to seek and share wholeness and freedom—God's desire for us ... and I think rightly.

Kristen Effler
Chattanooga, Tennessee
Summer 2014

Song of Hope

You were buried deep and hidden,
I was kept in silence.
Withdrawal were the words you spoke,
Mistrust my best defense.
His secret things He longs to share
With those who see them not.
Our secret things we cannot bear
Their darkness leads to rot.
But in the light of love,
With a song of hope,
There's a sword raised high
And a piercing cry … freedom!

We journeyed apart in our dance of fears.
As He watched over our steps and caught our tears,
He waited.
He knew within us the unknown treasures,
But our blinded hearts sought other measures,
Ill-fated.
His redemption He longs to give
To those who need His shield,
Yet rejection wouldn't let us live
As broken vessels healed.

But in His bright love,
With a song of hope,
Two swords raised high
A deliverance cry ... we cry freedom!

Now I see you and you see me
Naked and unashamed.
Now I touch you and you hold me
In a dance He has ordained.
With hurts no longer hostage, the past is what it was,
And risen from the ashes, a new-born love, because,
With a song of hope,
Two swords raised high
Come a victorious cry ... precious
freedom!

Kristen T. Effler
Chattanooga, Tennessee
January 2008

Acknowledgments

The Lord has always placed me in proximity to people who are in great pain. I have discovered that the agony expressed by others often triggers an inner anguish within me. I have always studied and sought the help of skilled counselors; all I have ever wanted is to learn more about myself and how I might best help others. My desire to understand and interpret my own "shadows" has been a lifelong journey for me ... and I am okay with that.

First and foremost, I want to acknowledge my wife, Kristen. She has seen the darkest side of me, so the brightest side rightly belongs to her. Early on in the writing of this manuscript, she said, "The world does not need another book on counseling. Write this one *straight*." Her wisdom has served me well.

Second, to my three grown children—Emily and her dear husband, John Michael, your imaginations and abilities to create are a blessing to watch. The world is a richer place because of you. Brady, more of this book belongs to you than any other; I am proud to be your dad. You have journeyed hard and valiantly. Kelly, Mom and I have been your roomates, friends, and cheerleaders; continue to live your life wide open—*live your dreams!* I know you will.

For the past fourteen years, it has been my privilege to teach pastoral counseling students at Lee University; they have been my lab rats, academic and emotional warriors, "early readers," and constant encouragers to get this material into book form. Well ... here it is!

Someone said, "There is no good writing, only good rewriting." I therefore acknowledge Sarah Webb, who served as the lead editor of this manuscript and who painstakingly "soldiered through" multiple rewrites and on through to the production phase of publication. I also want to acknowledge the editorial and production team at Westbow Publishers for putting this project into its final form. Dale Johnston wonderfully rendered *Shadows* with his personal artistic cover interpretation and also provided needed interior creativity. Thanks, Dale!

Gloria in excelsis Deo!
Bill Effler
Chattanooga, Tennessee
Fall 2014

Author's Introduction

Transcending My Shadows

The Parable of the Shadow

The beach has always been a place where the concerns of life seem to all but disappear for me. On one of these escapes, I stood momentarily, ankle deep, in the opal-colored ocean as the tide slowly swallowed the sand beneath my feet. I barely noticed the sun's final approach to the horizon. It was as if the sun's fading rays were offering me a gift at day's end. It was on this occasion that I discovered the "Parable of the Shadow."

As I had begun my late afternoon saunter on "shadow day," I walked directly into the sun; the South Carolinian breezes gently cooled my face. As I glanced back, I observed that the footprints that had marked my steps had been absorbed by the incoming tide. I also saw my shadow; it seemed so big. My heart became imprisoned by an imperfect replica, an emotional stalker that would not let me go. The "Parable of the Shadow" taught me that as long as I walk facing the "light," I will see no shadow. Conversely, when I *turn away from* the "light," I will be viciously reminded of whom I once was. That day, I came to realize that only "light" can provide direction, point to a desired destination, and silence the accuser's voice that maligns the true meaning and existence of who I am in Christ. Of greatest significance, my "shadow" is not who I am, nor how God sees me. Hence, part of my life's journey has been to learn how to come "out from the shadows."

My Shadowlands

Originally from southern California but living in northern California at the time, I thought I heard, "Move south." (I had no plans to move *back to* the Los Angeles area.) God said, "Wrong south." Having no prospects for full-time employment, no familial ties to the South, and no actual concrete direction, our family migrated to an unfamiliar land. Chattanooga, Tennessee, would become a place where shadows would edge into my life, yet the darkness would be transcended by a powerful light. God would move in ways that I had never experienced before. After moving from California to Tennessee, I opened a private counseling practice and was later invited to join a group practice of counseling professionals. Counseling was the initial way that I supported my family, but within one year's time, with no prior university teaching experience, I was extended the opportunity to teach at Lee University, in Cleveland, Tennessee, on a full-time basis.[1]

One of the classes I have taught these past fourteen years is a senior-level course called Pastoral Counseling. In looking back over my entire life, it is so interesting to see how God has used everything (God never wastes anything) that I have been a part of—pastor, church and business consultant,[2]

---

[1] I am deeply indebted to Lee University for being part of God's illuminating presence in my life. I am, in part, the person I am today because of this caring community. I am a tenured associate professor of pastoral studies in the School of Religion at Lee University and serve as a strengths vocational advisor in the Center for Calling and Career.

[2] Over thirty years ago, the Reverend Dr. Bob Pitman invited me to join his church staff as minister of education. In later years, Bob would invite me

and intake counselor at a residential treatment facility[3]—to uniquely prepare me to teach this class. In my early years as an instructor, I persistently researched a wide variety of pastoral counseling textbooks[4] (and still do) that would best fit the students' needs. During my research, I developed and later put into written form an approach to counseling that I have titled "The Genesis Model" for pastoral counselors.[5]

The Genesis Model showcases eight specific principles. Each principle identifies a specific feature of God's character, which I have tailored to the counseling environment. *Out from the Shadows* presents a different path toward gaining personal growth and counseling skills. This journey is challenging and may cause you to ask questions never before considered. In fact, as I have written, God has taken me to places that I have never sojourned before; I have simply chased after His presence. My prayer is for a new level of freedom in your life—a freedom previously unknown, a fresh discovery of God's goodness. At the heart of the matter is this: are you willing to do what you have never before done so that you can have what you have only dreamed of? If so, read on.

Out from the Shadows is a cord of three strands. First, this volume is an *academic inquiry* for those engaged in counseling, mentoring, or guiding people. (The guidance I speak of here may be in the formal setting of a counseling office or the

---

to join a team of people that he had founded, called the Knox Fellowship. There I would serve as the vision casting director. The ministry of Knox Fellowship was committed to bringing revitalization to local churches. Through these many years, Bob has personally exemplified the maxim, "Don't give up on people that others have thrown under the bus."

[3] After pastoring for eighteen years, the Lord opened a door for me to labor at the Salvation Army Adult Residential Rehabilitation Center in Healdsburg, California, as an intake counselor. While there, Treatment Director Mike Speakman uncovered a "shadow-side" of myself I had never known existed. This setting was another place of deep healing for me and, in part, why I am committed to what is found in this book.

[4] A counseling bibliography is included at the back of the book.

[5] A diagram of this model is in the Appendix.

personal encouragement extended to a business colleague.) I offer both practical and professional direction to mental health providers, pastors, and laypersons who are regularly involved in "caregiving" relationships.[6] I have taken the necessary time to cite or reference scholarly sources[7] that pertain to counseling issues. I also direct readers to secondary sources so that further study and reflection can be accomplished. I have relied heavily on the disciplines of biblical scholarship[8] and positive psychology.[9] During my writing, when I had questions that fell into either of these disciplines, I consulted biblical scholarship and successful mental health practitioners so as to ensure accurate information.[10]

Second, my academic inquiry in the field of pastoral counseling is supported with clear *biblical application*. When I was first asked to teach the pastoral counseling classes at Lee University, I thought, *"How might I develop lectures, identify topics, and create a curriculum that would be most helpful to these future leaders?"* My heart responded, *At the beginning.* I questioned, "as *in* Genesis *beginning?"* Next came one of

---

[6] I served the Southeastern Tennessee Board of the Alzheimer's Association, training caregivers of Alzheimer's patients in the areas of burnout prevention and self-care.

[7] In the next chapter, I will discuss specific differences between licensed counseling professionals and pastors who counsel. I will also introduce basic counseling issues that specifically pertain to pastors.

[8] My own personal foundation stones in theology were deeply rooted in reformed theology. Today, I have integrated into both my theology and "praxis" thinking found in the charismatic, Pentecostal, and prophetic arenas.

[9] Martin E. P. Seligman is considered one of the early pioneers in the field of positive psychology. His contribution of the concept of "learned helplessness" and its interrelatedness to depression was developed under Dr. Aaron Beck at the University of Pennsylvania. See the glossary of terms for a more complete definition.

[10] I want to thank my colleagues in the School of Religion and in the School of Psychology at Lee University in Cleveland, Tennessee, for their insightful input. I am also very grateful for the guidance of Dr. Bill Leonard, Director of Ministerial Care for the Church of God, who is certified in Critical Incident Stress Management.

the quickest answers to prayer I have ever had: *Yes, you will find your needed direction in the book of Genesis ... and more.*

The first two chapters of the first book of the Bible outline a wonderful eight-step approach for those who counsel. The reader will find in the table of contents that Chapters Five through Twelve are a stage-by-stage unpacking of each counseling phase as described in Genesis Chapters 1 and 2.[11] The Genesis Model for counseling is unapologetically biblical[12] and painstakingly practical; it is deep in Scripture and wide in application. This "deep and wide" approach is dedicated to my students, who are forever asking me, "How do we do ...?" or, "When do I ...?" I have also been asked, "Have you actually *done* this?"

Third, this book is a *personal reflection.* This manuscript represents the better part of thirty years of cumulative professional and personal experience. I document not only practical ideals I have learned about counseling but also personal experiences where I have seen God move in powerful ways within the counseling relationship. As one journeys through life, if carefully listening, a whispering from God in the midst of public living will awaken a side previously unknown.[13] To be keenly aware of the activity of God[14] is to discover new aspects of one's own person. Every year I say to my counseling students, "This class is not about printed words you read in a book or counseling principles that you hear in the classroom. Rather, this class will be a mirror

> *To be keenly aware of the activity of God is to discover new aspects of one's own person.*

---

[11] See Table of Contents.

[12] I have chosen to use the New King James Version as my preferred translation, unless otherwise noted.

[13] Parker Palmer writes in his book *Let Your Life Speak,* "[Calling] is rooted in a deep distrust of selfhood and can only be corrected by an external force of virtue"(p. 10).

[14] The importance of being able to discern the activity of God in a counseling setting is described in every chapter of this book.

in which you learn to see yourself in an altogether different way." This is my heart's desire for this written work also.

During the writing of *Out from the Shadows*, my family and I experienced profound heartache as my twenty-five-year-old son was diagnosed with a rare form of cancer. Five months into his treatment, my wife, Kristen, awoke on New Year's Eve morning and said, "I am blind." Between Kristen's literal shadows and the "shadow of death" that threatened the life of our son, Brady, this book ceased becoming "another counseling book." I will convey our family's journey and exodus from our personal shadows over the duration of our time together.

> *Between Kristen's literal shadows and the "shadow of death" that threatened the life of our son, Brady, this book ceased becoming "another counseling book."*

My own initial graduate and postgraduate education in the field of theology and psychology was devoted to studying the developmental landscape of leaders, with an emphasis on masculine spirituality. I am grateful to Dr. Archibald Hart, both my master's and doctoral professor, who encouraged me to grow *deeper* in my personal faith and *look even more deeply* into my mental and emotional health.[15] I also want to acknowledge Steven Arterburn, Robert Hicks, Gordon Dalbey, Carol Gilligan, John Eldredge, Melanie Beattie, Dan Allender, Patrick Carnes, Henri Nouwen, Ruth Haley Barton, Brennan Manning and Larry Crabb, all of whom I have been in therapy with via their literary contributions.

---

[15] While at Fuller Theological Seminary in the early 1980s and later as a doctoral student in the 1990s, I was privileged to be a student of Dr. Archibald Hart. His contributions, especially in the area of masculine spirituality, addiction, and anger were groundbreaking; he encouraged me to always move past what was seen at the surface level. I share this same advice with my students today.

I profoundly want my readers to know that I approach both counseling and this writing as a "wounded healer."[16] In the words of Isaiah, I know "the Spirit of the Sovereign Lord is on me to set captives free."[17] Of equal importance, I too have been "the brokenhearted, the prisoner, the poor, the captive, the ruined, and the city long ago forgotten" who stood in tremendous need of a caring friend.[18] My audience for this book includes anyone who has a desire to bring peace to a hurting world. It has been a privilege to spend countless hours with persons who, although emotionally incarcerated, struggled to locate the key to their freedom. Their prison cells were fashioned from labyrinths of mental lies or emotional anguish. The people who chose personal freedom over self-imposed imprisonment have been an inspiration to me. Finally, I have deliberately and intentionally changed particular details in my examples so as to ensure complete anonymity. Any similarity the reader may find in the content of this book to actual events is purely coincidental.

---

[16] Henri Nouwen has had a profound influence on my life. He is the author of *The Wounded Healer* (New York: Doubleday, 1979).
[17] Isaiah 61:1 (NLT)
[18] Isaiah 61:1–2,4 (NLT)

Chapter 1

Mental Health Practitioners and Pastors Who Counsel: What's the Difference?

"I have come to believe that by and large the human family all has the same secrets, which are both very telling and very important to tell. They are telling in the sense that they tell what is perhaps the central paradox of our condition—that what we hunger for perhaps more than anything else is to be known in our full humanness, and yet that is often just what we also fear more than anything else."

Frederich Buechner, *Telling Stories*

Introduction

It is easy to confuse the services a pastor may call "counseling"[19] and those offered by a licensed clinical mental health professional (i.e., psychologist, psychiatrist, social worker, or marriage and family therapist). In some aspects,

---

[19] Some pastors may describe their approaches to counseling as spiritual guidance, mentoring, or encouragement, and some will use the specialized term *spiritual direction*. See David G. Benner, *Strategic Pastoral Counseling: A Short-Term Structured Model*. (Grand Rapids, MI: Baker, 1992.)

1

these two branches of counseling are similar; yet in others they are significantly different. This chapter seeks to describe rudimentary differences between pastors who counsel in their churches and the counseling services of licensed mental health professionals.

Licensed Mental Health Practitioners

One need go only as far as the Internet to discover an ample quantity of mental health providers.[20] Clinical psychologists, psychiatrists, social workers, and marriage and family therapists are licensed and regulated by various governmental boards and professional associations. Clinical counselors are mandated to meet certain basic educational and training requirements to obtain their licenses. This training is directly related to the scope and limitations of their practice and may or may not include some expression of religious content.

A key difference between pastors who offer counseling and licensed mental health providers is the range and emphasis of each professional's education.[21] Licensed therapists receive specific training as it relates to individual or family development (i.e., marriage counseling, relationship issues, sexuality, substance abuse and addiction, personality theory, life-span development, crises intervention, and vocational counseling). In addition to generalized areas of human behavior, areas of specialized focus or interest[22] (e.g., family

---

[20] In 2008, the US Department of Labor estimated that there were 120,000 mental health counselors in the United States with a projected 37 percent increase by 2020.

[21] In 1893, Henry Drummond instructed his theological students, saying, "The study of the soul in health and disease ought to be as much an object of scientific study and training as the health and diseases of the body." Quoted in Wayne Oates, *The Art of Pastoral Counseling* (Nashville: Broadman Press, 1959), 15.

[22] Other examples of specialized or focused training in counseling include counseling persons with autism, gender identity, ADHD, anger, and

counseling, counseling with teens, geriatric counseling, critical incident counseling) are also included in the training of a mental health professional. A variety of mental health professionals may provide services that include medication, residential care, and the utilization of various forms of testing.

David Benner summarizes the differences between licensed mental health providers and pastors that counsel by saying, "While pastors may have taken a course or two in pastoral psychology or counseling and possibly an internship or supervised experience in clinical pastoral education, their typical exposure to psychology is somewhat limited. Without advanced specialized training in psychotherapy, they should not, therefore, attempt long-term approaches to counseling that seek to change underlying personality structures or resolve deep-seated unconscious problems and conflicts."[23]

In trying to bring integration to professional counseling theory with a Christian-based orientation, researchers Shawn Patrick, John Beckenbach, and James Sells comment,

> Research exists that discusses the importance of spirituality in counseling, no research exists that specifically examines the boundaries between counseling and pastoral counseling. Since through research this issue has not been previously clarified, one can instead look towards academic definitions held by each profession to gain some clarity. Wicks and Parsons (1993) sum pastoral counseling as, " ... a response by a baptized person to the call to help others in a quite defined way." This "way" includes training in psychology and theology, understanding of clients' problems, creating the foundation for growth, and opening clients to receive God's grace (Wicks & Parsons, 1993). This view of pastoral counseling suggests

---

eating disorders.
[23] Benner, *Strategic Pastoral Counseling*, 32.

the pastoral counselor receives a specific training which includes understanding of mental and spiritual health. Also, the pastoral counselor must gain a specialized knowledge of clients and client concerns, all with the goal of assisting the client towards healing. As the quote suggests, healing is also a function of being prepared to receive God's grace.[24]

Another way to bring clarification to the differences between licensed counseling professionals and the counseling services offered by a pastor is to cite a concrete counseling scenario. One hallmark of a pastor who counsels is his or her readiness to include spiritual resources in the primary intervention.[25] For example, in working with a person who has intense anger, a pastor might help this person understand this issue by approaching the anger issue *spiritually*. A person might, for instance, come to understand that he becomes angry when he feels threatened or unsafe. The pastor might then encourage him to explore other sources of safety that he might draw upon (a sense of the presence of God, for example) rather than to use inappropriate expressions of anger to protect himself. It is not outside the practice of pastoral counseling training to also explore (in this case, anger) how anger was exhibited in the person's family when he was a young child.[26] Most

> *One hallmark of a pastor who counsels is his or her readiness to include spiritual resources in the primary intervention.*

---

[24] *Exploring the Boundaries between Counseling and Pastoral Counseling.* A Delphi Study, Department of Counseling, Adult and Health Education. Northern Illinois University. See Professional Issues in Counseling; an On-line Journal

[25] These resources will be described in Chapter Three, "Pastoral Counseling Defined."

[26] The impact that family-of-origin issues have in a person's life can be tremendous, for both positive and negative reasons. It is very difficult to determine to what extent a person's life challenges directly relate to

assuredly, a pastor would also share Scripture as one possible key that could unlock this person from his emotional prison.

On the other hand, a clinically trained and licensed psychotherapist addressing the very same issue, anger, might approach the client somewhat differently. The therapist might help the client understand the biological dynamics that are in play at the release time of their anger (learning to recognize the physical warning signs that anger is rising because of brain chemistry),[27] psychological implications (possible errant or irrational thought processes and/or emotional dynamics that underlie anger), and relational repercussions (relational tensions that trigger or maintain the anger and possible relational loss or harm).

A hybrid, specialized category within the professional mental health arena is that of Licensed Pastoral Counselor (LPC).[28] A licensed pastoral counselor usually has an undergraduate education, at least three years of education in a graduate program or seminary, and ongoing supervision by an experienced counselor. This individual will value religious ideals and teaching[29] and will incorporate spirituality into his or her therapeutic treatment. Behavioral science theories and methodologies[30] may also be integrated into the counseling

---

family-of-origin issues. However, to overlook this important element in an individual's personhood would be very short-sighted.

[27] We know that one part of the brain is called the amygdala. The function of the amygdala is analogous to an alarm clock. In the case of anger, the amygdala "rings out" or "sounds off," telling the body that something is not right.

[28] This degree requires both an undergraduate degree and graduate degree; ordination or recognition of a denomination or governing institution; documented completion of a supervised experience; and 375 hours of pastoral counseling with 175 hours of supervision. See the website for the American Association of Pastoral Counselors for more complete information. It should also be noted that this designation or certification of counseling is not recognized universally and needs to be verified on a state-by-state basis.

[29] *Religious values* can include any biblical ideal as presented in Scripture.

[30] Two examples of these methodologies include *cognitive emotive therapy,* which explores irrational distortions of thought that lead to emotional

setting. Most LPCs are certified or licensed by professional organizations, are often ordained persons of faith (ministers, rabbis, or priests), and are certified by one or more of the following clinical organizations:

- The American Association of Pastoral Counselors
- The American Association for Marriage and Family Therapists
- The Association for Clinical Pastoral Education
- The National Board for Certified Counselors and Affiliates

Pastors Who Counsel: Ten Reasons that Create a Need for Pastoral Counseling

We live in an increasingly conflicted world.[31] Regardless of age, social status, or religious orientation, people live with heightened levels of pain and anxiety.[32] Some research indicates that people who describe themselves as religious have just as many problems as those who claim no religious orientation.[33]

---

unrest, and *rational emotive behavior therapy,* which uncovers unhealthy emotions and replaces them with productive, rational alternatives. See the Glossary of Terms for further information.

[31] An estimated 22.1 percent of Americans age eighteen and older (about one in five) suffer from a diagnosable mental illness (National Institute of Mental Health, January 2001).

[32] One in every eight Americans age eighteen to fifty-four suffers from an anxiety disorder. This totals over 19 million people. Depressive disorders affect approximately 18.8 million American adults, or about 9.5 percent of the US population age eighteen and older in a given year. This includes major depressive disorder, dysthymic disorder, and bipolar disorder (NIMH. "The Numbers Count: Mental Illness in America," Science on Our Minds Fact Sheet Series).

[33] "Religiosity and Major Depression in Adults at High Risk: A Ten-Year Prospective Study." *American Journal of Psychiatry.* doi: 10.1176/appi. ajp.2011.10121823. Also, it is not uncommon for me to get mail from both present and former pastoral students who today describe their lives as "very far away from God."

Five foreseeable scenarios that lead people to seek help from their pastors include times of personal crisis (death of a loved one, unforeseen disappointment), need for guidance or spiritual growth (decision making, encouragement/assurance), problems in relationships (marriage or family counseling), ongoing or recurring issues (addiction, job loss, finances), and wanting someone to talk to (one of life's most basic needs). Because of this initial and partial list of counseling issues that pastors can predictably expect, there is a very real need for clergy to have the ability to recognize and interpret emotional and existential needs as they are presented in the counseling environment. Below, the reader will find in greater detail five additional counseling scenarios that pastors encounter on a regular basis.

First and foremost, pastoral counselors need to familiarize themselves with counseling literature that pertains to *divorce*. Divorce is nearly as common within church communities as it is among people who claim no religious affiliation.[34] Geographically, we know that divorce rates are markedly higher in what has been called the Bible Belt.[35] Also, some

---

[34] "While it may be alarming to discover that born again Christians are more likely than others to experience a divorce, that pattern has been in place for quite some time. Even more disturbing, perhaps, is when individuals experience a divorce, many feel their community of faith provided rejection rather than support and healing." George Barna commented that these results raise "questions regarding the effectiveness of how churches minister to families." Barna Project Director Meg Flammang comments, "We would love to be able to report that Christians are living very different lives and impacting the community, but ... in the area of divorce rates, Christian and non-church divorce rates continue to be the same." (Barna Research Group, 1999-DEC 21, at http://www.barna.org/)

[35] According to the *Boston Globe*, an AP report stated that the divorce rate in these conservative states is roughly 50 percent above that of other states. The ten Southern states with some of the highest divorce rates were Alabama, Arkansas, Arizona, Florida, Georgia, Mississippi, North and South Carolina, Oklahoma, and Texas. (*Boston Globe* 2004-OCT 31, http:/boston.com.)

studies show that divorce is very much a reality for many pastors.[36]

Second, pastors confront questions regarding *decision making.* It is common for a pastor to hear a statement such as, "I am considering (blank), and I don't know what to do. What do you think?" Research shows that the criteria for how self-professing Christians make a decision shows little difference from that of non-Churched individuals.[37]

Research shows that the criteria for how self-professing Christians make a decision shows little difference from that of non-Churched individuals.

Third, pastors can expect to deal with various expressions of *compensatory behavior*—any behavior or activity (e.g., habit, addiction, lying, isolating) that helps a person ease or alleviate discomfort.[38] CNN Health reported,

The prescription drug overdose epidemic just recently began appearing on the national radar.... In the United States someone dies of a prescription drug-related overdose about every 19 minutes. This epidemic affects every state in the nation and has hit hardest in places like Washington, Utah, Florida, Louisiana, Nevada and New Mexico. Kentucky and the Appalachian Ridge, generally, is one of the regions to feel the greatest devastation. Kentucky is

---

[36] A national survey of Protestant clergy, conducted in 1993 and 1994 by the Hartford Seminary, found that 25 percent of clergywomen and 20 percent of clergymen have been divorced at least once. (Cited in *Los Angeles Times*, July 1, 1995.)

[37] "We rarely find 'substantial differences' between the moral behavior of Christians and non-Christians." (http:/barna.org)

[38] In 2010, approximately 7.0 million persons were current users of psychotherapeutic drugs taken nonmedically (2.7 percent of the US population). Among adolescents, prescription and over-the-counter medications account for most of the commonly abused illicit drugs by high school seniors. See "Compensatory Behavior" in the Glossary of Terms for further understanding.

the fourth most medicated state in the nation, and it has the sixth highest rate of overdose deaths.[39]

A fourth counseling issue (very much related to the prevalent misuse of drugs and alcohol) with which pastors contend is the continued *demise of the nuclear family.* Again, CNN reported that, "according to 2010 Census data, more than 86,000 children in Kentucky are being raised by someone who is not their biological parent, mostly grandparents, and many blame those fractured families on prescription drugs."[40] Between 1980 and 1994, the birth rate for unmarried women ages fifteen to forty-four increased from twenty-nine to forty-six per 1,000. By 2011, children born to unmarried women constituted 41 percent of all births.[41] Further, we know that one in two children will live in a single-parent family at some point in childhood, one in three children is born to unmarried parents, one in four lives with only one parent, one in eight is born to a teenage mother, and one in twenty-five lives with neither parent.[42] These statistics on the demise of the nuclear family result in the following behaviors: (1) 75 percent of children/adolescents in chemical dependency hospitals are from single-parent families. (Center for Disease Control, Atlanta, GA); (2) 1 out of 5 children have a learning, emotional, or behavioral problem due to changes in the family system (National Center for Health Statistics); (3) more than one half of all youths incarcerated for criminal acts lived in one-parent families when they were children (Children's Defense Fund); (4) every seventy-eight seconds a teen attempts suicide; every ninety seconds one succeeds (National Center for Health Statistics); and (5) 63 percent of suicides are individuals from

---

[39] CNN Health, December 14, 2012.
[40] Ibid.
[41] 2012 Childtrendsdatatbank. org
[42] *The State of America's Children, 1998 Yearbook,* Children's Defense Fund

single-parent families (FBI Law Enforcement Bulletin—Investigative Aid).[43]

A fifth counseling reality that pastors will face has happened in our nation during the writing of this manuscript. Recently, our country has experienced horrific violence due to a shooting in a shopping mall in Oregon that left two dead and a second shooting in an elementary school in Connecticut with more than twenty fatalities. I include the counseling topic of violence for three reasons: (1) violence is a common reality (domestic violence, self-inflicted harm) in church communities; (2) during these horrific times, people will ask their pastors, "Where is God in this?" and pastors *must* have answers for this specific spiritual question, and (3) violence and injustice will continue to occur in any place where the church is silent. If pastors do not make the subject of violence and the confrontation of it a matter of priority, especially from the pulpit, our society will continue to get what it has always gotten—more violence.

> *The counseling that pastors, priests, and rabbis offer is about life direction, not psychotherapy.*

Divorce, decision making, compensatory behavior, the demise of the nuclear family, and various expressions of violence are five additional issues a local pastor will handle in the counseling office.[44] Like mental health professionals, ordained pastors (in churches), chaplains (e.g., Armed Forces, Police Department), and people working in Christian nonprofit organizations (e.g., rehabilitation centers)[45] are

---

[43] Rainbows is a nonprofit organization dedicated to helping teens and families during grief and loss.

[44] This is by no means an exhaustive list and is meant only to be seen as a starting place to expose the reader to a variety of counseling issues that will arise for pastors.

[45] One example of a Christian nonprofit organization that has a proven, successful track record in the area of substance abuse counseling is the Salvation Army, which has resident Adult Rehabilitation Centers all over the United States. A second example would be Teen Challenge, a resident

regulated or supervised by various governing structures with whom they are affiliated. Pastoral counseling performed by a pastor, priest, rabbi, or staff member of a particular organization utilizes scriptural resources as *the primary means* to help individuals resolve and bring to closure some type of trial in daily living. The counseling that pastors, priests, and rabbis offer is about life direction, not psychotherapy.[46]

Pastoral counseling has evolved even in my lifetime from a purely religious and spiritual counseling approach to counseling that integrates or includes the behavioral sciences.[47] Pastors or persons whose ministries emphasize counseling recognize the clear need for in-depth ongoing theological and psychological education coupled with hands-on training.[48] Pastors who spend a significant amount of time counseling often choose to enroll in additional postgraduate classes in counseling, attend professional conferences, and regularly connect with other mental health professionals for personal enrichment and development so as to keep pace with the world in which they live and work.[49] In looking at a pastor's educational background as compared to that of a licensed mental health professional, one can see

> *Pastors or persons whose ministries emphasize counseling recognize the clear need for in-depth ongoing theological and psychological education coupled with hands-on training.*

---

treatment program that seeks to help men and women attain freedom from substance abuse. I have worked with both of these programs.

[46] *Psychotherapy* is a general term that involves the treatment of emotional, behavioral, personality, and psychiatric disorders by a psychologist, psychiatrist, or another mental health provider. (Definition from the Mayo Clinic Hospital, Rochester, MN.)

[47] Giblin, P. (1996). Spirituality, marriage, and the family. *The Family Journal: Counseling and Therapy for Couples and Families, 4*, 1, 46–52.

[48] "While many individuals have the attributes to become extraordinary counselors, skills have to be cultivated and nourished if clinicians are to reach their full potential." (Gerald Juhnke, *Counseling Today*, December, 2012)

[49] See Phil Monroe, *Facing Ministry Challenges*, AACC 2011 Conference.

commensurate yet distinctly different education and training. I argue here that pastors can execute pastoral counseling with high levels of competency and effectiveness; lives will be changed because of their faithful, disciplined, and God-honoring pastoral presence.[50]

> *Pastors can execute pastoral counseling with high levels of competency and effectiveness; lives will be changed because of their faithful, disciplined, and God-honoring pastoral presence.*

Dr. Siang-Yang Tan, in his book *Lay Counseling: Equipping Christians for a Helping* Ministry, comments, "I ... strongly recommend that more biblical or biblically based models and approaches to lay Christian counseling be further developed and refined in the future. A key element in such models or approaches based on biblical truth should be the significance of the ministry of the Holy Spirit, including appropriate spiritual gifts and spiritual power in effective Christian caring and counseling ministries."[51]

Siang-Yang Tan argues that lay counseling is to be constructed on a biblical foundation and reliant on the person and presence of the Holy Spirit. These two vital aspects, the authority of Scripture and the presence of the Holy Spirit, are two precise litmus tests that establish the cutting-edge difference between mental health practitioners and pastors who counsel. Just as pastors desire to counsel, guide, mentor and encourage people in their counseling relationships through the power

> *The authority of Scripture and the presence of the Holy Spirit, are two precise litmus tests that establish the cutting-edge difference between mental health practitioners and pastors who counsel.*

---

[50] Pastors who continue to receive training and education in the area of mental health can be very effective in the services that they offer, yet many pastors feel ill equipped in handling some of the situations that come their way (Kollar, *Solution Focused Pastoral Counseling*).

[51] Siang-Yang Tan, *Lay Counseling: Equipping Christians for a Helping Ministry* (Grand Rapids, MI: Zondervan Publishing, 1991), 228.

and presence of the Holy Spirit, so licensed mental health professionals base their counseling practices upon their specific educational training and supervisory relationships. I want to be clear that I am not advocating a bifurcated image of these two professional approaches. However, each discipline, with counseling provided by a pastor and counseling executed by a mental health expert, has its own clear foundation or origin. The time has long since come for pastors who counsel to stop saying that psychologists are "of the devil" (I have heard this!) and for mental health professionals to stop discrediting or minimizing the work done by pastors by saying, "A pastor does not offer *real* counseling."

The Context for Pastors that Counsel

I have identified the educational preparation of a counselor, Christian or otherwise, as a significant element that helps explain the difference between what pastors seek to accomplish while counseling and the counseling that is provided by mental health professionals. Having said this, I feel it would be helpful, particularly for pastors, to describe the context that "births" the pastoral counseling opportunity.

As a pastor, I came to discover that the pastoral counseling context can differ from that of a mental health counseling context. There were times in my own ministry when I heard, "Pastor Bill, can I make an appointment to see you?" Later, much to my surprise, I learned that I actually had said something in a sermon that created a desire within my parishioners to explore personal concerns. Yes, pastors, some people actually do listen to your sermons! I was also surprised in a second way. On numerous occasions, a church member, after a counseling appointment with me, would tell a friend about his or her experience. The new would-be counselee would then say, "He sounds so helpful and down to earth. I think I'd like to talk to him." Something in this seeker's life led to the decision to pursue counseling from a pastor. A pastor's sermon or a church member who tells a friend about a positive counseling experience are two ways people find their way to a pastor's office. More times than not, a pastor is absolutely unaware of the emotional catalyst that is operating within the seeker. This is an important truth for pastors to know.

Dr. David Benner provides a diagram in his book *Strategic Pastoral Counseling*[52] that illustrates the context for pastoral counseling. I have adapted Benner's diagram (found below) to suit my own purposes so as to explain three common experiences for those who seek guidance from a pastor; I call them entry points. Entry points precede a pastoral counseling session. I will use Acts 8: 26–40 as my biblical context. The story of Philip and the man from Ethiopia demonstrates how the pastoral counseling stage is set by the activity of the Holy Spirit and is consummated by the willingness and availability of God's servants.

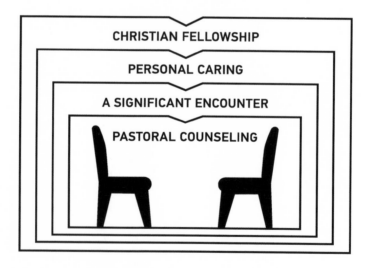

Acts 8:26–41: The Context for Pastoral Counseling

Christian Friendship

Scripture has many references that pertain to the subject of Christian friendship. Perhaps the first allusion to the idea of human friendship in Scripture is found in Genesis where God creates a partner or "friend" for Adam.[53] Proverbs 18:24 says, "a true friend stays closer than a brother." Also from Proverbs is this quote: "A friend loves at all times, and a brother is born for adversity."[54] Jesus referred to his disciples as friends.[55] Writing from the Island of Patmos, John writes of Jesus saying, "Behold, I stand at the door and knock. If anyone hears my voice and opens the door, I will come in to him and we will share a meal together as *friends*."[56] Further, the gospel writer John says that Christian friendship includes loving one another, sacrificing for one another, remembering what is important to another, modeling the aspect of mutuality, taking our confidences to one another, and working together on things of eternal significance.[57] When a person experiences any *one* of the above-mentioned Christian friendship qualities, people in need are helped.

Christian friendship and the potential of a transformed life begin with being where God needs us to be.

In the story of Philip and the man from Ethiopia, we read that Philip was instructed by an angel of the Lord to go south, down the desert road that runs from Jerusalem to Gaza. While on this journey, Philip received a second instruction from the angel of the Lord:

---

[53] Genesis 2:18 (NLT)
[54] Proverbs 17:17 (ESV)
[55] John 15:15
[56] Revelation 3:20 (NLT)
[57] John 15:14–17.

"Go over and walk beside the man …"[58] This is an example of establishing the first entry point in the above diagram. In the spirit of Christian friendship, Philip walks alongside a total stranger. Christian friendship and the potential of a transformed life begin with being where God needs us to be. If a person does not listen to God's leading, transformation can either be delayed or lost completely.

Personal Caring

Experiencing Christian friendship, validated by genuine personal caring, prepares an individual for the next entry point, number three—*a significant encounter.* Philip's story illustrates how Christian friendship, entry point number one (being present), can lead to entry point number two (personal caring). Once Philip was close enough to the man from Ethiopia, Philip could then establish what the man needed. Refamiliarize yourself with the illustration on the previous page. The context for pastoral counseling begins when a person is present in Christian friendship and continues by personal caring. A powerful way to demonstrate personal caring is by knowing the right questions to ask at the right time.

> *Do not assume that because you have spent time with a person and met some of his or her needs that the person you are talking with wants a closer relationship with you.*

Philip inquires of the traveler, "Do you understand what you are reading?"[59] The man becomes frustrated and says, ""How can I, unless someone instructs me?"[60] Luke then records that the man "urged Philip to come up into the carriage."[61] I want to pause here to make a very important behavioral observation.

---

[58] Acts 8:29 (NLT)
[59] Acts 8:30 (NLT)
[60] Acts 8:31a (NLT)
[61] Acts 8:31b (NLT)

Always, *always* wait for an invitation to get closer to a person. Do not assume that because you have spent time with a person and met some of his or her needs that the person you are talking with wants a closer relationship with you.

Significant Encounter

Luke records how Philip, beginning with the very Scripture that the man had been reading, answered the man's questions.[62] The story is clear that Philip spent time with the man, and he most likely talked about other matters pertaining to spiritual significance. The story culminates with Philip's baptizing the man.[63] To say the man encountered God would be an understatement. This is Luke's story, but this may not happen to us in just this fashion. A person may establish a Christian friendship and meet some of the needs of a friend or acquaintance. However, there will be other occasions where there is more transpiring in a person's life than a minister or friend or work colleague can address. Christian friendship, followed by deeper personal caring, may result in both persons realizing that the individual in greater need may benefit further by talking with a pastor. It is at this juncture that we then move to entry point number four, pastoral counseling.

Pastoral Counseling

Dan Montgomery describes pastoral counseling as a helping relationship between a religiously affiliated counselor and an individual, couple, or family who is seeking assistance for a specific need. Pastoral counselors include ordained ministers and consecrated professionals licensed in the field of counseling and therapy. The word *pastoral* indicates that

---

[62] Acts 8:35
[63] Acts 8:38

the services that are provided will include spiritual viewpoints and will keep in mind the values of the counselees, regardless of their faith affiliation. A respect for the faith dimension of human experience is an important contribution of the pastoral counseling movement to the mental health field. Pastoral counseling assumes that a counselor is committed to helping address emotional wounds, resolve conflicts, facilitate life transitions, and clarify values and purpose all through the lens of spiritually based principles.[64]

Final Thoughts: Mental Health Professionals and Pastors Who Counsel

People today live with increased levels of anxiety and will seek help through a variety of counseling models until their needs are met,[65] including ordained pastors and licensed mental health professionals. Both types of counselors must be equally prepared for a variety of problems that challenge people in our culture of increasing conflict.

There is another aspect of this "who goes to counseling?" puzzle. It must also be noted that not everyone will consider going to a counselor, whether it be a mental health expert or a clergy person.[66] There are well-established and deeply researched reasons that some people will not consider

---

[64] Dan Montgomery is a licensed therapist with over thirty years of counseling experience and is the coauthor of *The Self Compass: Charting Your Personality in Christ* (Montecito, CA: Compass Works, 2007).

[65] Seventy-eight percent of Americans said they would go to a counselor if he or she could help manage stress, and 54 percent of Americans said they would see a psychologist to prevent the day-to-day stress that can build up from becoming a problem (2012 US Census records). Bowdoin College reports that approximately 40 percent of its students seek out counseling while at school.

[66] See "Avoidance of Counseling: Psychological Factors That Inhibit Seeking Help" by David L. Vogel, Stephen R. Wester, and Lisa M. Larson, *Journal of Counseling & Development,* Fall 2007, Volume 85.

counseling. Research has identified five common reasons for this, which include social stigma ("What will people think?"), treatment fears (the concern the seeker has about how they would be treated in the counseling setting), fear of emotion (anxiety over expressing oneself or concern about not being able to express oneself), anticipatory risk ("What might I stand to lose?") and self-disclosure (the telling of a previously unknown fact about oneself).[67]

Brace yourself—my final reflections for this chapter are really a series of challenges or questions to those who say they practice "Christian counseling." During the writing of this particular portion of *Out From the Shadows,* I had meaningful, insightful, visceral, and constructive conversations with colleagues in the field of mental health. Committed Christian pastors who counsel are fortified with faith in Jesus Christ, guided by the Holy Spirit, and grounded in Scripture. Yet, based on the research that has been identified in this chapter, the number of mental health cases in our nation does not decline. Why?

If people are seeking a faith-based orientation to counseling, why do those seeking peace and freedom not find peace and freedom? Why is the divorce rate just as high within the church community as compared to the world in general? Why is it that a churchgoer goes to see his pastor at ten o'clock *sharp* for a counseling appointment and walks out of the same office at eleven o'clock *dull*? Is the lack of success seen in Christian counseling today due in part to Christian counselors' not keenly and appropriately utilizing their God-given skill set? What is the disconnect between what counselors say they believe about God's ability to set captives free and the established empirical statistics that reveal a staggering amount of people who still live in great pain?

---

[67] Ibid.

I believe that Christian counselors, in particular, need to take a long, hard look at how they practice that which they call counseling. Scripture tells us that Jesus is "the same yesterday, today and forever".[68] This prophetic promise is true. The same power that was available to the early church is available to the modern church and to the modern-day Christian counselor as well. However, contemporary challenges like autism,[69] varying forms of self-harm (e.g., cutting, eating disorders)[70], post-traumatic stress disorder,[71] and issues concerning gender orientation are not explicitly addressed in Scripture. What is a Christian counselor to do? The answer to this final question is expressly found throughout the remaining pages of this book. Those who call themselves Christian counselors must fundamentally learn anew the meaning of the word *disciple*. *Disciple* means "learner." Christian counselors, in an act of humility, must recognize that the field of the sciences has much to teach them. And in similar fashion, those in the ecclesiological community have much to teach a world that stands in great need of hearing good news.

> *Christian counselors, in an act of humility, must recognize that the field of the sciences has much to teach them. And in similar fashion, those in the ecclesiological community have much to teach a world that stands in great need of hearing good news.*

---

[68] Hebrews 13:8 (NLT)
[69] See Glossary of Terms
[70] See Glossary of Terms
[71] See Glossary of Terms

Chapter 2

Pastoral Counseling: Defined

"If we are going to deeply help people on the path to spiritual growth, we have to know where we came from and where we are heading."[72]

How People Grow,
Henry Cloud and John Townsend

Two Different Words: Pastoral and Counseling

My undergraduate, graduate, and postgraduate education primarily prepared me for my eighteen-year career in pastoral ministry. During this same period of time, I took coursework and attended conferences that systematically addressed how to help people in a caregiving or counseling setting. I have also personally benefitted from professional counseling on numerous occasions.

I document this personal information because, woven together, it provides the tapestry by which I weave my personal approach to counseling. I am neither a licensed mental health

---

[72] Henry Cloud and John Townsend, *How People Grow* (Grand Rapids, MI: Zondervan, 2001), 26.

professional nor a licensed pastoral counselor.[73] I realize my own limitations as a nonprofessional counselor.[74] (Having boundaries or knowing one's counseling limitations is critical for people who offer non- licensed help to those in need). As previously stated, one of my intentions in writing this volume is to offer practical guidance to people who enjoy helping others. Under the tutelage of experienced supervision, sound academic resources, and other expressions of ongoing education (e.g., classes, conferences), people can learn how to offer legitimate help to those needing and wanting help.

As is the case with most counselors, when I meet someone who is seeking some form of guidance, I introduce myself by telling them who I *am not.* I am clear that I am not a licensed therapist or credentialed counselor. Very few people inquire about my education or experience (this still surprises me) because they have been referred by a friend who had a prior positive experience with me. In a first session with an inquirer, I outline what can be expected from our time together.[75] I emphasize the vital importance for *nonlicensed pastors who counsel to be just as clear as I have just stated above.*[76] This is very

> *"I believe the (pastoral) counselor's task is to look for the writing of the Spirit in the counselee's life.... This is what ministers are expert at doing."*

---

[73] LPC was identified in Chapter One as a recognized designation for professionally trained counselors, but it is widely embraced throughout the United States.

[74] William Oglesby writes on the importance of knowing when to refer a person to someone else who has more experience in his book *Referrals in Pastoral Counseling* (rev. ed.; Nashville: Abingdon, 1978).

[75] See Siang-Yang Tan, "Lay Counselor Training," in *Christian Counseling Ethics: A Handbook for Therapists, Pastors and Counselors* (Downer's Grove, IL: InterVarsity Press, 1977)

[76] A pastor at a counseling conference where I was speaking shared with me that he informs and requires everyone that he sees to sign a waiver that releases him from any liability. I think this is a very good idea and also says a great deal about the culture we are living in today. I have seen *Christians* file lawsuits against other Christians for counseling services

important. Charles Kollar differentiates clearly between what therapists accomplish in counseling and the services pastors offer when he comments, "I believe the (pastoral) counselor's task is to look for the writing of the Spirit in the counselee's life.... This is what ministers are expert at doing."[77]

This chapter, by design, is intentionally short. I will not offer a deeply nuanced or technical definition of pastoral counseling. Rather, I will provide clear descriptions and identify different features for what pastors traditionally refer to as "counseling." This chapter (1) identifies a biblical passage that offers a textbook description of pastoral counseling; (2) describes what pastoral counseling looks like in very concrete ways; (3) enumerates varying pastoral functions or behaviors while in the counseling relationship; (4) outlines character traits that pastors can look for when identifying possible "lay helpers" in their congregations; and (5) concludes with a comprehensive definition of pastoral counseling.

A Pastoral Counseling Foundational Text

A signature and summary text from Scripture that numerous pastoral counseling experts have cited over the years in previously released academic works has been 1 Thessalonians 5:14–15. These two verses utilize seven Greek verbs that directly apply to the ministry of counseling, and they are *parakaleo, noutheteo, para mutheomai, antechomai, makothumeo, horate,* and *agathon*. Note their appearance in the cited Scripture, found below.

> And we urge [*parakaleo*] you, to warn [*noutheteo*]
> those who are idle [*lazy*], encourage [*para mutheomai*]

---

that were rendered. This is a very sad but true reality. See Appendix B: Resources for a waiver or release form for pastors in churches.

[77] Charles A. Kollar, *Solution Focused Pastoral Counseling* (Grand Rapids, MI: Zondervan, 1997)

the timid. Help [*antechomai*] the weak, be patient
[*makothumeo*] with everyone. Make sure [*horate*]
that nobody pays back wrong for wrong, but always
try to be kind [*agathon*] to each other and to everyone.

These seven words have a very practical application to
counseling. Pastors will discover that (1) some people need to
be *urged or challenged* because their lives lack determination;
(2) there will be those who need to be clearly *warned* about
choices that they are considering or the lifestyles in which they
are involved; (3) people who lack self-confidence will need their
pastor to come alongside them and *encourage* them; (4) some
people seek the aid of a pastor because they need *practical help*
of some kind (help that would not necessarily be considered
counseling); (5) the apostle Paul instructs counselors to be *patient*
with everyone; and (6) there will be specific (or more serious)
situations in which *absolute surety and/or self-confidence* will
need to be demonstrated by the pastoral counselor. Issues like
self-harm, domestic abuse, and spiritual questions come to mind.
Some people will respond very positively when a Christian
counselor exhibits a sound level of faith or boldness,[78] and (7)
being kind to those who come for counseling can yield much
fruit in the reestablishment of healthy and productive living.

Perspectives on Pastoral Counseling

Pastoral counseling is viewed as the following:

- A specific category of counseling or caregiving that is
  offered by a local church pastor

---

[78] Many people cite John 8:32, where Jesus says, "You shall know the truth
and the truth will set you free." The emotional reality of this text is that upon
first hearing the truth, the newly identified truth usually makes a person
angry. If people would read to the end of John 8, they would discover that
the very people who were described as "believers" at the beginning of the
conversation with Jesus wanted to kill him by the end of the same chapter!

- Something in which every pastor received instruction, either in their undergraduate education or postgraduate training[79]
- A part of a pastor's ministry that every church expects its pastor to perform[80]
- Something most church members will avail themselves of during their lifetimes
- An approach to counseling used by staff persons working in nonprofit organizations
- An approach to counseling by an informed layperson who enjoys helping others
- *A specialized or designated aspect of ministry* that is performed in a full-time capacity as described or outlined in a pastor's job description (e.g., Minster of Pastoral Care, Minister of Counseling, Visitation Pastor).

I know of the multiplicity of demands on a pastor's calendar and therefore today define pastoral counseling in the following ways: (1) biblically based,[81] (2) short term,[82] (3) need and solution focused,[83] and (4) directed under the leading of the Holy Spirit.[84]

---

[79] Research shows that a majority of pastors feel ill-prepared to do pastoral counseling. See Charles A. Kollar as previously cited.

[80] When I am asked to teach our Youth Ministry majors classes on counseling youth, I tell the students that as much as 60 percent of youth ministry is in some way connected to counseling.

[81] Pastoral counselors first and foremost refer to the Bible as the foundation from which they build a counseling relationship. Additionally, pastors also utilize other academic fields so as to ensure thorough and effective counseling.

[82] "Short term" (referring to the number of sessions a pastor will see a person) will vary from pastor to pastor. For my purposes here, I suggest three or four sessions. This would not include crises or emergency counseling (e.g., death).

[83] *Solution Focused Pastoral Counseling* by Charles Kollar is an excellent counseling resource for pastors. I will draw on his expertise and apply his findings later when describing the Genesis Model.

[84] See John Kie Vining's text *Pneumatic Based Counseling* for one understanding of counseling that firmly relies on the guidance of the

The Practice of Pastoral Counseling

Below is a non-exhaustive "skill set" for the pastor who engages in a significant amount of counseling. This skill set is to be best understood as how a pastor practices pastoral counseling.[85] Some may ask, "Must one demonstrate competency in all of these practices?" The answer is, "Of course not, but keep working at it." Pastors practice their skill in counseling based on the following:

- Unconditional (John 13:4–5), sacrificial (John 15:12), and whole-hearted (Luke 10:27) love
- Words of encouragement (Hebrews 3:13) through support, nurturing, listening, correction, and prayers for healing (James 5:13–16)
- The goal of building others up (Ephesians 4:14) so full maturity can be achieved (Ephesians 4:15)
- The use of Scripture (2 Timothy 3:16–17)
- Their spiritual gifting (1 Corinthians 12; Romans 12)
- An unshakable dependence on the Spirit (John 14:16–17)
- Having firm personal boundaries (2 Timothy 2:22)
- A desire to carry another's burdens (Galatians 6:2)
- A sensitivity to context (e.g., culture, gender, maturity)
- An ability to bring correction when needed (2 Tim. 2:25)

Holy Spirit. See also "Theophostic Counseling" in the Glossary of Terms for a broader definition of Spirit-based counseling.

[85] A further resource for the skills and competencies of pastoral counselors is *Christ-Centered Therapy* by Anderson, Zuehlke, and Zuehlke (Grand Rapids, MI: Zondervan, 2000).

Cultivating Lay Counselors:
A Pastoral Perspective

Many practitioners in the field of professional and lay counseling[86] have offered excellent instruction in answering the question, "Can one describe the emotional, educational, practical, and mental makeup of a person who is effective in helping another person?" Tan's research identifies nine criteria that should be considered when answering this question. The following qualifiers are meant to be seen as guidelines when selecting people as lay counselors.[87] When these criteria are not considered, Benner is right to conclude that "a pastor [or lay counselor] must know themselves and be able to reflect on their behavior with a degree of objectivity and honesty. Without this self-scrutiny, pastoral counseling will seldom be more than a ritualistic exchange of clichés."[88]

> "a pastor [or lay counselor] must know themselves and be able to reflect on their behavior with a degree of objectivity and honesty. Without this self-scrutiny, pastoral counseling will seldom be more than a ritualistic exchange of clichés."

I include Dr. Tan's emphasis here because this professional mental health expert's insights serve as an excellent guideline for a pastor who might want to recruit and develop a lay counseling ministry in his or her church. In growing churches in particular, there will be an increase in the number of people who seek counseling from the pastoral staff. When this happens, pastors must find

---

[86] See Wayne Oates, *An Introduction to Pastoral Counseling*, originally published by Broadman Publishing in 1959; Tan, *Lay Counseling*; Gerald Egan, *The Skilled Helper* (Brooks/Cole Publishing, 1975); John Eldredge, *Waking the Dead* (Nashville: Thomas Nelson, 2003); and Anderson, Zuehlke, and Zuehlke, *Christ-Centered Therapy*.
[87] Tan, *Lay Counseling*, pp. 100–103
[88] Benner, *Strategic Pastoral Counseling*, 38.

capable people in their congregations who can be extensions of their ministry.

Tan's description of an effective "people helper" includes the following nine qualities: (1) spiritual maturity that bears the evidence of a life that is filled and marked by the person and power of the Holy Spirit (I would add that one cannot assume today that because someone has been attending church it necessarily means that he or she is a committed Christian. I am confident that Tan would include in his understanding of spiritual maturity the ability to articulate one's faith story, which would pinpoint a time of conversion.); (2) psychological stability as indicated by *not being* emotionally volatile but rather vulnerable and transparent; (3) love for God and interest in people as demonstrated by genuine warmth and caring for others; (4) spiritual giftedness, particularly exhortation, wisdom, knowledge, and discernment; (5) some life experience, implying maturity, not youth; (6) previous training in helping people would be helpful but the lack of it is not necessarily a deal breaker; (7) sensitivity to gender and educational and cultural background; (8) availability and teachability that is clearly confirmed by humility; and 9) ability to maintain confidentiality and protect the privacy of others.[89]

Conclusion

At this point in our journey together, pastoral counseling has been defined in several ways. I have stated what pastoral counseling is not,[90] cited one biblical text that specifically

---

[89] See Tan, "Care and Counseling in the 'New Church Movement,'" *Theology, News and Notes, 33*, 4 (1986); 9–11, 21

[90] You may want to review Chapter One, which clearly lays out the differences between the services a pastor performs in his or her office as compared to what a licensed and experienced mental health professional offers.

relates to counseling (a practical application was also provided), and provided possible skill sets for pastors who counsel and a secondary skill set for lay counselors. Concluding this chapter, the reader will find a comprehensive definition of what pastoral counseling has come to mean to me.

Pastoral counseling is a time-limited relationship[91] that offers biblical and practical solutions to persons seeking help or guidance from another. The possible solutions to identified concerns are co-created through the partnering of counselor and counselee.[92] The pastoral counselor points out the activity of God in the counseling relationship for the purpose of developing the counselee's dependence on God's grace and faithful presence. The culminating goal of pastoral counseling is for the seeker to become increasingly dependent on the person and power of Jesus Christ and thereby rely less and less on the counselor.

> *The culminating goal of pastoral counseling is for the seeker to become increasingly dependent on the person and power of Jesus Christ and thereby rely less and less on the counselor.*

---

[91] "Time limited" is understood to mean three or four sessions. However, this is not a hard and fast number and will vary from pastor to pastor.
[92] The praxis or "how to" co-create solutions of pastoral counseling will be explained in the "Genesis Model" portion of this text.

Chapter 3

A Focused Theology for Pastoral Counselors: Sin and Salvation

> As God's revelation to us, the Bible is the final authority for our psychospiritual life. The Bible therefore should be allowed to inform the disciplines of psychology and counseling.[93]

The Significance of Sin

In the mid-1980s, I was on staff in a Presbyterian church in San Mateo, California. My job title as an ordained associate pastor was Minister of Education.[94] It was during this time that our church solicited an outside resource person to help us develop what would later be called Discipleship Counseling. Our church leadership was encouraged by our consultant [95]

---

[93] William T. Kirwan, *Biblical Concepts for Christian Counseling: A Case for Integrating Psychology and Theology* (Grand Rapids, MI: Baker Book House, 1984), 42.

[94] In those early days of ministry, as Minister of Education, I came to realize how uneducated I really was.

[95] Dr. Gary Sweeten was a licensed counselor who was instrumental in helping our church develop a fully orbed counseling ministry. Our counseling ministries were supported by senior leadership, and funds

to build our counseling ministries on a rock-solid theological foundation. Four initial pivotal ideas from Scripture formed part of the base upon which all approaches to counseling would be established. These first four biblical ideas pertained to the nature of sin: Adamic sin,[96] rebellion, bondage, and stronghold. Today, I refer to these four terms as "The Chain." This chapter will define these terms from a biblical and behavioral vantage point. I cannot overemphasize the importance of having a firm grasp on each of these. Because the subject of sin is one sorely neglected by both the pulpit and many evangelical pastoral counselors, I take intentional time here to unpack this theological term.[97] First, briefly consider these insights from the psychiatric community as it pertains to sin.

In 1990, *Life* Magazine published an article naming the one hundred most significant individuals of the twentieth century. Many of the names are familiar, but one may be new to you—Karl Menninger. You may not recognize his name unless you are a student of modern psychiatry. Dr. Menninger wrote a number of very influential books, probably none more influential to modern behavior than his 1973 publication entitled *Whatever Became of Sin?* In this book, Dr. Menninger wrote, "The very word 'sin' seems to have disappeared.... Sin was a central point in every civilized human being's life plan and lifestyle. Why? Doesn't anyone sin anymore? Doesn't anyone believe in sin?"[98] Later in this

---

were budgeted for this expanding ministry by our elder board. Our lay counselor training included basic approaches to counseling and more developed approaches that included inner healing and deliverance ministry. As time went on, we developed a curriculum and ultimately hired a full-time counselor in a staff position.

[96] Also referred to as original sin.

[97] One published work that I have found particularly useful is *Fallen: A Theology of Sin*, edited by Christopher Morgan and Robert Peterson (Wheaton, IL: Crossway Publishing, 2013).

[98] Karl Menninger, *Whatever Became of Sin?* (Hawthorn Books, 1975), 14. The author is recognized as a premier psychiatrist who founded

same work, Menninger writes about sin, saying "There needs to be a revival concerning the idea of sin."

Two years before his death in 1990, Menninger wrote to a colleague, saying,

> Long ago I noticed that some of our very sick patients surprised us by getting *well even without much of our "treatment."* We were very glad, of course, but frequently some of them did something else even more surprising. They kept improving, got "weller than well" as I put it, better behaved and more comfortable or reasonable than they were before they got into that "sick" condition. *We didn't know why. But it seemed to some of us that kind of the "sickness" resulted in some kind of conversion experience,* like trimming a fruit tree, for example.[99]

In his later years, Menninger seems to have argued that sin, as the Bible defines it, had been replaced by the sciences with a focus on symptomology.[100] *When a counselor is looking only at symptoms, God has been subtly taken out of the picture.* Author John Eldredge places an accurate theological perspective on the relationship

> *When a counselor is looking only at symptoms, God has been subtly taken out of the picture.*

---

the prestigious Menninger Clinic (psychiatric) and the Menninger Foundation. Menninger postulates that regardless of what sin is called (from either a secular or a spiritual mind-set), this behavior erodes one's emotional and psychological being. On a national scale, it corrupts culture and leads to moral decay.

[99] An initially private but now published letter to Dr. Szasz, "Reading Notes," *Bulletin of the Menninger Clinic, 53,* 4, July 1989, pp. 350–352 (emphasis added).

[100] An orientation in counseling where counselors focus on the presenting symptoms of a client while overlooking the root causes of the identified symptom. To describe symptomology, I use the analogy of root issues (systematic cause of a problem) and fruit issues (what is the presenting issue in the counseling setting).

of humanity's choice to "sin" and resulting behavioral effects when he says, "The Evil One lied to us about where true life was found ... and we believed him. God gave us the wondrous world as our playground, and he told us to enjoy it fully and freely. Yet despite his extravagant generosity, we had to reach for the one forbidden thing. And at that moment something in our hearts shifted. We reached, and in our reaching we fell from grace."[101] If one merely talks about unproductive or unhappy living and is only attentive to outward indicators or resulting effects in a person's life, one has reduced the client-patient relationship to superficial behaviors, hereditary factors, a person's environment, and life choices. This is a woefully inadequate and non-biblical way of viewing sin and a heartless and sterile way of relating to a person in need.

In addition to identifying what I have come to call "The Chain," our mentors helped us identify a second theological term that I would study more thoroughly and become more deeply acquainted with in later years. Besides understanding and diagnosing varying aspects of sin, our advisors enabled us to better understand a correct, three-pronged biblical understanding of salvation. I view sin and salvation as "bookend issues" for pastoral counselors. I intentionally focus (and yes, limit) my theological orientation to counseling by addressing only sin and salvation.[102]

---

[101] John Eldredge, *Epic: The Story God Is Telling* (Nashville: Thomas Nelson, 2004).

[102] I realize the limitations of addressing only sin and salvation as the theological foci for pastoral counseling. However, over the years, I have come to believe that these two concepts are the theological and behavioral bookends to nearly all of what a pastoral counselor will face.

The Chain: Adamic Sin, Rebellion, Bondage, and Stronghold

Prior to Adamic sin and after all of God's created order was complete, God declared his work "very good."[103] Then, God rested.[104] However, instead of acting with their flawless nature, the man and the woman willfully disobeyed God's instruction. Humanity's once-perfect relationship with their Creator was forfeited. Both the man and the woman would live with an inferior and marred substitute rather than God's beautifully intended original design.

Traditional Christian teaching has historically taught that Adam and Eve's choices resulted in humankind's being eternally separated from God.[105] The apostle Paul writes, "When Adam sinned, sin entered the world ... and death spread to everyone."[106] In short, everyone sins and has the propensity to sin. Even on a person's best day, sin is "crouching at their door" [107] and waiting to undo the strongest of persons.[108] Paul later conveys that the sinful nature as introduced by Adam and Eve degenerated God's originally given values, desires, and goals. A sinful orientation prompts humankind in such a way

> *In short, everyone sins and has the propensity to sin. Even on a person's best day, sin is "crouching at their door" and waiting to undo the strongest of persons.*

---

[103] Genesis 1:31 (NLT)

[104] Genesis 2:3

[105] Louis Berkhof identifies Augustine as the originator of the concept of original sin: "The early Church Fathers contained nothing very definite about original sin.... It is especially in Augustine that the doctrine of original sin comes to fuller development. According to him, the nature of man, both physical and moral, is totally corrupted by Adam's sin, so that he cannot do otherwise than sin. This inherited corruption of original sin is a moral punishment for the sin of Adam." *Systematic Theology*, 244–245.

[106] Romans 5:12 (NLT)

[107] Genesis 4:7 (NLT)

[108] 1 Peter 5:8

that people do not love what is good, but rather their hearts are deeply inclined toward evil.[109] Only *after* making a decision to disobey God do people see that they *could* have chosen differently in a particular situation but chose not to. It may come as a surprise to some that the idea of original sin as described above is a theological topic under significant debate. Today, the doctrine of original sin is seen in some theological quarters as a later understanding that was created by the early church fathers. Let me be clear—this is not my position. G. K. Chesterton remarked, "The doctrine of original sin is the only Christian doctrine that can be proved by just looking over 3,500 years of human history."[110]

Paul's letter to the Romans, specifically Chapters 5–8, is a comparison between Adamic sin and results that can occur when one makes godly choices. One can see how making godly choices is far more preferable.

The Results of Original Sin	The Results of Making Godly Choices
Slavery (much of Romans 6)	Freedom (much of Romans 8)
Death (crucifixion; 6:5)	Life (resurrected living; 6:5–8)
Being controlled by the world (6:12)	Being submitted to God (6:13)
Old nature (7:5; works-oriented living)	New nature (7:6; Spirit-directed living)
Destructive desires (7:14)	Thankful attitudes (7:25)
Condemnation (8:1)	Acceptance (8:1–2)
Living aimlessly (8:5)	Living with convictions (8:38)

---

[109] Romans 7:21–23
[110] G. K. Chesterton, *Orthodoxy*, Chapter 2

Consider now, a second way of understanding Adamic sin. In their book *Christ Centered Therapy*,[111] authors Neil Anderson, Terry Zuehlke, and Julianne Zuehlke illustrate the before-and-after effects of Adamic sin in both a behavioral and scriptural way. Found below is an adaptation of their work which I found particularly helpful.[112] I use this with counselees (often duplicating it and offering a copy to them) to help them understand the spiritual and existential significance of the illustrated ideas.

PRE-FALL MAN		POST-FALL MAN
Righteous	NATURE	"by nature objects of wrath" —*Ephesians 2:3*
Truthful, right	MIND	"darkened in understanding" —*Ephesians 4:18*
Alive	SPIRIT	"separated from the life of God" —*Ephesians 4:18*
Safe, secure, free	EMOTION	hardening of heart, lost sensitivity —*Ephesians 4:18, 19*
Free to choose	WILL	sensuality, impurity, lust for more —*Ephesians 4:18*

Rebellion

Original or Adamic sin is a dynamic that is part of every human being's personhood or nature. Scripture teaches, "All have sinned and fallen short of the glory of God."[113] We also know, "Yet God, with undeserved kindness, declares that we are righteous. He did this through Christ Jesus when he freed

---

[111] Anderson, Zuehlke, and Zuehlke, 134

[112] On occasion, I have simply shown this chart to a person in counseling so they can see a comparison of where a person often lives and how God wants him or her to live.

[113] Romans 3:23 (NIV)

us from the penalty for our sins."[114] Adamic sin is the first link in the chain of sin.

Rebellion is the second of the four links in the chain of sin. Generally speaking, I define rebellion as established opposition toward a person or an identified authority, and a refusal to obey rules or accept normal standards of behavior or ideology. *Behaviorally speaking*, I describe rebellion as "in-your-face sin." Rebellion asserts, "I am going to do what I do and get what I want." Rebellion is the type of behavior exhibited by a person who knows the better or healthier choice to make but intentionally selects a poorer alternative. By its nature, rebellion tends to be the following:

- A behavior practiced by people new to the faith (the deeper process of sanctification has not had time to fully develop)
- Situational
- A non-ritualized or an irregularly practiced behavior
- A behavior that can also be described as periodic or capricious

I want to comment to parents (and grandparents) about rebellion and youth under the age of twenty-five. To parents with a child who may be "acting out," do not "freak out." A one-time poor decision (Parent: "What were you thinking?" Child: "I don't know. I guess I wasn't.") or a minor speed bump along life's travels (e.g., first driving ticket or a young person who expresses little to no interest in spiritual things) does not perpetually predispose a person to ending up in a particular distasteful life orientation or situation.

> *In an effort to discover who they are, today's youth have yet to realize that choices have consequences.*

---

[114] Romans 3:24 (NLT)

In the rebellion stage, rebellious teens experiment with many different behaviors. In an effort to discover who they are, today's youth have yet to realize that choices have consequences. Parents must allow consequences to become invaluable teachers. In formative years, kids have not firmly established what they believe. A smorgasbord approach to life is the common code of conduct with young adolescents through the early years of adulthood.[115] I do not want to be misunderstood here—I am not approving or excusing a distasteful level of behavior; rather, I am merely describing an orientation to life at a specific age. Parents need to remember that during the rebellion stage (overt, covert, or attitudinal), experimentation has not resulted in their children making their final decisions on the behaviors or choices with which they are experimenting.[116]

If rebellion is correctly identified and the person seeking help is willing to make changes in his or her life to eradicate "less-than-best" choices, productive living can take place. The psalmist writes, "Oh, what joy for those whose rebellion is forgiven, whose sin is put out of sight!"[117] However, if rebellion goes unnoticed or unchecked, the person in rebellion will move into the third link of the sinful nature. Counselors should remind persons seeking help that mastery at anything, good or bad, comes only after much practice. Stated another way, what we feed thrives; what we starve dies.[118] Again, a person who continues in rebellion against God (or any

---

[115] It is right to observe here that the behavioral sciences identify "arrested emotional development" as a disorder that describes a person who continues to age chronologically but whose emotional make-up of their internal world continues to be that of an adolescent. This is to say that a person ages but never grows up.

[116] For more researched and practical insights on the subject of teens, faith, and rebellion, see *Sticky Faith* by Kara Powell and Chap Clark (Zondervan, 2011).

[117] Psalm 32:1 (NLT); see also Ezekiel 18:31, Proverbs 17:11, and Psalm 107:17.

[118] This saying is not original with me.

established authority) can expect to experience greater losses and deeper pain. Life will become increasingly difficult. If a person becomes entrenched in rebellious behavior, his or her life will ultimately become unmanageable.

Bondage

Sin is part of our nature; whether we call it human nature, fallen nature, second nature, or old nature, sin is a part of who we are. The person who *repeatedly* makes poor choices, especially against God's clear directives, has moved into the third link of the "sin chain." This third link is referred to as *bondage*. If a person continues practicing unhealthy and unproductive behaviors (i.e., continued experimentation; no longer "periodic" behavior), this person will eventually reach a destination (bondage, or worse) beyond what was ever intended. Yes, decisions lead to a destination, and a person's destination will ultimately result in a given destiny. The New Testament writer James asks his readers, "Don't you realize that friendship (ongoing fellowship) with the world makes you an enemy of God?"[119] In the bondage stage, writes James, a person is no longer a friend of God but rather an enemy.[120] Peter writes about the severity of this third stage as he warns, "Abstain from fleshly lusts which *war against* the soul."[121] Paul concurs with Peter as he writes, "The flesh lusts against the Spirit."[122] The good news, however, is that even the greatest enemy of

> *Yes, decisions lead to a destination, and a person's destination will ultimately result in a given destiny.*

---

[119] James 4:4 (NLT)
[120] Ibid.
[121] 1 Peter 2:11 (KJV)
[122] Galatians 5:17 (KJV)

God can be reconciled to God through Christ because of Christ's redeeming work on the cross.[123]

It is fair to ask, "What is the route or path from rebellion to bondage?" To answer this question, I use the image of a door (think of the door to your house) to explain the development of bondage. Three common beliefs or behaviors[124] allow or give admission to the developing condition of bondage. The goal of the counselor is to identify and address the doors that have exposed a person to the reality of being in bondage and how they were opened. It is vital to recognize and understand how the counselee forfeited peace, productivity, and freedom.

The Door of Unforgiveness

Unforgiveness is one of the main tools the Devil uses against God's people. It not only cuts a person off from God's forgiveness[125] but also turns a person over to being tormented by the Enemy.[126] If a person harbors bitterness against those who have wronged him or her, Scripture instructs that the person must forgive them.[127]

> *The more serious the sin and the longer the unhealthy behavior is allowed to go unchecked, the greater the need for professional help.*

---

[123] Ephesians 2:15

[124] And certainly, there are many others.

[125] Mark 6:15

[126] Matthew 18:23–35

[127] A tremendous resource on the subject of forgiveness is R.T. Kendall's book, *Total Forgiveness* (Great Britain: Houdder & Stoughton, 2001). This should be in every counselor's library. For inner peace to be fully restored to a person, there must be confession (acknowledgment of sinful or wrong behavior), repentance (asking God or another for forgiveness), and the reestablishment or recovery of a reconciled relationship. This door, unforgiveness, is an increasingly common reality in our culture and is found in people of all ages.

The Door of Unconfessed Sin

Any committed sin, especially repeated or ongoing sinful behavior, gives the enemy a *legal right* to affect or bother a person. Unconfessed sin lengthens the shadow to all kinds of trouble, including demonic harassment. The Apostle Paul writes to the Ephesians, saying, "Don't let the sun go down on your anger, lest the enemy gain a foothold."[128] Unconfessed sin is a guaranteed way of quenching the activity of the Holy Spirit in a person's life. The more serious the sin and the longer the unhealthy behavior is allowed to go unchecked, the greater the need for professional help. Scripture teaches, "If you confess your sins, He is faithful and just to forgive us,"[129] but if a person attempts to hide his sin, the enemy has permission to place him in bondage.[130]

The Door of Self-Condemnation

Words have the power of life and death.[131] If a person states, "I'll never amount to anything" or "I want to die," that person has essentially cursed him- or herself. The gospel writer Matthew warns, "For by thy words thou shalt be justified, and by thy words thou shalt be condemned."[132] When people experience deep emotional disappointments, especially in childhood, it is natural that they lock themselves behind an emotional system of coping. This newly identified way of "doing life" prevents them from interacting with reality.

In his book *Pain and Pretending*,[133] Rich Buhler makes a strong case for what is referred to as "necessary pretending."

---

[128] Ephesians 4:26–27 (NASB)
[129] 1 John 1:9 (ESV)
[130] Proverbs 28:13
[131] Proverbs 18:21
[132] Matthew 12:37 (KJV)
[133] Rich Buhler, *Pain and Pretending* (Nashville: Nelson Publishers, 1988).

What I refer to here is more than, "Fake it until you make it." Let me illustrate. When a young child experiences a significant trauma, particularly under the age of seven or eight, the young child is nearly forced to *pretend* that the trauma did not occur. This pretending for the child is a common coping mechanism that children utilize in order to emotionally manage the painful event. In the case of an older person, pretending is not the primary default mechanism used to cope with deep disappointment. The more mature person (post adolescence) will use a variety of other coping mechanisms (e.g., suppression,[134] substance abuse, projecting, and avoidance of the issue or event) to distance him- or herself from a painful reality.

Some may ask, "What are the behaviors exhibited by someone in bondage?" Nancy Groom, in her book *From Bondage to Bonding*,[135] describes in great detail the life of a person who lives in bondage. Groom says a person in bondage has a life marked by the following:[136]

- Excessive compulsivity (an inability to stop any form of compensation)
- Addictions (any expression of self-medicating)
- A family history of dysfunction
- An absence of unconditional love (from one or both parents)
- A resignation to helplessness
- Inclination toward worthlessness
- Controlled by others (an inability to establish boundaries)

---

[134] Suppression is the conscious or unconscious withholding of information (related to of a painful event).

[135] Nancy Groom, *From Bondage to Bonding* (Colorado Springs: NavPress, 1991).

[136] This is by no means a complete list. Several of these identifiers will be discussed in the remainder of this book.

- Profound victimization (she also uses the word *self-forfeiture*)
- False legitimacy (entitlement thinking)

In his book *The Bondage Breaker*,[137] Neil Anderson offers an insightful biblical corrective to any type of captivity when he states, "When you sin you may feel sorry, but feeling sorry or even telling God you're sorry, isn't confession. *You confess your sin when you say what God says about it.*... 'I treated that person unkindly and that was wrong.'"[138] When an authentic confession is made, the person making the confession can be assured that God not only forgives but forgets the sin as well.[139]

In summary, a person in bondage (1) recognizes that something is not right; (2) will seek help, and (3) still has a degree of remorse for his or her wrong behavior. What I am about to convey is of critical importance—the element of remorse *is the pivotal dividing line, the differential,* between bondage and the deepest and darkest of shadows. Remorse is what a person experiences after making a poor decision—a deep regret for a wrong that has been committed.[140] A person in the state of bondage still *feels something.* The person in the last link in the chain of sin *feels nothing.*

Stronghold

The fourth link in the chain of sin is stronghold, and it is the most serious and difficult of the four links to address in a

---

[137] Neil T. Anderson, *The Bondage Breaker* (Harvest House Publishers, 1990), 81 (emphasis added).

[138] Another outstanding resource on the subject of confession or apology is Gary Chapman's book *The Language of Apology.* What I found most helpful in this text is the differentiation Chapman makes between the "apology language" of men as compared to that of women.

[139] Jeremiah 31:34; 1 John 1:9

[140] *The Free Dictionary,* s.v. "remorse," accessed January 2010, http://www.thefreedictionary.com/remorse

counseling environment. I use this definition of *stronghold*: "a place dominated and defended by a particular group of people that hold to particular characteristics and ideologies."[141] When an individual arrives at this place (and let me say, it takes intentionality to get to the depths of this place), he or she

- No longer has any control of his or her life
- Has no sense of remorse (that is to say, does not feel bad for what he or she is doing or has done)
- Will ask advice from those he or she knows can be manipulated (or lied to!)
- Does not seek help from legitimate sources of help

I have been asked on numerous occasions, "What hope is there for those caught in the vice-like grip of stronghold?" I respond, "As long as there is life and breath, there is hope." I want to conclude this section on stronghold by elaborating on *how to prevent this level of sin* from ever occurring in the first place. Prevention—what a concept!

1. **Ready and Resist.** *All believers are to ready themselves and resist any satanic assault in whatever form that it may present itself.*[142] Part of being ready is to know that we are in conflict.[143] Every Christian should be well aware of the enemy's threefold attack plan: to steal (temporary loss), kill (not necessarily physical death; this could be the death of a dream), and ultimately, to destroy (certainly this would include physical death). The devil does not play games, and neither should we.

2. **Establish.** *All believers are to establish themselves by utilizing the full wardrobe of God's spiritual*

---

[141] *New Collegiate Dictionary, twentieth edition*
[142] Ephesians 6:11
[143] John 10:10a

equipment. We are to be battle-ready![144] All believers are to cover their thought lives with the helmet of salvation; protect their hearts with the breastplate of righteousness; wrap their lives with the belt of truth; be equipped with God's Word, the sword of the Spirit; and learn to walk out life's difficulties by wearing the sandals of peace.

3. **Endure.** *All believers are called to endure the attacks of the evil one.* To endure means to stand strong for a season, a period of time and testing. The book of Revelation records that five of the seven churches listed were "overcomers," or churches that endured very difficult times. For these churches, there would be a particular blessing because of their clear endurance. Scripture promises, "And these signs will follow those who believe" [145]

4. **Displace.** *All believers will victoriously displace anything that is not of God.* Displacement begins by inviting God to increase in every area of a person's life. Just as falling water finds its way to the lowest areas, so the Spirit of God finds its way to the lowest places of our lives that need to be washed clean! This spiritual displacement begins with the same attitude that John the Baptist articulated when he said, "This is a time for him (Jesus) to increase and for me to decrease."[146] Where this level of submission is, the devil is not!

5. **Occupy.** *All believers are to have nothing in their lives that the devil can exploit.* Maturity teaches that there is to be no pocket of rebellion, corruption, or immorality in which Satan can find refuge to build darkened influence or strength. Scripture teaches,

---

[144] Ephesians 6:13–17
[145] Mark 16:17 (NIV)
[146] John 3:30 (NLT)

"do not give the devil an opportunity to work."[147] A description of King David's first military victory and *occupation* is found in 2 Samuel 5. For David to "occupy" that which he was fighting, we discover that (1) David did not fight alone (v. 6), (2) David rose above the ridicule and insults of his opponents (v. 6), (3) David fortified the newly occupied city from the inside out (v. 9), (4) with his victory David increased in the favor of God (v. 10), and (5) the conclusion of his physical and spiritual conquest bestowed a new identity for that which he was fighting (v. 7).

Concluding Thoughts on Sin

Dietrich Bonhoeffer, in his book *Creation and Fall*,[148] observes that the tree with the forbidden fruit was placed in the center of the garden of Eden.[149] Why would God place a beautiful, productive tree in this garden setting and essentially hang a "Do Not Touch" sign on it? The reason, concludes Bonhoeffer, is that this is where God belongs in our lives—at the center,[150] not merely at a tangential boundary around the edges of our lives. God is neither an insurance policy that protects us against unforeseen disasters nor an emergency exit that is accessed to escape trouble.

If God were an "outer boundary God," humanity would be protected from all outsiders, yet this would place humanity at the center of all organizational reasoning—a scary thought! Sure, we would be protected from outside evil forces, but we would probably destroy ourselves from the inside out. Again,

---

[147] Ephesians 4:27 (ISV)

[148] Dietrich Bonhoeffer, *Creation and Fall: A Theological Exposition of Genesis 1–3* (Fortress Press, 2004).

[149] Genesis 2:9, 16–17

[150] See Marguerite Shuster's article in *Christianity Today* entitled, "The Mystery of Original Sin," April 2013.

the prophetic placement of the Tree of the Knowledge of Good and Evil at the center of Eden tells us that it is God who brings us life and meaning. One way we return to the center of our lives is to "bring every thought captive"[151] to God. When we submit our thought-life to God, we can become empowered to accomplish the deepest desires of our hearts.

When people in pain return to *the center,* they will find the One, who will reorder and reestablish those things that have been lost. People formerly living in the shadows will have heard their Savior's invitation, "Come to me all who are weary and carry heavy burdens and I will give you rest."[152] They will have heard the prophet's plea, "Come to me all who are thirsty and I will give you drink."[153] As Romans 8 assures us, "We know that the whole creation has been groaning as in the pains of childbirth right up to the present time; we wait eagerly for our adoption to sonship, the redemption of our bodies. For in this hope we were saved. But hope that is seen is no hope at all. Who hopes for what they already have? But if we hope for what we do not yet have, we wait for it patiently. In the same way, the Spirit helps us in our weaknesses."[154]

The Significance of Salvation

Salvation is a word commonly found on the lips of those who profess to be believers of God. This same word is also frequently understood in a limited fashion. A more thorough understanding of salvation is conceptualized in three expressions.

The Greek word for *salvation* is "sozo,"[155] and it is found over one hundred times in the New Testament. *When the word*

---

[151] 2 Corinthians 10:5 (NIV)
[152] Matthew 11:28 (NLT)
[153] Isaiah 55:1 (NLT)
[154] Romans 8:22–26 (NIV)
[155] The New Testament Greek Lexicon (also keyed to Kittle, *Theological Dictionary,* Eerdmans's Publishing, 1976)

salvation *(or sozo) is spoken, it is most commonly referred to in terms of repenting of sin, turning to God, and being baptized so that salvation from this wicked generation can be realized.*[156] The gift of God's salvation for lost humanity is secured when anyone accepts Jesus' substitutionary death on the cross for their sins. The gospel writer Matthew records, "The Son of Man is come to save (sozo) that which was lost."[157] The Apostle Paul wrote, "If you confess with your mouth Jesus is Lord and believe in your heart that God raised Him from the dead you shall be saved [sozo]."[158] Other ways of understanding salvation (sozo) can include to be rescued from danger or destruction; to make well; to restore to full health; and to be delivered from the penalties or evil that obstructs the reception of God's grace.[159]

A second understanding of salvation incorporates the idea of being "saved from" physical challenges, afflictions, and illnesses. Matthew records a time in Jesus' ministry that illustrates this second aspect. Jesus was on his way to help someone in need when a woman who had suffered for twelve years with a blood disease reached through the crowd and touched his robe. She was healed immediately. Turning and seeing the woman, Jesus said, "Daughter, take courage your faith has made you well (sozo) and at once the woman was made well (sozo)."[160] This story illustrates that salvation (sozo) has both spiritual (faith) as well as physical (healing) components. New Testament scholar George Eldon Ladd identifies the parable of the lepers[161] to illustrate that salvation is more than salvific in nature. A proper understanding of salvation will include both a physical and attitudinal element to

---

[156] Acts 2:38–40
[157] Matthew 18:11 (NASB); Luke 19:10
[158] Romans 10:9 (HCSB)
[159] New Testament Greek Lexicon; King James Version
[160] Matthew 9:22 (NASB)
[161] Luke 19:11f.

its composition; salvation should include a grateful response. Ladd correctly observes that a greater blessing was bestowed on the Samaritan who returned (after being *physically* healed) to thank Jesus than on the other nine who *did not return* to thank him.[162]

A third aspect of salvation is related to being "saved from" circumstances that torment an individual on an ongoing basis, issues that repeatedly occur in a person's life that will prevent the person from experiencing an abundant life.[163] Examples of a lingering or repeating issue are any behavior (e.g., the use of pornography, anger, laziness), substance (e.g., any addiction, alcohol, drugs, prescription medications of any kind), or memory (e.g., unresolved trauma, PTSD) that plagues a person. These unfortunate realities inhibit a person from walking through life with God, and others, in complete, fearless, "naked" intimacy.[164] One biblical account authenticating the understanding of being set free from ongoing, tormenting issues is found in the Gospel of Luke. This story chronicles deliverance and freedom as Luke tells us of a man who *had been* tormented throughout his life by demons. After the man's release, Luke records, "And those who had seen it (the man's deliverance) reported to them how the man who was demon-possessed had been made well (sozo)."[165]

---

[162] George Eldon Ladd's major contribution to biblical scholarship may be his understanding of the kingdom of God. Concerning the kingdom of God and its interrelatedness to salvation, Ladd contends for an understanding of salvation that is *more than* just a gift from God (and it is!) sometime in the future. Salvation, argues Ladd, is realized sometime in the future, but moreover, *salvation is also to be seen as an ongoing gift* that is to be lived out in community and experienced in the present by all true believers. "The gift of *present fellowship*," (emphasis added) writes Ladd, "is in anticipation of the eschatological consummation" on the final day.

[163] John 10:10b

[164] Genesis 2:25 (NIV)

[165] Luke 8:36 (NASB)

Conclusion: Between the Bookends

After careful reflection, I have concluded that every counseling situation in which I have been involved existed because of the seeker's sin or sin that was perpetrated upon the seeker by another. Further, the remedy to the seeker's pain and subsequent freedom would be experienced only when the person in pain accepted the free gift of salvation as described in this chapter. In the words of Bryan Chapell, "Jesus wants to liberate us from the unappeasable demands of human merit. Thus, he must turn us away from the mistaken belief that perfection or performance will gain his favor."[166] Therefore, sin and salvation can be seen as the "theological bookends" for any Christian counselor.

For a final time, I underscore that sin and salvation are the theological beginning and ending points for the Christian counselor. Merely acknowledging sin will not help a person escape the inner depravity that is a part of the human condition. It is only by accepting the free gift of salvation that is offered in Jesus Christ that we become more than who we presently are and, with God's grace, become all that God intends.

---

[166] Bryan Chapell, "Repentance That Sings," in Christopher Morgan and Robert Peterson (eds.), *Fallen: A Theology of Sin* (Wheaton, IL: Crossway Publishing, 2013), 268.

Chapter 4

When the Counselor Needs Counsel

"To live a spiritual life we must first find the courage to enter into the desert of our loneliness.... The movement from loneliness to solitude, however, is the beginning of any spiritual life because it is the movement from the restless senses to the restful spirit, from the outward-reaching cravings to the inward-reaching search, from the fearful clinging to the fearless play." [167]

"Receiving from God is a problem for many of us, and so we resist it; we resist spiritual nurture. We are much more comfortable performing for God than receiving from God, and receiving has been perceived as some kind of weakness."[168]

---

[167] Henri Nouwen, *Reaching Out: Three Movements of the Spiritual Life* (New York: Doubleday, 1966).
[168] Jeff VanVonderen, Dale Ryan, and Juanita Ryan, *Soul Repair* (Downer's Grove, IL: InterVarsity Press, 2008), 42.

A Short Story

I was thinking that my writing was nearly done; my scheduled trip to Israel with university students was just five days away. But I was becoming uncomfortable—something was missing. That *something* is this chapter.

After talking with a dear friend about my growing discomfort, I called Bob, a gifted counselor and pastor friend who has taught me much about the ministry of counseling[169] and who helped me emerge from my own "shadows." After I described my inner turmoil, Bob asked me, "Have you read anywhere in all your research anything that approaches the question, 'When does the counselor need counseling?'" I told him I hadn't. I went on to tell him that I was keenly aware of counseling ministries and retreat venues that dealt with the restoration of pastors and was familiar with researched literature that pertained to signs of what was typically referred to as burn out,[170] but Bob said, "That is not what I am talking about."

> "In all the counseling I have done with counselors, the majority told me that they felt as though they had no one to talk to."

He said there was a reason that hard-copy, researched data on counselors' needing counseling would be nearly impossible to find.[171] Continuing, he said, "In all the counseling I have done *with counselors*, the majority told me that they felt as though they

---

[169] Bob Sanders served as an ordained pastor for over forty years and held a doctorate in pastoral studies. Bob's academic work emphasized psychology and the implementation of the person and work of the Holy Spirit. I am honored that Bob read portions of this manuscript and offered his helpful professional critiques before his death just prior to publication.

[170] These services are by and large interventions of help, *but only after* there is a recognized need for such.

[171] Again, there are specific venues uniquely positioned to help people in ministry (and that includes counselors) with life issues, but these organizations most often are helpful to caregivers and pastors *only after* there has been a professional or personal "meltdown" of some fashion.

had no one to talk to." If counselors felt as though they had no one in whom to confide, of course, there would be virtually little or no data available on the topic of "pre-meltdown conditions."[172] My mind went into overdrive, and by evening's end, I knew I had to write this chapter.

> *Aboard, aboard for the wind fills the shoulder of your sail... And this above all:* **to your own self be true** *and, it must follow, as the night the day, Thou canst not then be false to any man. Farewell, my blessing season this in thee!"[173]*

Perhaps you recognize the above lines from William Shakespeare's play *Hamlet*, where Polonius offers this parting piece of wisdom to his son Laertes before the young man heads off to Paris. Once there, he is safe from his father's well-intentioned but lengthy discourses. Being true to self is a first step or starting point for a counselor's mental health.[174] In order for counselors to be tethered or grounded mentally and emotionally, they must first deeply understand the core or very essence of their beings—their personalities and behavior. The *American Psychological Association* defines *personality* as "the unique psychological qualities of an individual that influence a variety of characteristic behavior patterns (both overt and covert) across different situations and over time."[175] In their book *Safe People: How to Find Relationships That*

---

[172] I will address the term *pre-meltdown conditions*; at present, let me emphasize how critical it is to know the signs and signals of impending disaster *prior to* the meltdown.

[173] Shakespeare, William. Hamlet, Act one, scene 3

[174] My graduate and postgraduate studies of greatest impact were under the tutelage of Dr. Archibald Hart, whose research on the mental health of the emerging minister helped shape my appreciation for the hidden inner workings found in every person, but particularly people in places of ministry.

[175] American Psychological Association; 750 First St. NE; Washington, DC 20002-4242

Are Right for You and How to Avoid Those That Aren't,[176] researchers Townsend and Cloud explain in pronounced detail the personalities, behaviors, characteristics, and more deeply nuanced issues of *unsafe people*. I reference this research because it has helped me to not only recognize this behavior in others but also within myself.

Earlier, I used the term *pre-meltdown conditions*.[177] This term describes behaviors and activities that can be seen in a person *prior to* poor decision-making, physical fatigue, and emotional depletion.[178] Pre-meltdown conditions in a counselor's life are easily observable and can be seen in the literature presented in Townsend and Cloud's "unsafe people" research. Townsend and Cloud state that these unsafe people (to which I add a counselor headed for meltdown) demonstrate the following behaviors or belief orientations: (1) erroneously believe they have their lives all together, when in actuality they do not; (2) resist input; (3) will apologize for certain behavior, but will not alter the behavior; (4) will lie/ not tell the complete truth; (5) prefer and increasingly choose isolation *from people* versus connecting *with people*; (6) function in an authoritarian role rather than one of equality, and (7) live with a strong sense of self-sufficiency. Each of these pre-meltdown conditions merits commentary at length, but for now I merely catalogue them as noted. One must ask then, how do pre-meltdown conditions develop? What is the point of origin of these beliefs and behaviors? When these pre-meltdown indicators are allowed to develop, what is the

---

[176] Henry Cloud and John Townsend, *Safe People* (Grand Rapids, MI: Zondervan, 1991).

[177] See the Glossary of Terms.

[178] When a person is physically exhausted, the probability of poor decision making multiplies exponentially. This level of fiendish work, much like a hamster on a wheel, will soon render the individual physically and emotionally bankrupt, leaving little mental and emotional currency available to invest in things that deeply matter.

anticipated trajectory? I believe I have some answers for these questions.

Blind Spots

Think of your car and its side-view mirrors. The mirrors allow the driver to see if there are any cars adjacent to the car being driven. Once a driver checks the mirror and sees that the lane is clear, the driver can change lanes. *Wrong.* Experienced drivers will also look over their shoulder to be assured that there is not a car in their *blind spot.* Lesson: mirrors do not reveal everything. Following is a two-part diagram of developmental blind spots and corresponding explanations.

Diagram 1 illustrates the trajectory of movement that can be seen in a person's life that ultimately will enable him or her to move from "things unseen and not understood" to a clarity of life greater than they could have imagined. The reader will also observe in the diagram that a person will initially not see, seek, or accept help of any kind. After a season of confusion, which is usually marked by disappointment at some level, a person will suspect that the way he or she has been approaching or "seeing" life was not correct. In every sense of the phrase, he or she has been "vision impaired." It will take a counselor, a "watchman on the wall,"[179] to guide that person into a state of reality and consciousness, eventually removing blind spots.

---

[179] Ezekiel 3:17–19 (NLT)

The counselee
knows he does
not know.
Continued
losses occur.
The struggle
of inadequacy
intensifies.

A person has
a growing
discomfort
that something
is not right.

Conscious

A person does
not know what
he does not
know.

Suspected

Reality

Unconscious

Reality

Reality

Has blind
spots; a person
will experience
loss and have
difficulty
taking
direction when
it is offered.

Life is marked
by confusion
and a sense of
being "stuck."
Losses
continue.

Has come
to the place
where help is
authentically
asked for.
These people
learn the
truth about
themselves
and, namely,
loss does not
define them.

**Questions
help and still
avoids help.**

Avoids help.

Seeks help.

Diagram 1 ⟶

RESISTANCE
Unproductive living

When writing this material on blind spots, I initially thought about the blind spot concept only from the counselee's perspective—that is, an issue that prevents a counselee from experiencing a healthy and productive life. However, the counselor can also have blind spots, or at least a season of blurred vision. Therapist Joseph McCann comments that self-deception (or having a blind spot) is a major problem increasingly seen in clinical practices.[180] Another mental health professional, Daniel Via, confirms McCann's research, saying that the reason for the existence of a blind spot is because a person sees him- or herself as being well integrated, having an issue-free life, and capable of making sound judgments, yet this "blind-sided person" lives far from reality.[181]

If a counselor has a false understanding of self, marked by skewed projections, diminishing professional boundaries, defensiveness, and an inability to properly frame reality, the counselor may be headed for a meltdown (or any number of the seven previously mentioned pre-meltdown conditions). The blinded counselor's primrose path can be likened to a fun house at a county fair with mirrors that grossly distort a person's true self. Christian writer Thomas Merton says, "We conceal the truth of our misery from ourselves, our brethren and from God. A very real extension of self-deception is keeping from others what a person may really need others to see [the most]."[182] Henri Nouwen wrote, "It seems easier to be God than to love God, easier to control people than to love

---

[180] Joseph T. McCann, *Malingering and Deception in Adolescents* (Washington D.C.: American Psychological Association, 1998), 23.
[181] Dan O. Via, Jr., *Self-Deception and Wholeness in Paul and Matthew.* (Minneapolis, MN: Augsburg Fortress, 1990), 1.
[182] Matthew Brett Vaden, Discovering the True Self: Thomas Merton and Contemplation. *Edification: The Transdisciplinary Journal of Christian Psychology,* 5, 1:56.

people, easier to own life than to love life."[183] Ralph Keyes, in his work *The Post-Truth Era: Dishonesty and Deception*,[184] states that our culture no longer feels any remorse for lying and has abandoned many sacred forms of tradition. Our "post truth" culture is consumed with deception on nearly every societal, economic, religious, and vocational front; deception is an equal-opportunity predator. When the counselor, or anyone, comes out of the "distorted fun house," he or she will discover—and often too late—that he or she failed to hear even the most direct of cautions from well-meaning friends and family. Our photo-edited society has made it easy for a counselor (and really, anyone) to portray a veneered image of integrity, sincerity, and power on the outside, all the while living in the "shadowlands" of a tormented existence.

> *Our photo-edited society has made it easy for a counselor (and really, anyone) to portray a veneered image of integrity, sincerity, and power on the outside, all the while living in the "shadowlands" of a tormented existence.*

I now advance an unvarnished challenge to counselors. God hates deception, in any form. I am sure my readers are well aware of the well-known early church leaders Ananias and Sapphira. Both lied to Peter about an offering that they had given to the church.[185] Let me clarify the wrongdoing here—*the* cardinal issue for both the husband and wife was not "pulling a Judas" by withholding some of the money for themselves; rather, the more serious issue was giving the illusionary impression of being godly givers when, in actuality, they were not. Ananias and Sapphira had the mental blind spot of thinking they could get away with their

---

[183] Henri Nouwen, *In the Name of Jesus* (New York: Thomas Nelson, 1992), 59–60.
[184] Ralph Keyes, *The Post-Truth Era: Dishonesty and Deception in Contemporary Life* (New York: St. Martin's Press, 2004), 1.
[185] Acts 5:1f.

carefully planned extortion. The original story of Ananias and Sapphira relates to a "misappropriation of funds," but an analogy to counselors can be easily made. Counselors misappropriate relationships, like Ananias and Sapphira misappropriated funds, anytime they allow themselves to become emotionally consumed by their clients, thus leading to an unhealthy relationship.

Diagram 2 illustrates the transition from resistance (the left side of the diagram) to the acceptance of help with migration toward a healthier way of approaching life (the right side of the diagram). The key to traversing the vertical line that separates unproductive living from productivity and "crazy successful" living is a *teachable spirit*. If a counselee (or counselor!) is not receptive to hearing the invitation of Jesus—"Come to me all those who are weary and carry heavy burdens, and I will give you rest"[186]—little can be done. However, an individual who accepts the invitation to come and release must then adopt the quality of life that Jesus offers.[187] According to Jesus, coming, releasing, and learning at His feet will result in "rest."[188]

---

[186] Matthew 11:28 (NLT)
[187] Matthew 12:29
[188] Matthew 12:29. I devote the entire thirteenth chapter to the subject of rest. Rest is a big deal—to God!

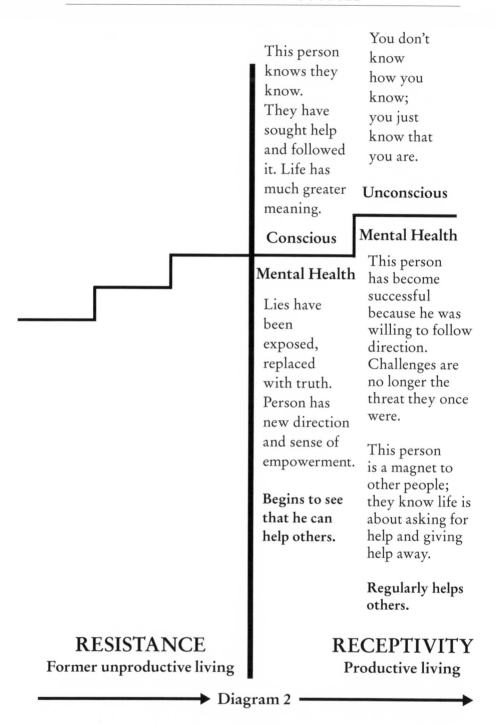

This person knows they know. They have sought help and followed it. Life has much greater meaning.

You don't know how you know; you just know that you are.

Unconscious

Conscious

Mental Health

Mental Health

Lies have been exposed, replaced with truth. Person has new direction and sense of empowerment.

Begins to see that he can help others.

This person has become successful because he was willing to follow direction. Challenges are no longer the threat they once were.

This person is a magnet to other people; they know life is about asking for help and giving help away.

Regularly helps others.

RESISTANCE
Former unproductive living

RECEPTIVITY
Productive living

Diagram 2

Relational Blind Spots

Blind spots in a counselor's life can be lethal. They can be any of the following:

- Intellectual (possible errant ways of thinking)
- Chemical (possible organic/biological imbalances in the brain)
- Familial (an unawareness of needs in the home)
- Vocational (not realizing that downsizing or layoffs are imminent)
- Emotional (counseling is an emotionally draining ministry and one that should not be pursued without great intentionality)

To specifically develop the concept of a counselor's blind spots, I will explicitly identify three common counseling relationships that can erode a pastor's mental and professional health.

The Uninformed Counseling Relationship

The uninformed counseling relationship can be described as a scenario that the pastor has *previously* faced (e.g., death of a congregational member) and that has with which he or she is well acquainted. The presenting concern, as told by the counselee, is familiar to the pastor. The pastor may reason, with no ill will or arrogance intended, "I can handle this." *The pastor feels very informed but, in reality, is not at all.* I tell my counseling students to proceed with caution *particularly if* a similar situation was successfully navigated earlier. In this case, *there is even greater need to slow down.*

> *The pastor may reason, with no ill will or arrogance intended, "I can handle this." The pastor feels very informed but, in reality, is not at all*

63

The New York Yankee great Mickey Mantle once said, "It is amazing that I have played this game all my life and still know so little about it."

The most common mistake an inexperienced counselor makes is moving too quickly. Great experience or expertise with a given concern is no reason to think that one can again successfully address and master it a second or third or fourth time. When a counselor makes an assumption based on a positive past experience and adopts a "cut to the chase" or "get 'er done" mentality, risks run high for missing unique details in the present situation that were not part of the former circumstances.

> *The most common mistake an inexperienced counselor makes is moving too quickly.*

The Pain-Driven Counseling Relationship

Meeting with people who are experiencing or facing a spectrum[189] of pain is what pastors and counselors accept as part of their calling. I use the word *spectrum* intentionally because when a person is in any type of pain (e.g., loss of a job), the pain is commonly viewed by the counselee as extreme, acute, all-encompassing, or fatal. The person in pain has little ability to see their pain in terms of a spectrum. When I am listening to someone in pain, I try to embrace or validate his or her pain by asking questions, clarifying details, and offering some level of encouragement and assurance to the counselee. However, pain can become infectious and contagious.

Codependency[190] has been defined as becoming self-absorbed in a person or situation (e.g., *pain*) and thereby

---

[189] When thinking about the word, spectrum, think of a rainbow. Applied to a counseling situation, spectrum can be understood to mean a range of conditions, feelings, thoughts or variables that exist between two points.
[190] See Melody Beattie. *Codependent No More* and *Beyond Codependence*. (Hazelden Publishing, 2011). See Glossary of Terms in back of book for additional information.

losing sight of one's own life. Pastors who find their personal lives superseded by a counselee's pain, rather than meeting their next obligation for the day, have become infected by a pain-driven relationship. Those who fall into this scenario are often people pleasers, have poor boundaries, tend to be very reactive, project a portrait of competence, and yet have their own fair share of deeply rooted painful memories.

The Adrenalin-Saturated Counseling Relationship

We live in an adrenalin-saturated culture. People are driven by anything that excites them: social media, the latest fad, "retail therapy" (shopping), the newest and fastest phone upgrade, and the list goes on. If a person is going to attempt counseling on any level, he or she must become aware of the effects that adrenaline has on the body.[191] An analogy may be helpful here.

Adrenalin-saturated relationships are like driving on the European autobahn, which has no speed limit. However, a car does have a limit. It is called a gas tank. Counselors can become involved in highly dramatic or adrenalin-saturated (also referred to as "high-maintenance") relationships. Often, the counselor will go faster, faster, and faster … and if the counselor does not monitor his or her emotional gas tank, he or she will become stranded—out of emotional gas.

An experienced counseling mentor, using the above analogy, reminded me that insomnia is a side effect of excess adrenaline operating in the body, which can ultimately result in hospitalization. Think about this with me. Because the adrenalin-saturated counselor is so "jacked up" or stimulated by certain specifics in the counseling relationship, he or she cannot get to sleep. What is the counselor doing in the time of

---

[191] Body chemistry, our brains, and healthy living will be ongoing topics throughout this book.

sleeplessness? Thinking about the counseling situation while the counselee sleeps away.

Adrenalin-saturated counseling relationships are also like a popular roller coaster ride at an amusement park. You wait a long time in line, and you get bored. You need something, anything, to make the time pass. Then, the adrenalin-saturated counseling relationship walks into your office. Remember, you have been bored. The counseling conversation commences slowly (chug, chug, chug uphill). Then an unexpected drop comes, and hairpin turns follow. You are jerked all over the place at faster speeds followed by gasps of air and not-so-silent thoughts of, *How did I ever get into this in the first place?* and *When does this ride end?* Remember, you paid a park entrance fee for all of this drama!

It may sound strange to you, but some people actually seek out these types of relationships. Anytime a person needs to go to a place, a relationship, or a job or needs to do anything in order to be "amused," there is something wrong in that person's core. I was talking one time with a very prominent person whom I respect highly. I asked this individual, "What are you going to do during your vacation?" They described a wonderfully serene scenario and then commented, "I really do not need any added excitement in my life right now." I responded, "That sounds very healthy to me. Enjoy!" I promise you, for the counselor who needs a dysfunctional relationship to make the time pass, there are covert "shadows" operating in that person's life—shadows that need to be exposed, illumined, and filled with God's light.

A Short Course on Christianity

The book of James, specifically 4:1–7, offers the best short, biblical behavioral inventory to safeguard the everyday Christian counselor from the drama of roller-coaster relationships.

James begins by posing a question: "What causes quarrels and fights among you?" (James 4:1). For the counselor wishing to adhere to certain core beliefs and values, the first application question is, Do you know what makes you angry? In interviewing well over five hundred people, I discovered that nearly 60 percent of them *could not* articulate, quickly, what made them angry. It is a very worthwhile exercise to stop, even now, and think through this first question.

Next, James posits the statement: "You want what you do not have" (James 4:1). A second inventory question that is designed to prevent getting on an emotional roller coaster or relational autobahn is, Do you know what you want? I know this question sounds rudimentary, but when it is over looked, people can make decisions in haste that will result in a lifetime of regret.

In addition, James calls out his readers by saying, "You want what you do not have so you scheme and kill to get it" (James 4:2). My application question is, When you experience disappointment, how do you handle the cruel blow? Do you deal with or address this situation constructively or destructively? I believe one of the truest reflections of a person's inner self is shown at a time when the individual does *not get* what he or she wanted or thought he or she deserved. People who resort to "scheming" and "killing" in order to get what they want need to remember that there is no right way of doing something that is insidiously wrong.

James continues, "And even when you ask, you don't get what you want because your motives are all wrong—you want only what will give you pleasure" (4:3). Years ago, I heard someone say that thanklessness is not being content with what you do have, greed is wanting more of what you already have, and jealousy is wanting what others have. Again, the key idea hinges on what motivates you. Question of application: Do you know what motivates you? James 4:4 warns, "Don't you realize that friendship with the world makes you an enemy of God?"

I really like application question number five: What do you think about? (James 4:5). This is such a challenging question to me personally. I would flesh this question out specifically by asking, What do you think about when there is absolutely no pressure? or What do you daydream about? Graham Cooke[192] teaches, "There are two general ways of approaching decision making and the future. The first position is a 'present past' orientation. This person is firmly rooted in his or her current life but spends a fair amount of time second-guessing what happened to him or her in the past. The second type of person is more of a 'present-future' type of individual. This person also has a fairly grounded understanding of who he or she is but approaches the future with far less emphasis on what has happened in the past". Again, here, I invite the reader to ponder this question: What do you think about? Why not pause now and daydream ... *just a little.*

In James 4:6, we read, "But he gives us even more grace to stand against such evil desires." My question of application here is, Do you find yourself "standing up" under the pressures of your life as God would have you stand? Or do you find yourself, in the words of the psalmist, as one of those who will "follow the advice of the wicked, or *stand around with sinners,* or join in with mockers"?[193]

James draws his inventory to a close with this statement: "So humble yourselves before God. Resist the devil, and he will flee from you. Come close to God, and God will come close to you" (James 4:7–8a). The application question is, Do you have a responsive and teachable spirit when God invites you to flee from your flesh and draw close to Him? These thoughts beg little explanation.

---

[192] Graham Cooke is an author and a publisher with over twenty books that bear his name. His books and teaching materials are on the subjects of prophetic ministry, spiritual warfare, intimacy with God, leadership development, evangelism, and spirituality.
[193] Psalm 1:1

Below, you will find a bulleted inventory list that will serve as a good preventive for the Christian counselor to stay out of trouble.

1. What makes you angry?
2. Do you know what you want?
3. How do you handle disappointment?
4. What motivates you?
5. What do you think about?
6. Do you actively resist evil?
7. Do you draw close to God?
8. Do you have a teachable spirit?

A Final Tool

Every year in my counseling class on the first day of lecture, I pass out what I call the One-Minute Manager, shown below. After students have completed this instrument, I interpret the statements by way of basic existential issues. In Appendix A in the back of this book, readers will find this tool along with an explanation of each of the questions and of how to administer the inventory.

The One-Minute Manager

Instructions: Take 'three minutes' to read the sentence on the left and check (+) either "yes" or "no" on the blank placed to the right of each sentence. The total number of "yeses" or "no's" is not what is important in this exercise.

	YES	NO
1. I exercise on a regular (at least twice a week) basis.	_____	_____
2. I get at last six hours of sleep on a regular basis, and awaken rested.	_____	_____
3. I have had a complete physical within the last two years.	_____	_____
4. I have fairly disciplined or healthy eating habits.	_____	_____
5. I know what makes me happy, content or satisfied.	_____	_____
6. I have at least one person I can sit down and be completely honest.	_____	_____
7. I have a "survival mode" as compared to a "sky is the limit" view of life.	_____	_____
8. I have a difficult time talking about my feelings.	_____	_____
9. I usually accomplish the majority of my responsibilities on time.	_____	_____
10. I place a high value on attaining personal success or identified goals.	_____	_____
11. I have a hard time dreaming or imagining my life in the future.	_____	_____
12. I do not give up on challenges easily.	_____	_____

13. I prefer working with other people, as   _____ _____
    compared to working by myself.

14. I have been told I am a good listener.   _____ _____

15. I have had a life experience that I avoid   _____ _____
    talking about.

16. I value harmony more than success.   _____ _____

17. I seem to have an easy time connecting   _____ _____
    and relating to people.

18. I am clear in my mind about my
    ultimate life purpose.

19. I work first and play later.

20. I have specific goals for the future that
    I want to accomplish.

PART II

To Do:
The Genesis Model
for Counseling

Chapter 5

Introducing the Genesis Model

Creator as Counselor

Early in my career as a pastor, I had the privilege of being invited to a dinner party in Dallas, Texas, with a group of thirty other church educators. We were told that after our Texas-style barbecue, we would be having an evening speaker. The speaker, as it turned out, was none other than Zig Ziglar. Zig, as he preferred to be called, was a highly successful Christian businessman, best-selling author, motivational speaker, master of one-liners, and captivating storyteller. I still remember Zig saying, "I know the day my business career took off. It was the day I learned that the answer to many questions that people have is in knowing the right question to ask in return." He went on to say that people are not so much interested in a download of information as they are in having a meaningful conversation. I think the same principle holds true for counseling. When a counselor is the one doing all the talking, he or she is no longer counseling. Zig Ziglar's wisdom shared nearly thirty years ago is as true today as it was when I was first introduced to it. Another writer confirms Ziglar's philosophy this way: "The person with the greatest ability to listen and ask insightful questions will have the greatest depth of influence with others."

I will offer, as previously stated, a "deep and wide" approach to Christian counseling; this manuscript will be deep in Scripture and wide in application. But still, I want the reader to have a sense that we are engaged in conversation—talking with one another. Chapters Five through Twelve identify the eight-step approach to the "Genesis Model of Pastoral Counseling." Below I offer a brief sketch of each principle so the reader can get a sense of where I am headed. Undoubtedly, there will some of the steps that will carry greater meaning for one person than another.

Genesis Principle 1: The God Who Is

Genesis Principle	God is before all things. God is active before there is ever a need for a counselor.
Genesis Principle Applied	Counselors must know it is God, not them, who is leading the counseling environment. Counselors must determine if the counselee authentically knows God as described throughout the Bible.

Genesis Principle 2: The God Who Creates

Genesis Principle	God creates all that is called into existence.
Genesis Principle Applied	Counselors are to be creative, especially in providing a safe place for counselees to share themselves and their concerns.

Genesis Principle 3: The God Who Speaks

Genesis Principle	God speaks into existence all that is created.
Genesis Principle Applied	Counselors are to listen to God for words to speak into the lives of their counselees.

Genesis Model Principle 4: The God Who Illumines

Genesis Principle	God illumines that which was in darkness.
Genesis Principle Applied	Counselors are to "shed light on the darkened areas of a counselee's life and illuminate lies that are thought to be truth or untruths that have been spoken over the life of the counselee.

Genesis Model Principle 5: The God Who Sees

Genesis Principle	God sees what has been created.
Genesis Principle Applied	Counselors are to "see" clearly that which is before them.

Genesis Principle 6: The God Who Separates

Genesis Principle	After creating light and declaring it "good," God then separated the light from the darkness.
Genesis Principle Applied	Counselors are to aid counselees in freeing themselves from the mental, emotional, and existential darkness that plagues them.

Genesis Principle 7: The God Who Blesses

Genesis Principle	Scripture records that on the seventh day, God blessed the work of His hands.
Genesis Principle Applied	Counselors need to speak appropriate words of blessing over the newly created person.

Genesis Principle 8: The God Who Rests

Genesis Principle	Scripture declares that after Creator God's work was complete, God "rested."
Genesis Principle Applied	God's counselors, at the end of their work, are to rest.

Chapter 6

The God Who Is

"In the beginning, God ..."

Genesis 1:1

Christianity did not come in order to develop the heroic virtues in the individual, but rather to remove self-centeredness and establish love.

Soren Kierkegaard

Biblical counseling must insist that the image of God is central to developing a solid view of personality.... Our greatest need is that repentance, not insight, is the dynamic in all real change.

Dan B. Allender

Genesis Principle 1

Genesis Principle: God is before all things. God is active before there is ever a need for a counselor.

Genesis Principle Applied: Counselors must know it is God, not them, who is leading the counseling environment. Counselors must determine if the counselee knows God as He is described throughout the Bible.[194]

---

[194] Norma Dearing writes in *The Healing Touch*, "Healing our image of God is one of the most basic and necessary healings of all. A distorted image of God stands in the way of approaching Him, making it all but impossible to want to receive His healing touch" (Grand Rapids, MI: Baker, 2002, p. 47).

Introduction

The Bible does not attempt to defend the existence of God or to prove the reality of His being. The Scriptures take for granted that God exists. The psalmist wrote, "The heavens tell of the glory of God and their expanse is declaring the work of His hands."[195] The prophet Isaiah declares, "Woe to him who argues with his Maker! Does a clay pot argue with its maker? Shall the clay say to him who forms it, 'What are you making?' Or shall your handiwork say, 'He has no hands'?"[196] In Job, we find these weighty questions from Creator God: "Where were you when I laid the foundations of the earth? Tell Me, if you know so much. Who determined its measurements and stretched out its surveying lines? To what were its foundations fastened?"[197]

In his writing to churches in Rome, Paul says the following about the God of all creation:

> For since the creation of the world His invisible attributes are clearly seen, being understood by the things that are made, even His eternal power and Godhead, so that they are without excuse, because, although they knew God, they did not glorify Him as God, nor were thankful, but became futile in their thoughts, and their foolish hearts were darkened. Professing to be wise, they became fools.[198]

And to the church at Colosse, Paul writes of "the God of creation," saying, "For by Him [God] all things were created that are in heaven and that are on earth, visible and invisible, whether thrones or dominions or principalities or powers.

---

[195] Psalm 19:1 (NASB)
[196] Isaiah 45:9 (NLT)
[197] Job 38:4–6 (NLT)
[198] Romans 1:20–22 (NKJV)

All things were created through Him and for Him. And He is before all things and in Him all things consist."[199]

This initial chapter will offer a five-part understanding of God and His character in light of a counseling environment: (1) the activity of God, (2) the name of God, (3) the voice of God, (4) the goodness of God, and (5) the plan of God.

The Activity of God

Genesis 1:1 reads, "In the beginning *God ...*" I enter every counseling relationship believing that God has been active in the life of the counselee and that God has orchestrated the counseling appointment that I am about to enter into. The counselee may think that coming to counseling was his or her idea (or someone else's); I think otherwise. Henry Blackaby says in his book *Experiencing God*[200] that the initial step to experiencing God is to know that God is already active in a person's life. I apply this principle *especially when I have no history* with the person to whom I am talking. If a counselor believes that God is always active in a person's life, then the counselor's goal is to establish how this has been occurring. The psalmist affirms Blackaby's assertion.

> *I enter every counseling relationship believing that God has been active in the life of the counselee and that God has orchestrated the counseling appointment that I am about to enter into.*

> If I go up to the heavens, you are there; if I make my bed in the depths, you are there. If I rise on the wings of the dawn, if I settle on the far side of the sea, even there your hand will guide me; your right hand will hold me fast. If I say, "Surely the

---

[199] Colossians 1:16–17 (NKJV)
[200] Henry Blackaby and Richard Blackaby, *Experiencing God* (Nashville: Broadman & Holman Publishers, 1994).

darkness will hide me and the light become night around me," even the darkness will not be dark to you; the night will shine like the day, for darkness is as light to you.[201]

However, there is an entire segment of people today who believe the contrary. There are many who believe in a "silent God"—a god who is capricious, plays favorites, or flat-out ignores human pain. During times of loss or disappointment, people need to be reminded that neither *their goals nor themselves are out of reach of God's great provision.*[202] John Eldredge has his finger on the pulse of our contemporary culture as he writes,

> You are the son of a kind, strong, and engaged Father, a Father wise enough to guide you in the Way, generous enough to provide for your journey, offering to walk with you every step. This is perhaps the hardest thing for us to believe ... [and the lack of this belief] is the core issue of our shared dilemma. We just don't believe it. Our core assumptions about the world boil down to this: We are on our own to make life work. We are not watched over. We are not cared for. When we are hit with a problem, we have to figure it out ourselves, or just take the hit. If anything good is going to come our way, we're the ones who are going to have to arrange for it. Many of us have called upon God as Father, but, frankly, he doesn't seem to have heard. We're not sure why. Maybe we didn't do it right. Maybe he's about more important matters. Whatever the reason, our experience of this world has

---

[201] Psalm 139:8–11 (NIV)
[202] Andy Stanley goes into great detail about this reality in his book *The Principle of the Path* (Nashville: Thomas Nelson, 2008).

framed our approach to life. We believe we are fatherless[203].

As God has been working in a seeker's life to the extent that they he or she has made an appointment, I then "join" both God and the seeker in the counseling environment. As I enter a new counseling session, I am guided and helped by John the Baptist's statement, "This is the time for him (Jesus) to increase and for me to decrease."[204] In every sense, I need God to increase His activity in the counseling relationship while giving me cues through the leading of His Spirit as to the direction I am to go. At the same time God is increasing, I know that I am to "decrease."[205] *To decrease* does not mean that a counselor does or says nothing. One way I decrease is to ask God to show me what He needs me to see. God will bring revelation as we seek Him. I have faith that God will reveal the things I need to know in order to help the person I am seeing. I rest in Jesus' great promise, "Blessed are the pure in heart, for they shall see God."[206]

A foundational prayer of mine is that the counselee would see and hear and come to believe that the very God who was active in the creation of the world would be just as present in

---

[203] John Eldredge, "Fatherless." Ransomed Heart daily reading, June 14, 2014. This is a free online publication.

[204] John 3:30 (NLT)

[205] My "decreasing" or listening process is a part of what has been described by some Christian mental health practitioners as a pneumascriptive or theophostic counseling (see John Kie Vining, *Spirit-Centered Counseling*). Dr. Ed Smith was an early pioneer of this orientation to counseling in the early 1990s. In Smith's words, "I grew weary of teaching people to find tolerable recovery but rather find deliverance from the Lord." For further reading see *Healing Life's Hurts through Theophostic Prayer*, p. 39 (New Creation Publishing, 2002, 2005) and Fernando Garzon (ed.), *Pursuing Peace: Case Studies Exploring the Effectiveness of Theophostic Prayer Ministry* (Xulon Press, 2008). I will delve more into theophostic counseling later in this book.

[206] Matthew 5:8 (NIV)

those things that are of concern to the counselee. Many times in the counseling relationship, it is not words that people need to hear as much as they just need a place to be. This counseling orientation—counselor as an "active presence" rather than a dispenser of information—is yet another description of pastoral counseling. I draw on the gospel writer John to support this approach to caregiving. John wrote these familiar words.

> *Many times in the counseling relationship, it is not words that people need to hear as much as they just need a place to be. This counseling orientation— counselor as an "active presence" rather than a dispenser of information—is yet another description of pastoral counseling.*

In the beginning was the Word ... And the Word became flesh and dwelt among us, and we beheld His glory, the glory as of the only begotten of the Father, full of grace and truth. John bore witness of Him and cried out, saying, "This was He of whom I said, 'He who comes after me is preferred before me, for He was before me.'"[207]

These verses can very well be the basis of what I call incarnational counseling. One way a counselor can "join God, where God is active" is for the counselor to appropriate five different principles found in these verses.

People need to see the following in their counselor:

- A tangible presence of God (words becoming flesh)
- An established presence of God ("word dwelt among us"—sojourning with the seeker through difficult times)
- The gracious and truthful presence of God ("grace and truth," *in this order!*)
- One who bears witness to the Word ("John bore witness," not the world's spin)

---

[207] John 1:1, 14–15 (NIV)

- The humble presence of God (God is the preferable source for all comfort and wisdom, *not the counselor*)

In light of these five counseling behaviors the reader may want to re-read the above passage from John so as to further incorporate these ideas into the heart. A Christian counselor will follow and be committed to these biblical ideals. I know when I have needed the *active* guidance, discipline or encouragement from an outsider these five principles were practiced by those who have spoken into my life.

The Name of God

So, if God is active, who is this God? We are all known by our names. Some people carry names that are family names handed down by their parents. For instance, my middle name, Benson, is my mother's maiden name, the last name of her parents. And my first name, William, means "strong protector." In a similar way, the very names ascribed to God carry significant meanings. What is God's name? Does God have a middle name, too? Each name of God referenced throughout Scripture gives us a glimpse into the character and nature of the God of the Bible.

We know the Bible begins with God's creating all things. The word *God* in Genesis 1:1 is the Hebrew word *Elohim*.[208] This "first" name of God stresses God's majesty, omnipotence, and power. The *-im* ending on the name *Elohim* is the Hebrew plural ending.[209] It may sound strange to you, but *Elohim* can actually mean "gods." However, when used as a name for God in the Bible, Elohim is always used with singular verbs, which indicates only *one* God. Therefore, *Elohim* is a plural name with

---

[208] James Strong, *New Strong's Concise Dictionary of the Words in the Hebrew Bible* (Nashville: Thomas Nelson, 1995).
[209] Ibid.

a singular meaning. The Bible presents God as a trinity. The concept of a triune God has always been difficult to understand (a single God who is a Father and a Son and a Holy Spirit). This plurality of persons in the Godhead—Father, Son, and Spirit— were all engaged in the creative work at the beginning of time (see Prov. 8:27; John 1:3, John 1:10; Eph. 3:9; Heb. 1:2; Job 26:13).

Elohim is used throughout the Old Testament, over 2,300 times, and comes from the Hebrew root meaning "strength" or "power."[210] In Genesis 1:1, we read, "In the beginning *Elohim* created the heavens and the earth." The *El* portion of this Hebrew word is often combined with other words for descriptive emphasis. When God reveals Himself, using a name, He is essentially telling us what God is like.

Some of my personal favorite names of God include the following:

- *Elohay Kedem*—God of the Beginning (Deuteronomy 33:27)
- *Elohay Mishpat*—God of Justice (Isaiah 30:18)
- *Elohay Selichot*—God of Forgiveness (Nehemiah 9:17)
- *Elohay Mikarov*—God Who Is Near (Jeremiah 23:23)
- *Elohay Mauzi*—God of My Strength (Psalm 43:2)
- *Elohay Yishi*—God of My Salvation (Psalm 18:46)
- *Elohim Kedoshim*—Holy God (Leviticus 19:2, Joshua 24:19)
- *Elohim Chaiyim*—Living God (Jeremiah 10:10)
- *Elohay Elohim*—God of Gods (Deuteronomy 10:17)
- *El HaGadol*—The Great God (Deuteronomy 10:17)
- *El HaKadosh*—The Holy God (Isaiah 5:16)
- *El Yisrael*—The God of Israel (Psalm 68:35)
- *El HaShamayim*—The God of the Heavens (Psalm 136:26)
- *El Yeshuati*—The God of My Salvation (Isaiah 12:2)
- *El Immanu El*—God Is with Us (Isaiah 7:14)

---

[210] Ibid.

The name of God is an important concept to remember. God's character, at the very core, is benevolent. It is in God's heart to give or provide.[211] God does not withhold any good thing from His children. It has been my experience that when a person comes to me seeking help, the themes of identity (who a person is) and industry (what a person is to do in life) commonly come into play. The twin observations of identity (being) and industry (doing) come from research done by Hebrew scholar John Parsons. He observes,

> "The relation between a name and a function is of fundamental importance. In the Hebrew mindset, naming and being are linked together to form a unity. The right use of a name denotes a right relationship with the thing being named."[212] Parsons continues by saying that Yeshua is so vital to our correct understanding of reality that without it we are virtually lost, since we are told explicitly there is salvation in no other *name*, "for there is no other *name* under heaven by which we must be saved."[213]

It is critical for Christian counselors to be sure that those whom they are helping have an accurate point of reference, especially about the nature and character of God. If a person who needs help does not *begin* with a correct understanding of God at the outset of the counseling experience, he or she most likely will not *end* in an authentic or true relationship with God when the counseling experience ends. Stephen Covey seems to convey this same idea when he writes, "To *begin* with the end in mind means to *start with* a clear understanding of destination."[214]

---

[211] John 3:16
[212] John Parsons, "Introduction to the Hebrew Names of God." Hebrew4Christians Ministries
[213] Acts 4:12 (NLT)
[214] Stephen Covey, *The 7 Habits of Highly Effective People* (New York: Free Press, 1989, 2004), 98 (emphasis added)

Key Counseling Principle: Some people have problems in their lives because they have a "wrong God" or "small God" concept.[215] A false understanding of God prevents people from living productive lives; some people do not *correctly* know God. Part of the answer to personal freedom is in *introducing people to a God whom they have never met*. I have identified a few names of God above. The greatest advantage for a person seeking help will include getting to know God authentically. A counselor could offer the partial list of names as shown above or go online for a more comprehensive list.[216] In studying the names of God, any person can get to know God better.

The Voice of God

God existed before the universe. God created the universe. *The universe came into existence because God spoke it into existence*. The phrase, "Then God *said* ..." occurs eight times in the creation story found in Genesis 1. The reader of Genesis will note an entire series of commands *spoken* by God. Thus, the connection between a *spoken* command and a corresponding result cannot be missed.[217] In similar fashion, there is no mistaking the connection between instruction and obedience. John the Beloved knew of this formula for success when he wrote, " Happy is the one who reads this book, and happy are those who listen to the words of this prophetic message and obey what is written in this book! For the time is near when all these things will happen..."[218] *By His voice* God

---

[215] See Appendix A at the end of the book for a list of false God images that I have compiled.

[216] Henry Blackaby offers his own list of the names of God in his book *Experiencing God*.

[217] In Chapter Eight, I will specifically address how God speaks to counselors and counselees. After all, wouldn't a person rather hear from God than a counselor?

[218] Revelation 1:3 (GNT)

fashioned the world into existence, filled emptiness, brought illumination, ordained order, and ultimately pronounced goodness to all that had been created. Psalm 19:1–4 (NIV) is a wonderful hymn about all of God's work.

> The heavens declare the glory of God;
> the skies proclaim the work of his hands.
> Day after day they pour forth speech;
> night after night they reveal knowledge.
> They have no speech, they use no words;
> no sound is heard from them.
> Yet their voice goes out into all the earth,
> their words to the ends of the world.

Key Counseling Principle: There is existent power in the *spoken* word. I am more careful and deliberate about what I say today because of my strong belief in this principle.

While in Israel, I was on an elevator with a group of our students. The elevator was malfunctioning; it would go up three floors, not open, stop, and then go all the way down to the basement and stop while still not opening. This repeated at least twice. During this temporary spell of electrical insanity, some of my students were saying things like, "This is terrible!" "We will never get to our floor," and "We might spend the whole night in this overheating elevator." I reminded them to be more careful with the use of their words. The neurotic elevator finally opened at the lobby, and the students ran out. Before the doors closed, I said, "See you on the sixth floor." The doors closed, and I prayed, "God, empty this elevator of the ill-spoken words and get me to the sixth floor." The elevator immediately bulleted its way up to the sixth floor, and the doors opened. I laughed (an expression of praise) all the way to my room.

Further, words spoken by people, *especially about themselves*, become self-fulfilling prophesies—prophesies that are actually curses. The last comment here concerning God's voice comes from the book of James: "Everyone should be quick to listen, *slow to speak*, and slow to become angry" (1:19 NIV, emphasis added). My wife once said, "Most people do this in reverse." That is to say, people are *quick* to speak (they interrupt), *slow* to listen (they are close-minded), and *quick* to become angry (they take offense). If you want a surefire way to *not* hear the voice of God, do James's instructions *in reverse*.

The Goodness of God

Seven times in the creation account, we find the phrase, "God saw that it was *good*." We know that the number seven is the number that represents perfection.[219] This sevenfold evaluation by God, "It was good," indicates that God was well pleased with His finished work (Genesis 1:4, 10, 12, 18, 21, 25, 31).

Concerning goodness, Paul says, "And we know that all things work together for good to those who love God, to those who are the called according to His purpose."[220] The biblical writer James testifies, "Every good and perfect gift is from above, coming down from the Father of the heavenly lights, who does not change like shifting shadows."[221] And the psalmist declares, "Oh, give thanks to the LORD, for He is good. His love endures forever."[222] God is good because He has created good things. God sees His work as good and, yes, even *perfect*.

The goodness of God is a very crucial concept for people to grasp. If people can see God's goodness in what they see around them, then they might tend to seek after the very God that created such goodness. However, Scripture is very clear that people living in the shadows have a difficult time

---

[219] See E. W. Bullinger, *Number in Scripture*, http://philologos.org/__eb-nis
[220] Romans 8:28f (KJV)
[221] James 1:17 (NIV)
[222] Psalm 107:1 (NKJV)

believing that there is a God of goodness. When people are in pain, it is difficult for them to see, hear, or believe that God is good. This is normal and predictable. I am reminded of C. S. Lewis's *Narnia* tales, when the children ask about "this Lion of Narnia." "Is he safe?" they inquire. Mrs. Beaver answers, "Safe? Who said anything about safe? Course he isn't safe. But he's good. He's the King, I tell you."[223]

In a counseling session, I take every occasion to share and teach about the goodness of God, and I do not debate a person's sense of negative reality. Some people have been raised in homes where the positive is rarely expressed. Paul describes a "negative orientation to life" when he says that the whole world lies under a curse, a curse of its own negative reasoning. In the book of Romans, Paul writes, "For all creation is waiting eagerly for that future day when God will reveal who his children really are. [20] Against its will, all creation was subjected to God's curse. But with eager hope, [21] the creation looks forward to the day when it will join God's children in glorious freedom from death and decay."[224] To the Corinthians, Paul says, "For the message of the cross is foolishness to those who are perishing, but to us who are being saved it is the power of God."[225]

If a person does not believe in the inherent goodness of God—that is to say, that God is for them—the counseling process is greatly hindered. Albert Ellis, an American psychologist, developed Rational Emotive Behavior Therapy (REBT)[226] in the mid-1950s. This therapeutic approach has been outlined, developed, and interpreted by many academics

---

[223] C. S. Lewis, *The Lion, the Witch, and the Wardrobe* (New York: Harper Collins Publishers, 1950).

[224] Romans 8:19–21 (NLT)

[225] 1 Corinthians 1:18 (NLT)

[226] Rational emotive behavior therapy (REBT) is focused on resolving emotional and behavioral problems. This approach to pastoral counseling is very appropriate and encouraged because of the short-term nature of pastoral counseling.

and practitioners in the mental health field over the years. Below I offer my own interpretation of Ellis's REBT using an A–G outline. This approach to any type of counseling can help disarm an overly pessimistic person.

- **Adversity** is a reality of life and must be acknowledged.
- **Beliefs** are developed by the person based upon an experience he or she is reporting. If these beliefs are not factual, they will need to ultimately be challenged by the counselor.
- **Consequential feelings** (most commonly, negative) develop. Emotionally based beliefs activate brain chemistry, resulting in varying stages of maladapted living.
- **Deciding what to do** is *jointly identified by the counselor and counselee.* If an active plan can be identified by the counselee, the counselee will feel a sense of empowerment over what was perceived to be a hopeless situation.
- **Empowered by the counseling process,** a person will choose to remain in a negative orientation or consider positive workable options. The counselor must plan for *both* responses.
- **Follow up** by the counselor will ensure success (and accountability) so that identified outcome goals can be realized and the identified adversity can be defeated.
- **Give away to others.** A counselee should be encouraged to help other people who may be struggling in life. This step is a recommended way to ensure ongoing success over negativity.[227]

---

[227] This adapted seventh step in Ellis's REBT approach to mental health is actually a modification of the Alcoholics Anonymous approach to getting clean and sober. AA documents their final step to recovery this way: "Having had a spiritual awakening as the result of these steps, we

Keep in mind these words from Winston Churchill for they are a fitting summary: "The pessimist sees difficulty in everything; the optimist sees opportunity in every difficulty."[228]

Key Counseling Principle: It is important to remember that just as God is the author of life, there is another "author,"— an author of death and destruction.[229] From the time Adam chose to disobey God until this day, people have been making choices that are fatal. In spite of ongoing selfish choices, Christ still loves us! The ultimate expression of the goodness of God is most clearly seen in the gift of God's one and only son. Jesus came into the world not to judge the world but to save it and give us eternal life. If we accept this wonderful gift, our lives will be marked with more goodness than selfishness. If we accept God's gift, we will begin to see changes in our lives. One of these changes will be that we will increasingly seek after God's goodness and good things for others as well.

The Plan of God

From the beginning, God had a plan for His creation. He placed both man and woman in this world, working side by side, to bring order to that which had been created.[230] Work, or labor, was not part of the curse due to the fall; rather, *work was always part of God's plan.* Work can give meaning and purpose. In Hebrew, the word for "order" is *kybosh*.[231] Perhaps you have heard the saying, "I am going to put the kybosh

---

tried to carry this message to alcoholics and to practice these principles in all our affairs."

[228] Original source unknown

[229] John 10:10a

[230] Genesis 1:28

[231] There are varieties of understandings concerning *kybosh* or *kibosh*—to end, stop, conquer, or tread upon.

on this." This means that a person is going to actively and intentionally "work" at putting an end to something.

Counselors are to help counselees identify and subdue anything that would not result in a fruitful life (i.e., chronic negativity). A counselor is to help a person put to death anything that would prevent him or her from achieving God's best plan for his or her life. That which leads to death rather than life must be eradicated. Any sin, any errant behavior, and any errant thinking does not glorify God and must be subdued. A rather terse statement in the book of James speaks to the eradication of any ungodly orientation to life: "You adulterous people, don't you know that friendship with the world means enmity against God? Therefore, anyone who chooses to be a friend of the world becomes an enemy of God."[232] After identifying that which needs to be "kyboshed," James then identifies a solution to this problem. He advises, "Humble yourselves before God. Resist the devil and he will flee from you. Draw close to God and he will draw close to you."[233]

Jesus' words about pruning, found in John 15, provide a clear example of putting the kybosh to sin. Jesus' horticultural analogy of God's plan for productivity does more than bring order to life. Jesus tells us that an ordered life will result in lasting abundance. In John 15, Jesus speaks of three different types of fruit. First, He talks about the vine that bears *no* fruit.[234] I liken this plant to the empty precreation chaos. It was to creation's initial emptiness that God spoke and filled. The fruitless vine of John 15:1 describes a life void of direction, having more questions than answers. This person needs to hear from God, needs order spoken into the chaos, and needs hefty doses of reality.

---

[232] James 4:4 (NIV)
[233] James 4:7-8 (NLT)
[234] John 15:1

Second, Jesus talks about a vine that bears *some* fruit. [235] This vine is a plant with some productivity. However, Jesus says that even this vine needs to be pruned *so that* it can be even be more fruitful. This vine is descriptive of a person with some signs of maturity. Yet, this same person needs someone to come alongside and encourage him or her to move to the *next level* of productivity. Paul writes to the *Christians* at Corinth saying, "I couldn't talk to you as I would a spiritual people. I had to talk to you as though you belonged to this world or as if you were infants in the Christian life. I had to feed you with milk, not with solid food because you weren't ready for anything stronger."[236] Because this second type of fruit (or person) lacks maturity, a full or abundant life has not been experienced.

A third vine described in John 15 is a vine that is producing "fruit that will last."[237] This plant has grown in good soil; has been pruned and cared for by the gardener; and has endured the withering heat of the summer and the cold blasts of winter. This vine has resisted anything that could have brought harm to any vineyard. [238] Yes, God has a plan. God's plan is calling forth gardeners' (John 15), guardians (Galatians 4:1–3), and shepherds (John 10:14). God is looking for wonderful counselors (Isaiah 9:6) who will tend to people's souls, people who will stand in the gap (Ezekiel 22:30) and repair the broken places in people's lives (Isaiah 61:4).[239]

> *The local church, scholarly academies, and Spirit-led counseling services need to rise up to meet increasing needs of a present-day culture that is filled with immense emotional complexity!*

---

[235] John 15:2

[236] 1 Corinthians 3:1–2 (NLT)

[237] John 15:16 (NIV)

[238] Song of Solomon warns about the "little foes" that ruin the vineyards (2:15).

[239] Isaiah 61:4. This entire chapter is one of God's calls on my life. It speaks of rebuilding ancient ruins and renewing places that have long been forgotten.

God also is calling forth *apostolic ministries* that will spearhead new expressions of caregiving; *prophets* who will declare the timing of God's restorative healing; *evangelists* who will be the bringers of good news; *pastors* who will act as a ship's rudder in order to enable individuals to navigate the channels of daily living; and finally *teachers* who will illuminate the deeper truths of God in ways that will set captives free for the long term. The local church, scholarly academies, and Spirit-led counseling services need to rise up to meet increasing needs of a present-day culture that is filled with immense emotional complexity!

Key Counseling Principle: The "Vinedresser's plan" for increasing fruit production includes an elimination of any unhealthy growth. Branches that bear no fruit are cut off and thrown into the fire. Fruitful branches are not left untended but rather are pruned in order to help them bear more fruit. God's plan of pruning is not pleasant. Pruning exposes self-centered character traits. The Bible says, "Do not despise the LORD's discipline, and do not resent his rebuke, because the LORD disciplines those he loves, as a father the son he delights in."[240] Scripture offers wise counsel regarding the concept of pruning: "No discipline seems pleasant at the time, but painful. Later on, however, for those who have been trained by it, it produces a harvest of righteousness and peace."[241]

Pruning sculpts the plant (or person) into the image of Christ. While God cuts away, especially at the unproductive parts of our lives, He simultaneously provides nourishment to our roots. In times of (emotional or relational) drought, we, like plants, must spread our roots in search of water. Paul wrote, "So then, just as you received Christ Jesus as Lord, continue to live your lives in him, rooted and built

---

[240] Proverbs 3:11–12 (NIV)
[241] Hebrews 12:11 (ISV)

up in him, strengthened in the faith as you were taught, and overflowing with thankfulness."[242] To the woman at the well, Jesus said, "Everyone who drinks this water will be thirsty again, but whoever drinks the water I give them will never thirst. Indeed, the water I give them will become in them a spring of water welling up to eternal life."[243]

After considering the activity, voice, goodness and plan of God, it should be clear that it is not an easy task to help people who are going through a shadow time in their lives. But help is available. During my writing, I was reminded again of my role in God's plan in the life of another. I leave you with these wise words by Oswald Chambers.

> One of the hardest lessons to learn comes from our stubborn refusal to refrain from interfering in other people's lives. It takes a long time to realize the danger of being an amateur providence, that is, interfering with God's plan for others. You see someone suffering and say, "He will not suffer, and I will make sure that he doesn't." You put your hand right in front of God's permissive will to stop it, and then God says, "What is that to you?" ... When you do have to give advice to another person, God will advise through you with the direct understanding of His Spirit. Your part is to maintain the right relationship with God so that His discernment can come through you continually for the purpose of blessing someone else. Most of us live only within the level of consciousness—consciously serving and consciously devoted to God. This shows immaturity and the fact that we're not yet living the real Christian life. Maturity is produced in the life of a child of God on the unconscious level, until we become so totally surrendered to God

---

[242] Colossians 2:6–7 (NIV)
[243] John 4:13–14 (NIV)

that we are not even aware of being used by Him. When we are consciously aware of being used as broken bread and poured-out wine, we have yet another level to reach—a level where all awareness of ourselves and of what God is doing through us is completely eliminated. A saint is never consciously a saint—a saint is consciously dependent on God.[244]

---

[244] Oswald Chambers, "My Utmost for His Highest," November 16

Chapter 7

The God Who Creates

Unless the Lord builds the house its builders labor in vain.

Psalm 127:1

If we are willing to listen to our uneasiness, it might lead us to important questions that lurk under the surface of our Christian busyness.

Ruth Haley Barton

Genesis Model Principle 2

Genesis Principle:
God creates all that is called into existence.

Genesis Principle Applied:
Counselors are to be creative, specifically in providing *a safe place for counselees to share and their concerns.*

Scripture announces that God created the universe, *ex nihilo*—
out of nothing. Moses declares, "The earth was formless and
empty, and darkness covered the deep waters."[245] The first
feature attributed to God's character is creativity. This feature
is also to be a character descriptor of God's counselors. Job
confirms this quality of God's personhood as he says, "God
stretches the northern sky over empty space and hangs the
earth on nothing."[246] Isaiah also supports this assessment of
God: "The Lord, the everlasting God, Creator of the wide
world, grows neither weary nor faint."[247] The prophet Daniel
said, "Everything on earth is like nothing to Him, He does
as He wills with the host of heaven and the inhabitants of the
earth."[248] Every possible aspect of God's created order was
fashioned or designed by Creator God.

The signature piece of God's creative handiwork is
certainly the creation of man and woman.[249] Scripture records,

> Then God said, 'Let Us make man in our image,
> according to our likeness; let them have dominion
> over the fish of the sea, over the birds of the air, and
> over the cattle, over all the earth and over every
> creeping thing that creeps on the earth.' So God
> created man in His own image; in the image of
> God He created him; male and female He created
> them.[250] Then God blessed them, and God said to
> them, 'Be fruitful and multiply; fill the earth and
> subdue it; have dominion over the fish of the sea,
> over the birds of the air, and over every living thing
> that moves on the earth."[251]

---

[245] Genesis 1:2 (NLT)
[246] Job 26:7 (NIV)
[247] Isaiah 40:28 (NIV)
[248] Daniel 4:32 (NASV)
[249] Genesis 1:26f. (NLT)
[250] Genesis 1:26–31 (NLT)
[251] Genesis 1:28 (NLT)

This command by God is actually God's first "great commission."

The New Testament writers also affirm the creative feature of God's character. The earliest gospel writer, Mark, pens these words: "But from the beginning of the creation, God 'made them male and female.'"[252] John bears witness to the Creator God as he says, "You are worthy, O Lord, to receive glory and honor and power; for You created all things, and by Your will they exist and were created."[253] The Apostle Paul echoes John's conviction about God's creative nature as he says, "He is the image of the invisible God, the firstborn over all creation. For by Him all things were created that are in heaven and that are on earth, visible and invisible, whether thrones or dominions or principalities or powers. All things were created through Him and for Him. And He is in all things and before all things."[254] Paul also asserts, "For since the creation of the world His invisible attributes are clearly seen, being understood by the things that are made."[255] The writer of Hebrews states, in lyrical fashion, "You, LORD, in the beginning laid the foundation of the earth, and the heavens are the work of Your hands."[256]

But there is more to the creation account. Moses, the writer and compiler of the Genesis story,[257] writes, "Then God looked over all that He had made, and He saw that it

---

[252] Mark 10:6 (NIV)
[253] Revelation 4:11 (NIV)
[254] Colossians 1:15–18 (RSV)
[255] Romans 1:20 (RSV)
[256] Hebrews 1:10–12 (NKJV)
[257] Duane Garrett, in his book *Rethinking Genesis: The Source and Authorship of the First Book of the Pentateuch*, explains that Moses at Sinai "wrote all the words of the LORD" (Exodus 24:4) and must have written this part of Genesis when he communed with God on top of the mountain. He says that "Genesis 1 has *no parallel* anywhere in the ancient world outside the Bible. The creation myths from Egypt and Mesopotamia can hardly be set alongside Genesis 1 as a parallel in any meaningful sense. It must be regarded as an example of a genre unique to the Bible" (p. 191).

was very good. And the evening passed and morning came, marking the sixth day."[258] Everything God made was good. However, sin entered the world, and all that God had created was devastated. Paul understands this tragic turn of events this way: "They exchanged the truth of God for the lie, and worshiped and served the creature rather than the Creator."[259] And "just as through one man sin entered the world, and death through sin, and thus death spread to all men, because all have sinned."[260]

In spite of the fall, Paul is confident there will be a total redemption of God's originally created order. Paul writes, "Creation itself also will be delivered from the bondage of corruption into the glorious liberty of the children of God. For we know that the whole creation groans and labors with birth pangs together until now."[261] To people living in the southern part of Galatia, Paul says there will be complete ethnic reconciliation (for both the Jew and Greek), complete class or societal reconciliation (for slaves and free), and complete reconciliation between genders (as it relates to males and females).[262] In what has been termed the climax of Pauline soteriology,[263] Paul's conviction about the complete redemption of a fallen world is spelled out in Romans 8. A chapter often described as Life in the Spirit,[264] Paul declares, "There is no condemnation for those who are called in Christ Jesus"[265] and concludes this same chapter with clear "creational language," saying, "No power in the sky above or in the earth below—indeed, nothing in all creation will ever be able to

---

[258] Genesis 1:31 (NLT)
[259] Romans 1:25 (NASB)
[260] Romans 5:12 (NASB)
[261] Romans 8:21–22 (KJV)
[262] Galatians 3:28
[263] Norman C. Habel, ed., Cited in an unpublished paper by William A. Simmons; Lee University.
[264] Douglass Moo, Eerdmans Publishing, Pillar Commentary Series, 1988.
[265] Romans 8:1 (NIV)

separate us from the love of God that is revealed in Christ Jesus our Lord."[266] Even after the fall of humankind, Creator God will not be separated from His creation. Even though humanity's existence will be marked by extreme relational tension (Genesis 3:15), vocational frustration (Genesis 3:17; 4:12), spiritual and familial alienation (Genesis 4:16[267]), and an existential reality that is described as "homeless wandering" (Genesis 4:12), Paul declares, "We know that God causes everything to work together for the good of those who love God and are called according to His purpose."[268]

In a very preliminary way, after reading the salient elements of the creation story, we know the following:

1. In the beginning, creation was described as formless, empty, dark, and deep.
2. Scripture describes Creator God's *initial* relationship to the creational enterprise as proactive, decisive, and "need-meeting."[269]
3. All of creation was "very good."[270]

The Genesis principle as it relates *to the counselee* is fairly straightforward. People who seek counseling could be described as similar to creation's preilluminated dawn. I will consider the words Moses uses to depict initial creation and use these same four words to describe persons whom counselors see in their offices.

---

[266] Romans 8:39 (NIV)

[267] It is important to note that Cain [chose] to leave the Lord's presence and "settled" for a life that was far from what God would want or hope.

[268] Romans 8:28 (NIV)

[269] I use the term *need meeting* because God is actively committed to meeting the need for Adam to have a helpmate and, even after the fall, God meets the need for a more permanent "covering"(animal skin) for Adam and Eve.

[270] Genesis 1:31 (NIV)

Formless

First, these unfocused or emotionally out-of-shape people often lack boundaries. (A deficiency of boundaries is a common root cause for many problems.[271]) *Formless people* frequently do not know from whence they have come or where they are headed.[272] It is not uncommon at all for a formless person to say, "I really do not know" when he or she is asked, "What makes you happy?" or "What kind of job or relationship would give you a sense of peace?" These types of people are commonly empty, and sadly, they want someone else to "fill them up." Formless people have not learned what the psalmist declares: "The *boundary lines* have fallen for me in pleasant places; surely I have a delightful inheritance."[273]

Empty

Second, some people attempt to fill their lives with a variety of "things" *other than God*. Yet, in spite of this, success and ongoing happiness elude them. Paul says, "They have become *filled* with every kind of wickedness, evil, greed and depravity. They are full of envy, murder, strife, deceit and malice."[274] The antidote to these expressions of unhealthy behavior is to be "filled with the Spirit."[275] Various Greek scholars and Bible commentators[276] point out that the Greek present-imperative tense is used in this verse. The language found in this verse in

---

[271] See Henry Cloud and John Townsend's book *Boundaries* (Zondervan Publishing). (See also Glossary.)

[272] When a counselor asks a person in a first session, "Why are we here today?" the textbook response that is frequently heard is, "I don't know. I just felt like I needed to talk with someone."

[273] Psalm 16:6 (NIV)

[274] Romans 1:29 (NIV)

[275] Ephesians 5:18 (NIV)

[276] Peter T. O'Brien, *The Letter to the Ephesians* (Grand Rapids, MI: Eerdmans Publishing, 1999).

Ephesians implies an ongoing or continuous replenishment. There is a clear process to this "ongoing filling" or "continuous replenishment." Jesus invites his hearers, "If anyone is thirsty, let him come to me and drink. Whoever believes in me, as Scripture has said, streams of living water will flow from him."[277] Jesus says a replenishment of *any kind* involves a thirsting (there must be desire on the part of the counselee), a coming (this involves humility), a believing (this involves trust), and finally, the culminating promise of an overflow of living water.[278]

Dark

Third, a common statement made by people living a "shadowed" existence (i.e., behaviors or belief systems that are far less than God's best) is, "I can't see where I might be five years from now." More than just needing to see (having a vision), these people also need to understand (have factual information) as to why their lives are in their present states (taking personal responsibility for past choices). Jesus knew of the cultural and spiritual reality of darkness in his day as he told his disciples, "This is the verdict: Light has come into the world, *but men loved darkness instead of light because their deeds were evil.*"[279] Yet, for those trapped in darkness, a counselor will need to communicate one clear scriptural promise: "*The people walking in darkness have seen a great*

---

[277] John 7:37-38 (NIV)

[278] In Matthew 11:28–29, Jesus uses similar principles of replenishment when he says, "Come unto me, all ye that labor and are heavy laden, and I will give you rest. Take my yoke upon you, and learn of me; for I am meek and lowly in heart: and ye shall find rest unto your souls." The reader can see the importance of not only "coming" (humility) but also "learning" (the importance of teachability on the part of the counselee), the promise of rest (from one's own self-made plans) and a release or letting go of a self-imposed yoke of slavery.

[279] John 3:19 (NIV)

light; on those living in the land of the shadow of death a light has dawned."[280]

Deep

And fourth, people who are in deep trouble are often in this state because of well-established and clearly identifiable reasons. Some of these reasons may be by the seeker's own doing (e.g., irresponsibility, not listening to wise counsel, or deliberate ungodly behavior), while other, deeper issues may be purely circumstantial. This last descriptor of early creation ("deep"), is a significant counseling issue not to be overlooked. The issue of depth is noteworthy because counselees tell their counselors that they have "hit bottom" when, in reality, *they have not*. Scripture tells us that "deep [can] call to deep."[281] Only a voice that expresses the depths of God's wisdom can reach a person at his or her lowest point. People often make disastrous decisions because they live shallow and largely unexplored lives. The ancient philosopher Socrates said, "The unexamined life is not worth living."[282] People

> *People who have never deeply explored their lives or considered the possibility of trusting a counselor with intimate information will need no small amount of courage to enter the healing journey.*

[280] Isaiah 9:2–4, 6–7 (NIV)

[281] Psalm 42:7 (RSV)

[282] Socrates was a Greek philosopher who lived in Athens (469 BC–399 BC). In what is termed the Socratic dialogue, Socrates argued for the importance of talking with another person. Talking with a person who has an outside perspective can reveal blind spots (and we *all* have them). Counselors see the effects in the life of a person who lives with blind spots or issues of which he or she is not aware. Examining one's life reveals the hidden reasons behind well-established behavior patterns. Only through deeper examination will a person discover the subconscious programming that has often derailed his or her life. Unless a person becomes aware of

who have never *deeply* explored their lives or considered the possibility of trusting a counselor with intimate information will need no small amount of courage to enter the healing journey.

Paul wrote, "Remember this, a farmer who plants only a few seeds will get a small crop. But the one who plants generously will get a generous crop."[283] Paul is referring to a farmer who sows seed because he is expecting a harvest. I want to apply this image to a counselee who shares information with his or her counselor or therapist. A person in a counselor's office who shares selectively, like a farmer in the field who "sows sparingly," will receive a much smaller "harvest." An honest counselee *does not* offer "spin" or "smoke" by rationalizing, minimizing, or sharing only partial information. A person who authentically seeks help will leave no stone unturned as to the challenges he or she faces. *Like the successful farmer who sows generously and sees a plentiful harvest, the successful counselee communicates fully and sees very positive results.* Full disclosure of significant details of a situation goes a long way in achieving a successful counseling experience.

Summary

God's original creational state was described as dark, formless, empty, and deep. In a setting where there was no shape, substance, visibility, or bottom, God *created*. The question a counselor must ask him- or herself is, "What am I to create?" Arguably, a counselor (like God) may at times have very little with which to work. In some cases, a counselor, like God,

---

unhealthy patterns, life will continue to be an unconscious repetition of behavior that results in unhappiness. I have often said, "New decisions are based on new information. No new information, no new decisions. No new decisions, same unproductive way of living."

[283] 2 Corinthians 9:6 (NLT)

will need to create *ex nihilo*, out of nothing. When faced with a situation that could be described as empty, dark, shapeless, and deep, a counselor will need to establish or "create" a climate or an environment of safety for the counselee.

Why is safety so important for people who seek counseling? If you were to come to my office, you would see an ordinary street sign given to me many years ago that reads, "Sanctuary." This sign was acquired by someone whom my wife and I took into our home after he had been beaten up and abandoned. On the back of the sign are these words: "Thank you for giving me my first *safe place.*" If a counselor cannot create a place where people feel safe, the counselor has virtually nothing with which to work or build upon. A counselor can have good intentions, an education, practical ideas for helping hurting people, available professional colleagues with whom to consult, and belief in God, but if a hurting person does not feel safe with the counselor, the counseling relationship is doomed from the start.

> *If a counselor cannot create a place where people feel safe, the counselor has virtually nothing with which to work or build upon.*

The Creation Principle as It Relates to the Counselor

People who have never before consulted a counselor or are beginning anew with a different counselor have at least three unarticulated ideas in their minds: (1) a fear of the unknown or what to expect, (2) a lack of order or purpose, and (3) a diminished level of personal self-worth.

These people, at times, enter into counseling being somewhat suspicious of the process. They are fueled or empowered further by repeated negative experiences and increasing discomfort; observing other people, similar to themselves, going through difficulty; and a learned passivity[284] instead of proactively taking charge of their lives.

In a first counseling session, especially when any of the above is in play, I borrow from a medical model by asking the counselee, "On a scale of 1–5, how serious do you see your situation?" (Think of those signs in a doctor's or dentist's office with smiling and sad faces.) It is important for a counselor to determine the difficulty of the situation from both the counselor's and the counselee's vantage point. The level of difficulty will determine how the situation will be addressed and how many sessions it may take to resolve the conflict. When a counselor is facing an elevated level of mistrust, the optimum way of creating a safe place is by *listening*.

> *When a counselor is facing an elevated level of mistrust, the optimum way of creating a safe place is by listening.*

One other note about creating a safe place in a first session includes the topic of confidentiality.[285] If a counselee cannot be assured that what he or she is sharing in a counseling session stays with the counselor, the counselee will be reluctant to fully divulge intimate information. It goes a long way for counselors, *in a first session*, to assure counselees that they highly value confidentiality and that they would not violate their counselees' trust by using a counseling session as a sermon illustration.

Listening as a Tool to Creating a Safe Place

Scripture speaks of the importance of "hearing or listening." John tells us that there is a blessing for "the one who *hears* the

---

[284] Seligman refers to this as 'learned helplessness' (see glossary).
[285] See Glossary of Terms in the back of this book for more complete information.

words of this book and keeps them."[286] John also sends out the warning that *those who refuse to listen* will be considered to be disobedient disciples.[287] In his workbook *The Art of Hearing God*,[288] John Paul Jackson lays out several observations that are helpful for a counselor in creating a safe place for those needing help.

1. Authentic spiritual listening is profoundly "other focused."
2. The world today is starving to death for anyone who will listen.
3. Many good listeners, at one time, were the recipient of someone who took the time to listen to them.
4. The Golden Rule could be adapted to: "Listen to others as you would have them listen to you."
5. The individual with the greatest influence will be the greatest listener.

Listening is not something that comes naturally to people; we as a society, by and large, do not value listening. Children should be taught at an early age the importance of this highly valued quality in healthy and successful relationships. I want to identify five levels or categories of listening. *The level of listening a counselor practices will determine how safe a counselee will feel in the counseling environment.*

The first level of listening is ignoring. This type of listening, obviously, is rude and is guaranteed to create an unsafe place for the counselee. I want to advance an insight here to the ignoring phase of listening. If a person is available to listen to someone and agrees to meet with someone, yet is more interested in watching the time, this can be very harmful

---

[286] Revelation 1:3 (NRSV)
[287] John 8:47
[288] John Paul Jackson, *The Art of Hearing God* (Streams Ministries International)

to the person in pain. Ignoring the person through inactive involvement in the counseling situation is very damaging. My counsel here is that if a counselor or caregiver does not have the legitimate interest to listen in the first place, the counselor should not agree to meet with the person. One other practical note: I have three clocks hidden around my office because I want the people who see me to think I am on "their time" and not "my time." I encourage the careful placement of clocks in the counseling office so that the appointment time can be kept within limits without constant, obvious turning to check on the time.

The second type of listening is interruptive listening. This approach to listening is seen in people who finish other people's sentences for them. The interruptive listener is quick to analyze and frequently interject his or her own thoughts while another is talking. Interruptive listeners usually have unresolved needs in their own lives that overflow into their relationships. These people are commonly heard saying (interrupting), "That reminds me of a time when …"

A third kind of listening is informational. People who engage in information listening neither ignore others who are talking nor interrupt. The informational listener is comfortable with silence, listens to learn new things about other people, and may sense that he or she could possibly help the seeker or counselee in some way. The informational listener knows the importance of earning the right to be heard. There is an old saying that goes, "People don't care how much you know until they know how much you care." Informational listeners, by the active and sincere way they present themselves to the counselee, establish a safe place for counselees to share. And ultimately, because the counselor has listened, the counselor has earned the right to speak into a counselee's life situation.

The fourth type of listening is incarnational listening. The person who practices this type of listening knows the importance of their words' "becoming flesh."[289] Incarnational listening recognizes the validity of gaining new information while having no agenda other than just being present. The incarnational listener is aware of body language and eye contact and is in touch with the emotional climate of the counseling environment. Incarnational listening is very powerful and, when practiced optimally, goes a long way toward creating a safe place.

The final expression of listening is intercession-oriented listening and is by far the most meaningful type of listening a counselor can practice. This listening could also be described as multitasked listening as the counselor simultaneously listens to what God is saying and to what the person is conveying about his or her situation. This genre of listening is routinely used in what is referred to as Theophostic counseling.[290] See the chart below for a clear summary of the five listening types. The reader may want to pause now and evaluate them to determine what category he or she fits into.

---

[289] John 1:14 (NIV)
[290] See Glossary of Terms at end of book.

Types and Descriptions of Listening	
Ignoring	Not listening; rude and insensitive. *Wounds or hurts the counselee.*
Interruptive Listening	Finishes a person's sentences; often interrupts; has a time-driven agenda; is not comfortable with awkward silence. *Frustrates the counselee.*
Informational Listening	The beginning of a good listener; does not interrupt; listens to gain new information. *Creates an increased desire within the counselee to want to share or talk more.*
Incarnational Listening	Is very present with the counselee as seen in body language, eye contact, and empathetic voice. *The counselee feels understood, validated, and genuinely cared for.*
Intercessory Listening	Is profoundly multitasking as the counselor listens to both the counselee and God. A safe place is created, and the counselor earns a deep level of trust from the counselee. *The counselee feels safe and comes to trust the counselor.*

Creation: For Counselor and Counselee

At the outset of this chapter, I observed that "in the beginning," God's creative abilities were proactive, decisive, and "need meeting." When a safe place for counseling has been created by a counselor, a counselee will *want to* return and talk to the counselor. The counselor can develop an even more meaningful counseling environment by concluding the first session with the following strategies:

1. As a session comes to an end, a counselor can actually deepen an environment of safety by asking, "What is one idea or concept discussed in our time together that is significant or new to you?" This information allows the counselee to recognize *for themselves.*

2. There are times when I ask, "Is there something that we touched on that you would like to explore further in our next session?" The counselee's response to this question actually creates necessary anticipation and motivation for coming back for further help.

3. Another counseling strategy is for the counselor to validate or affirm the counselee's efforts toward addressing presenting issues. These encouraging observations actually empower the counselee. I have often heard after a session, "I think I am going to get through this!" Only a counselee who has been in a safe place and has received some constructive guidance for the future can make this statement. When a counselor can succinctly summarize what has taken place, the counselee can see and hear that something has been accomplished. This sense of accomplishment also breeds encouragement in the life of the one seeking help.

4. A final idea I offer here surrounds the concept of "starting small." There will be times when the counselee is hesitant to identify or establish any goals that would result in forward movement. When this fear-based scenario presents itself, the counselor should be reminded of the following:

a. Starting small encourages a person to get started, *period.* Counselees should be encouraged to know that they do not have to have every "i" dotted and every "t" crossed before getting started on what they want to accomplish. Starting small is not concerned with details; the emphasis in "starting small" is on the word *starting.*

b. Starting small also gives a clear initial *focus.* After a small or initial step forward has been taken, the counselor will want to move from "starting" to "starting with focus." The additional component of focus provides increasing clarity, meaning, and accountability. Focus always carries with it the ability to measure or verify success. I have heard numerous leadership practitioners comment, "If a goal cannot be measured, it is not an adequate goal."

c. Starting small and being successful can increase *self-confidence* when an initial obstacle is overcome; this same self-confidence can be tapped later to transcend obstacles. People who do not take the first necessary small step will never experience the increased exhilaration of confidence when bigger challenges are successfully overcome.

A Final Thought

I can in no way overemphasize the importance of counselors' creating a safe haven for counselees. A counselor can have good intentions, outstanding academic and professional credentials, and an established spiritual base from which he or she works, but if a counselor cannot create a safe place for the counselee, the counseling relationship will flounder and die. It is not my intention to conclude this chapter on a somber note, but this is the stark reality.

Chapter 8

The God Who Speaks

God speaks to those who take the time to listen
and God listens to those who take the time to pray.
Mario Tomasello

Every happening, great and small, is a parable
whereby God speaks to us, and the art of life is to
get the message.
Malcom Muggeridge

Genesis Model Principle 3

Genesis Principle: God speaks into existence all that is created.

Genesis Principle Applied: Counselors are to listen to God for words to speak into the lives of their counselees.

The third principle of the Genesis Model is presented in this chapter. Just as God *spoke* all of created order into existence,[291] counselors are to speak as ambassadors for God.

---

[291] See Genesis 1:3, 9, 11, 14, 20, 24, 26, 29

Some basic examples that speak to their counselees is to clarify (ask questions) what is being said by the counselee, offer direction (e.g., "Have you considered … ?"), speak words of encouragement ("Your follow through last week on [blank] was really good. That is a new level of discipline for you."), and bring correction ("You know we need to talk about … "). In every sense, counselors are God's ambassadors and *spokespersons* to a hurting world—or as one person once said to me, "You are Jesus with skin on."

Admittedly, an entire volume could easily be written on this single topic. I share the following story from a friend, which illustrates the "speaking power" of God's presence in a counseling relationship. Briefly, this family sought various types of help for behavioral concerns related to their child. They pursued help from a variety of counselors, well-meaning clergy, pediatricians, pharmacologists, and some of the finest and most renowned medical clinicians. Thousands of dollars later, their situation was not only unchanged—it was markedly worse. Ultimately, this family went to a Christian counselor who practiced a specific approach to Christian counseling. This method brought needed freedom and greater levels of peace. In my friend's own words, "This was an approach to counseling that utilized the *spoken words of God.* This style of counseling brought peace and healing to our family when dozens of other interventions failed." This orientation embraces the belief and practice that God speaks through His word (the Scriptures) and that God is still speaking to His people today through God's faithful servants. One supporting text that validates this counseling approach is found in 1 Corinthians, chapter two, verses one and six. Paul says,

> *This orientation embraces the belief and practice that God speaks through His word (the Scriptures) and that God is still speaking to His people today through God's faithful servants.*

Now we have received, not the spirit of the world, but the Spirit who is from God, that we might know the things freely given to us by God....I do speak with words of wisdom, but not the kind of wisdom that belongs to this world or to the rulers of this world, who are soon forgotten."[292]

Professionals in the Christian mental health field refer to this orientation of counseling as pneumatic or Theophostic counseling.[293] This approach to counseling routinely utilizes two spiritual gifts mentioned in Scripture. These spiritual gifts are: the gift of knowledge[294] and the discernment of spirits.[295] A clear example of the "word of knowledge" spiritual gift is found in the Gospel of John. Jesus, having a conversation with a woman, says to her, "You don't have a husband, for you have had five husbands and the man you're living with now is not your husband."[296] In this story. Jesus "shares personal information" with the woman that may not have been public knowledge.

The second spiritual gift commonly utilized in pneumatic counseling is the gift of discerning of spirits.[297] An example of

---

[292] 1 Corinthians 2:1, 6 (NLT)

[293] A pneumatic approach to counseling recognizes that the Holy Spirit is at the center of the counseling relationship and not seen as an optional add-on. Readers are encouraged to see John Kie Vining's text, *Spirit-Centered Counseling: A Pneumascriptive Approach*. See also R. T. Brock, *The Holy Spirit and Counselling, Vol. II, Principle and Practice* (Peabody, MA: Hendrickson, 1988); David Allender, *The Wounded Heart* (London: NavPress, 1990).

[294] John Wimber. The gift of knowledge is the supernatural revelation of a fact or situation that is not known by the natural mind. It is a disclosing of truth by the Holy Spirit that God wants to make known. (*Spiritual Gifts*, Vol. 1, Vineyard Ministry International)

[295] 1 Corinthians 12:10. This is not an ability or natural insight into a situation but rather a God-given gifting whereby a person discerns root causes of a spiritual nature in a person's life. This type of counseling often brings to a person deep release from past traumas or painful experiences.

[296] John 4:17-18 (NLT)

[297] Also called, the spiritual gift of discernment.

this gift is found in the story of the father with the demonized son.[298] The father knew something was terribly wrong with his son, but he needed someone who could help bring freedom and deliverance from such a significant challenge. On occasion, I have had friends and counselors feel as though they had "hit the wall" when it came to handling a person's problem. During these times, the Holy Spirit has guided me in asking the right questions, uncovering previously unknown information, and ultimately seeing the person(s) receive freedom from what had been a problem.

From the outset of this chapter on the spoken aspect of counseling, I want to be very clear about my intentions when I say that Christian counselors are to be God's ambassadors and spokespersons.

Before I Go Further

Speaking prophetically for God takes wisdom and great maturity. The apostle Paul seems to have valued this expression of spiritual gifting rather highly, as he once said, "Now I wish that you all spoke in tongues, but *even* more that you would prophesy."[299] The reader should also be reminded of a group of prophets in Jeremiah's day who put *their own words* into God's mouth and in so doing "falsely prophesied," or wrongly "spoke for God." Scripture records the Lord saying about these errant prophets, "The prophets of Samaria ... led my people Israel astray.... Do not listen to what the prophets are prophesying to you; they fill you with false hopes. They speak visions from their own minds."[300] The Lord warned the people that He would forsake all those who pervert His words.[301]

---

[298] Mark 9:17
[299] 1 Corinthians 14:5 (NASB)
[300] Jeremiah 23:13–16 (NIV)
[301] Jeremiah 16:36

When it comes to speaking for God, I would remind the reader of God's servant, Job. At the end of Job's story, we find an emotionally, physically, and spiritually threadbare servant. This is the very same man whom God described at the beginning of his life as blameless and full of complete integrity.[302] However, in Chapter 42, God refers to Job as a man who lacks wisdom and is full of ignorance.[303] Job admits that he has "misspoken" (a reference to his lament in Chapters 38–41) and will not speak again.[304] Job confesses that he had spoken of things that he did not understand and were, in fact, beyond his level of comprehension.[305] However, the story continues. God then rails against Job's three friends, Eliphaz, Bildad, and Zophar, saying, "I am angry with you because you have not spoken accurately about me, *as my servant Job has*" (emphasis added).[306] Do you catch the subtle innuendo here? It appears that Job had said at least some things correctly about God. At story's end, God abundantly blesses Job with even more than he had at the beginning of his life.[307]

We know from this biblical account that Job "misspoke" for God, and that God clearly voiced His displeasure with Job. Question, why did God restore to Job more than his original fortune? The answer is threefold. First, with humility, Job confessed his wrongful actions and repented.[308] Second, the Lord acknowledged that there was some part of Job's discourse that God deemed "right."[309] And third, Job was willing to censure himself and never speak again. Even though Job misspoke, God recognized the deeper parts

---

[302] Job 1:1
[303] Job 1:3
[304] Job 38:1–40:5
[305] Job 42:1–6
[306] Job 42:7 (NLT)
[307] Job 42:12
[308] Job 42:6
[309] Job 42:7

of Job's character.[310] A wonderful promise of Scripture tells us, "The LORD sees not as man sees; man looks on the outward appearance, but the LORD looks on the heart."[311] My colleague Dr. Rickie Moore says of this text, "Job prays *through*. It takes God-talk that is straight and firm enough to break through our forms and speak to the One who is no form, the One who breaks all forms, the One who breaks us. Yet the One who has broken me is the One who has spoken to me, revealing that I have spoken *straight to Him*."[312]

There have been times I have heard Christians say, "I am bored with my prayer life." I have been tempted to respond by saying, "Have you ever thought that God might feel the very same way?" A key principle in speaking for God is summed up in the condition of a person's heart and motives. Ambassadors for God, in any life-changing setting, must embrace pure motives and right intentions when they believe that God has called them to speak on His behalf.

Speaking for God in the New Testament

The Apostle Paul is very clear about the authority of his own ministry. Paul states unequivocally that he did not misuse his apostolic authority as God's messenger or spokesperson to the Gentiles. Paul exhorted the Corinthians that he neither wrongfully nor deceitfully shared the word of God.[313] Paul defended his apostolic mandate when he said, "When I came

---

[310] It is worth noting that there is no mention of Job's three friends' recanting their behavior or responding in any way to God's discipline.
[311] 1 Samuel 16:6–7 (ESV)
[312] Rickie Moore, "Raw Prayer and Refined Theology," (University Press of America, 2000). An article found in *The Spirit and the Mind,* on the occasion to honor Dr. Donald Bowdle. This is an outstanding article outlined by solid theological and linguistic insight.
[313] 2 Corinthians 4:2; see also 2 Corinthians 10:1 and 11:5–6

to you, I did not come with eloquence or human wisdom as I proclaimed to you the testimony about God."[314]

There was also a time in Paul's ministry when he clearly identified or "called out" false teachers, saying, "For such are false apostles, deceitful workers, transforming themselves into apostles of Christ. And no wonder! For Satan himself transforms himself into an angel of light. Therefore it is no great thing if his ministers also transform themselves into ministers of righteousness, whose end will be according to their works."[315] Paul's courageous presentation of the gospel is compared to the deception and trickery of other teachers.[316] This warning of "'later day false teachers and prophets" is made pristinely clear by Paul, late in his ministry, as he says, "For the time is coming when people will not put up with sound doctrine, but having itching ears, they will accumulate for themselves teachers to suit their own desires, and will turn away from listening to the truth and wander away to myths."[317]

God Speaking in Our Contemporary Context

Historically, Christians have believed that God has *spoken* to them in *the Bible.* In II Timothy 3:16, we read, "All scripture is given by inspiration of God, and is profitable for doctrine, for reproof, for correction, for instruction in righteousness." Each of these *applications of God's word* (reproof, correction, and instruction) is to be routinely used by counselors, *verbally.* Counselors are to share Scripture with their counselees in a way that is "profitable," resulting in instruction for righteousness. The apostle Paul said in his "sorrowful letter" of 2 Corinthians that his going to see the Corinthians and

---

[314] 1 Corinthians 2:1 (NIV)
[315] 2 Corinthians 11:13–15 (KJV)
[316] 1 Thessalonians 2:1–8 (NIV)
[317] 2 Timothy 4:3–4 (NRSV)

speaking to them was not intended to treat them with severity and tear them down, but rather to strengthen them.[318]

Christians have also been taught that God speaks to His people *through others*.[319] The Bible says that believers are "ambassadors for Christ."[320] A trustworthy civil ambassador says only what his or her government authorizes him or her to say. In his final commission to his disciples in Matthew's gospel, Jesus said, "I have been given all authority in heaven and earth. Therefore go, and make disciples of all people."[321] Acts 17 offers a second accounting of people who heard a spoken word that was given to them by an ambassador of Christ. The people living in Berea were called noble because they listened eagerly to Paul's message and also searched the Scriptures day after day to see if what Paul and Silas were teaching was the truth.[322] In other words, the people of Berea didn't merely trust an itinerant preacher (an ambassador for Christ or counselor) who came to minister to them; they verified that Paul and Silas were declaring God's truth and not spouting their own errant opinions. God calls the Bereans noble for doing their "due diligence." Christians today would be wise to follow the Berean's example of listening to a messenger from God and then confirming that message via Scripture as being truly authentic. It is encouraging to know that there is a blessing for this "hearing and doing" principle. In Revelation 1:3, we learn, "God blesses the one who reads the words of the prophecy to the church, and he blesses all who listen to its message and obey what it says."

---

[318] 2 Corinthians is referred to by New Testament scholars as Paul's sorrowful letter because it was written out of much affliction and tears (see 2 Corinthians 2:4).

[319] I realize there is a segment of believers today who do not believe that God speaks prophetically or through these types of expressions of counseling. All I will say here is that this is not my position.

[320] 2 Corinthians 5:20 (ESV)

[321] Matthew 28:18f. (NLT)

[322] Acts 17:10–12

Finally, today's counselors can speak to another person with Scripture that might apply to their identified concern or by sharing a specific truth that the counselor believes to be God's word (something that the counselee does not know or cannot see). This spoken aspect of Christian counseling always exalts Christ and never the counselor. Any instruction or direction that is spoken to another person in a counseling session should also bring practical assistance.[323] We know that the Holy Spirit always points to or exalts the person of Jesus and brings His fresh revelation to the person who is seeking guidance. The Bible tells us, "Where there is no revelation, the people cast off restraint; but happy is he who keeps the law."[324] Revelation is the discovered will of God given by a counselor to the counselee. Where there is no revelation of the activity of God in a person's life, the person will lead an unbridled and unrestrained life.

The culminating result of the "God speaks" aspect of the Genesis Model of counseling is that the seeker or counselee would build his or her life on the foundation of Christ because of the words that have been spoken to him or her. I often tell my counseling students that *the crowning result of all counseling* is to have people learn to live their lives independently dependent on Christ. A counselor's greatest satisfaction should come from seeing a person who was formerly in great need live his or her life with fullness and grace *apart from* the counselor. Christian counselors are to impart this foundational philosophy of dependence on Christ into the lives of their counselees. A personal goal that I had, even as a paid counselor in a professional counseling practice, was to "graduate

> *the crowning result of all counseling is to have people learn to live their lives independently dependent on Christ.*

---

[323] 2 Corinthians 14:7f.
[324] Proverbs 29:18 (NIV)

counselees" out from the counseling office.[325] Something I say early on in the counseling relationship is, "Thank you for the privilege of allowing me to be in this season of change with you. I also want you to know that my goal is to help you live independently from me."

I strongly believe and embrace the "God speaks" feature of the Genesis Model of counseling. Scripture is filled with examples that demonstrate the interrelatedness between a spoken word and behavioral change. There is power in words that are spoken—for both good and evil. God desires to reveal Scriptures to us for the purpose of bringing people to greater levels of righteousness, which is rewarding for both the counselor and the counselee. In addition to scriptural understanding, God desires to give His counselors pictures, images, impressions, and even dreams that can be used in the counseling setting. God, in His love and mercy, sends people into our lives that can offer prophetic insight and direction. It is entirely up to the counselee to listen to what is being spoken to them. The moment a person chooses to align his or her life with the prophetic purpose of God spoken by the counselor, the person in need will discover a life that he or she has never known before. It is through the "God speaks" stage in pastoral counseling that the counselee can discover that God has not left him or her without His divine guidance.

Moses: A Biblical Case Study in "Speaking for God"

That God desires to use a person in a *spoken way* in the life of another poses a unique set of challenges. When I hear God

---

[325] I fully recognize the tension that credentialed counselors have in needing to support their families through their practice. I was in this very situation. However, for me there is greater satisfaction with seeing someone live independently from me.

speak in a counseling setting, I have some routine responses. Frequently when I hear from God, I think *I can't say that!* or *Is that really you speaking, Lord?* I share these very honest personal experiences because I want the reader to know that these *personal responses* actually have a *biblical basis*. Let me offer a brief case study.

The setting is Exodus 3 and 4. We find that Moses had no confidence in his earthly ability to be a spokesperson for God (or a speaker, period!). Moses could have easily thought (negative self-talk) that being a murderer[326] disqualified him from being used by God. It is reasonable to think that when God spoke to Moses from the burning bush there was little else Moses could say other than, "But …"[327] I have seen this deficit-oriented pathology[328] at work in many of God's servants, especially as it relates to being able to hear from God. People often need added assurance when it comes to believing that God has spoken to them. God used two different signs or proofs that He was truly calling or confirming Moses to be his "mouthpiece."[329]

It is interesting that God used things that were "close at hand"[330] to prove to Moses that He was at work in his life. Through this initial twofold confirming experience (and there would be additional signs throughout Moses' journey), Moses would learn how to do what was being asked of him, *even if it made him feel uncomfortable.* The principle of God's using things that are found close to any servant is seen several times

---

[326] See Exodus 2.

[327] Exodus 3:11; this is actually my interpretive "but."

[328] *Deficit-oriented pathology* is when a person's first inclination in decision making is to reason why they cannot do what is presented to them. These people automatically see the glass half-empty rather than half-full. People also approach decision making with either a "present future orientation" (hope) or a "present past orientation" (often with regret). See Philippians 3:11.

[329] Exodus 2:2–5

[330] Exodus 4:2–7

in Scripture: an ox goad in Shamgar's hand to ensure military victory;[331] the stone launched from David's hand to defeat Goliath;[332] the jawbone of a donkey that was in Samson's hand to kill three thousand Philistines;[333] five loaves and two fish from the lunch of a little boy to feed a hungry crowd;[334] and Jesus' saying, "The kingdom of God is *at hand*"[335] (emphasis added).

In spite of God's miraculous activity in Moses' life, this friend of God had an excuse for not speaking for the Lord. Moses said, "O my Lord, I am not eloquent, neither before nor since You have spoken to your servant; but I *am* slow of speech and slow of tongue."[336] In short, Moses did not think he had speaking ability.[337] The first forty years of Moses' life in Egypt would have afforded him training in the wisdom and culture of the Egyptians, including being tutored in the discipline of rhetoric, or "argumentation." The apostle Paul substantiates this fact, saying, "Moses was learned in all the wisdom of the Egyptians, and was mighty in words and deeds."[338] In Moses' "silent years" while living on the backside of Sinai, Moses would have been relegated to speaking only to sheep.[339] Any form of eloquence learned in Egypt would have certainly atrophied. The old phrase "Use it or lose it" comes to mind. What Moses needed in order to

> *Maybe Moses thought God had made a mistake in choosing him. A key truth to remember here is that God had no Plan B. Moses was God's one and only plan.*

---

[331] Judges 3:31
[332] 1 Samuel 17:49
[333] Judges 15:15
[334] John 6:9
[335] Mark 1: 1f. (NIV)
[336] Exodus 4:10 (ESV)
[337] The phrase *not eloquent* literally means "heavy of mouth."
[338] Acts 7:22 (KJV)
[339] There were undoubtedly times when Moses thought leading sheep was far easier than leading people!

be God's mouthpiece was not an eloquence learned from Egypt's finest teachers or any validation that position or popularity or pulpit might offer. No, Moses needed a self-confidence that can only be given by God!

The drama continues. Moses remains faithful to his insecurity-based script. God does not let up; He will not accept Moses' excuses. Was Moses' inability in speaking ever an issue for God? Was Moses' past ever an issue for God? Maybe Moses thought God had made a mistake in choosing him. A key truth to remember here is that God had no Plan B. Moses was God's one and only plan. God's counselors must remember, especially in regard to "speaking for God," that God is sufficient no matter what real or imagined inadequacies a counselor may perceive *about themselves.* God's response to Moses was, "Who has made man's mouth? Or who makes the mute, the deaf, the seeing, or the blind? Have not I, the LORD? Now therefore, go, and I will be with your mouth and teach you what you shall say."[340]

The fact that Moses believed that he was not eloquent was completely beside the point. God's refusal to accept Moses' pathetic reasoning reveals something about the depth of the sovereignty of God—a divine sovereignty that is specifically revealed in the context of calling from without yet, must also be heard from within.[341]

> *God's refusal to accept Moses' pathetic reasoning reveals something about the depth of the sovereignty of God—a divine sovereignty that is specifically revealed in the context of calling from without yet, must also be heard from within.*

---

[340] Exodus 4:11–12 (ESV)

[341] In his book, Palmer states that vocation, or calling, does not come from willfulness. It comes from listening. The word *vocation* is rooted in the Latin word *voice.* Calling is not something you pursue, writes Palmer. It is something you *hear.* Parker Palmer, *Let Your Life Speak* (San Francisco: Jossey-Bass Publishers, 2000). See page 4f.

At this point in the narrative, Moses still does not grasp the significance of God's activity in his life. Unwillingness to cooperate with God's call continues as he says, "O my Lord, please send by the hand of whomever *else* You may send."[342] So the anger of the LORD was kindled against Moses, and He said,

> "Is not Aaron the Levite your brother? I know that he can speak well. And look, he is also coming out to meet you. When he sees you, he will be glad in his heart. Now you shall speak to him and put the words in his mouth. And I will be with your *mouth and with his mouth, and I will teach you what you shall do. So he shall be your spokesman* to the people. And he himself shall be as a mouth for you, and you shall be to him as God. And you shall take this rod in your hand, with which you shall do the signs."[343]

It is important to note that God was *not* angry when Moses asked, "Who am I?"[344] God was *not* angry when Moses asked, "Who should I say sent me?"[345] God was *not* angry when Moses disbelieved God's word and said, "Suppose they will not believe me or listen to my voice?"[346] God was not even angry when Moses falsely claimed that he was not and had never been eloquent.[347] But even God has a breaking point. God became angry when Moses was just plain unwilling to do what was being asked of him. Having an identity issue may be understandable ("Who am I?"). Not having proper authority to do a job is also

> Blatant unwillingness to serve does not cut it with God.

---

[342] Exodus 4:13 (NET)
[343] Exodus 4:14–17 (NLT); emphasis added.
[344] Exodus 3:11 (NLT)
[345] Exodus 3:13 (NLT)
[346] Exodus 4:1 (NIV)
[347] Exodus 4:10

understandable ("Who should I say sent me?"). Having concerns with one's possible lack of abilities is also easily understandable ("They will not listen to me"). But blatant unwillingness to serve does not cut it with God.

By Exodus 4, God seems to be willing to shore up Moses' insecurities by having Aaron go along with him into Egypt. However, as the story of Aaron (and Moses) later unfolds, we learn that Aaron was just as much a problem to Moses as he was a help. It would be Aaron who would instigate the worship of the golden calf, fashioning the calf and building the altar himself.[348] At one time, Aaron openly led a mutiny against Moses.[349] Aaron may have been a good communicator, but he was a man of thin character. God does not need ministers or counselors who are smooth talkers. God also does not need people whose ethics are based more on favorable conditions or convenience. God needs servants who are willing to respond to the prophetic call of the Almighty by simply saying, "Here I am Lord, send me."[350]

God Still Speaks

"So Moses went and returned to Jethro his father-in-law, and said to him, 'Please let me go and return to my brethren who *are* in Egypt and see whether they are still alive.' And Jethro said to Moses, 'Go in peace.'"[351] It was wise on Moses' part to make sure that it was clear for him to go. When the fire faded from the burning bush and the voice of God became silent across the desert in the cool of the evening, it came time for Moses to assume his new identity:

> *Serving God involves hearing from God before ever speaking for God. Being a messenger for God is no guarantee that people will listen.*

---

[348] Exodus 32:1–6
[349] Numbers 12:1–8
[350] Isaiah 6:8 (NIV)
[351] Exodus 4:18 (NASB)

spokesman for God. One may ask, "Did Moses have any idea what was ahead of him when he agreed to take the Lord's call?" or "Could he have imagined a vision of God on Mount Sinai or heard the voice of God thunder from heaven?" I wonder, what was it like to carry the tablets of stone down Mount Sinai? And did he ever conceive the level of ungrateful contentiousness that he would face as he led the children of Israel out of bondage? The story of Moses offers an unblemished example of a key leadership principle: serving God involves hearing from God before ever speaking for God. Being a messenger for God is no guarantee that people will listen. I remind readers that Moses' words to Pharaoh, (as scripted by God), although audibly heard by the Egyptian leader, were ultimately rejected because of a hardened heart. Moses' instruction and direction to the children of Israel were also heard but were often received with faithlessness, as they said to Moses, "It would have been better for us to serve the Egyptians than to die in the desert."[352]

Having the desire to be a voice for God is not wrong, but this desire may entail a season of obscurity before there is any level of recognition. And even then, the recognition that the spokesperson of God may get may not be what was ever expected!

Despite the many ways in which Moses came up short, he is still referred to as a "Friend of God."[353] Each of us should take encouragement from this. Just as God worked patiently and painstakingly in Moses' life, such will be the case for you and me. Scripture tells us that God spoke "face to face, clearly, and not in riddles"[354] *because Moses could be trusted.*[355] It was while Moses was tethered to

---

[352] Exodus 14:12 (NIV)

[353] Exodus 33:11

[354] Numbers 12:6–8 (NIV)

[355] Numbers 12:7 (emphasis added); there is an entire lesson here all by itself. One lesson is that God speaks powerfully and clearly to those who can be trusted!

the backside of nowhere, between obscurity and monotony, that he developed the ability to hear God and learn how to deliver the goods. I think parallel experiences to those of Moses produce similar hearing and speaking abilities in you and me.

Each of us can indeed hear from God and, dare I say, speak God's oracles as they are shared with us. Glory, let it be so! Having the desire to be a voice for God is not wrong, but this desire may entail a season of obscurity before there is any level of recognition. And even then, *the recognition that the spokesperson of God may get may not be what was ever expected*!

A cultural reality today is that many want to feel the warmth of the fire without experiencing the pain of the flame.

It grieves me to say that there are others who long to speak God's words, yet they cannot even recognize the voice of God when He is calling to them.[356] These same people lack the daily discipline of reflection and study of the Scriptures. If people desire to speak God's truth, God's truth must first burn within them, like it did for the prophet Jeremiah.[357] People cannot give that which they do not have. These types of people may read the Bible from time to time, but they rarely ever

> *A cultural reality today is that many want to feel the warmth of the fire without experiencing the pain of the flame.*

have the Bible *read them*. The Bible is not to be seen as only a book to be read but rather a mirror that reveals who we really are as individuals.

I close this chapter on God's counselors speaking into the lives of others with a cautionary word. Any person who draws close enough to hear God's voice or have a burning

---

[356] Even the learned rabbi, Saul, former student of Gamaliel, did not recognize the voice of God when God called to him on the Damascus Road (see Acts 9:5).
[357] Jeremiah 20:9

bush experience may experience something that he or she did not expect. In my personal experience, there was a time when God revealed to me that the portrait of my life more closely reflected the church of Sardis, to whom God said, "You have the reputation of being alive but in fact are dead. And that which is alive, is about to die."[358] Our ability to hear God and speak God's word effectively into the lives of others begins with a lifestyle of holiness, a mind-set of seeking hard after the truth of God, and a willingness to be a sent ambassador of God. God's counselors should join with the apostle Paul in praying, "I want to know Christ—yes, to know the power of his resurrection and participation in his sufferings, becoming like him in his death."[359]

---

[358] Revelation 3:1 (NLT)
[359] Philippians 3:10 (NIV)

Chapter 9

The God Who Illumines

As our bodily eyes are illuminated by seeing the light, so in contemplating God our soul is illuminated by him.

St. John Chrysostom

I am the light of the world.

Matthew 5:14

You are the light of the world.

John 8:12

Genesis Model Principle 4

Genesis Principle: God illumines that which was in darkness.

Genesis Principle Applied: Counselors are to "shed light" on the darkened areas of a counselee's life and illuminate lies that are thought to be truth or untruths that have been spoken over the life of the counselee.

First Steps Out from the Shadows

From "the beginning," we witness God's involvement in the counseling paradigm.[360] As God created the heavens and the earth, so counselors are to utilize every means in their innovative arsenal to be just as creative.[361] The biblical story of creation reveals that God spoke into existence all of created order. In similar fashion, counselors are to "speak order" into previously unordered lives.[362] Following the establishing of earth and sky, God ushers light upon all that has been created.[363] For the first time in the creation narrative, the totality of God's power comes into view; dawn is fully illuminated.

This chapter uncovers the hard counseling realities and challenges that God's illuminating presence brings to the counseling relationship. Three ways or three levels will be enumerated whereby God specifically brings "illumination" or insight to both counselors and counselees. In every sense, God's counselors are to be light bearers in the counseling session. I will conclude this chapter by answering an often asked question: "Why do some people refuse to change, especially after light has come into their shadows?"

The Emergence and Function of Light

Out of the darkness, out of the silence, out of the shapeless void of creation, God speaks, "Let there be light."[364] Light is the first element that is released into creation by Creator

---

[360] The sovereign activity of God is the sole emphasis of Chapter Four.
[361] The necessity of creational activity is the subject of Chapter Five.
[362] The importance of speaking truth is the emphasis of Chapter Six.
[363] Genesis 1:3, 14
[364] Genesis 1:3, 14 (NIV)

God.[365] An interesting observation about the concept of the entrance of light is that there appears to be a two-step approach[366] to light's existence and light's purpose in the creation story. In Genesis 1:3 we read, "And God said, 'Let there be light' and there was light. God saw that light was good." Yet, as *we read further,* we learn in Genesis 1:14–19 the following:

> And God said, "Let there be lights (plural) in the vault of the sky to separate the day from the night, and let them serve as signs to mark sacred times, and days and years, and let them be lights in the vault of the sky to give light on the earth." And it was so. God made two great lights—the greater light to govern the day and the lesser light to govern the night. He also made the stars. God set them in the vault of the sky to give light on the earth, to govern the day and the night, and to separate light from darkness. And God saw that it was good. And there was evening, and there was morning—the fourth day.

I observe from this text that light has a practical threefold purpose. Light separates light from darkness (v. 14); appears to be a sign (v. 14); and provides governance of the day and the night (v. 16) as each has its own particular light (i.e., sun and moon). One could say a counseling application to the above is that light separates light (truth) from darkness (error/deception); is a sign that *initially points* a person in the

---

[365] Light is seen by some scientists as the most foundational form of energy. Henry M. Morris, founder of the Institute of Creation Research, has written widely on the creation of light in respect to creationism and evolution.

[366] The only other time in the creation narrative that we have an accounting of a two-step process is in the creating of man and woman. God creates man and then, sometime later, God creates woman.

right direction; and governs or oversees a person as he or she *continues to walk* through life.

The God Who Illumines: The Difficulty of Principle Four

This fourth stage in the Genesis approach to pastoral counseling is my least favorite stage, and this is why. I can recall numerous occasions when I have invested much time and effort in a person, and the moment arrived for me to shed light on a sabotaging factor that had brought pain to the counselee. After I brought observation and insight to the counselee,[367] I heard words similar to, "I hear what you are saying, but I do not want to (make the necessary change)." My response? "Eeeeek!" (*Not* out loud, of course.) Pastoral caregivers are to shed light on lies, half-truths, faulty thinking, and false accusations, all of which have kept people in the dark. However, pastoral counselors must be aware of the biblical reality, that "the light has come into the world, and men loved darkness rather than light, because their deeds were evil."[368]

This fourth stage, where illumination is brought into darkness, is what I refer to as one of two "break points" in the counseling relationship.[369] As light shines forth in the darkened areas of a counselee's life, the counselee will either see the truth and make changes or choose *not* to change. At this break point, the person seeking help will either choose to

---

[367] Educators may be heard saying, "The light bulb of learning has been turned on."

[368] John 3:19 (KJV)

[369] At this first break point, the counselees "see" a new reality before them; this leaves the counselees with a decision to make. The second break point follows almost immediately. It is where the counselees must make the decision to separate themselves from unproductive behavior or thinking. It is entirely possible for some counselees to weigh the information that they have heard for quite some time before ever making a final decision.

live in the light or choose continued darkness. Naturally, you want to see people make necessary changes so they can live more productively.

However, there are people who ascribe to the orientation of, "Don't confuse me with the facts." When this happens, and it will, I need to state the obvious—no one can force another person to change. For a counselor to try and force his or her will onto the counselee would show a lack of respect and actually would be a violation of a person's boundaries. I will say more about the inability to change at the end of this chapter. For now let me simply say that there are very real reasons that people can actually see toxins in their lives and *choose not to change.*

Below please find a partial diagram of the Genesis Model. The following diagram illustrates "The Break Point." At break point, the counselee sees his or her situation differently because of new, illuminating data brought forth by the counselor. A decision now rests firmly in the hands of the counselee to continue to live the way he or she has been living or to choose a better alternative. This can be a very difficult stage for both the counselor and the counselee. In John's gospel, Jesus says *to believers,* "You shall know the truth and the truth will set you free."[370] Yes, Jesus is telling us the truth about truth. It must be pointed out here that an emotional reality is that when someone hears the truth for the first time, it frequently provokes anger. Many previously productive counseling relationships sadly break apart at this point. This is why I refer to stage four as the break point. Below you will find Diagram A as an illustration (read from bottom to top) of the first break point in the counseling relationship.

---

[370] John 8:32 (HCSB)

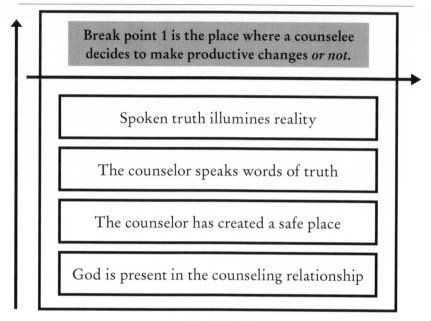

Break point 1 is the place where a counselee decides to make productive changes *or not*.

Spoken truth illumines reality

The counselor speaks words of truth

The counselor has created a safe place

God is present in the counseling relationship

Diagram A

Hard Truth: When a counselor secures a safe counseling environment, the counselee will, in turn, give his or her trust to their counselor. When a counselor earns trust from the counselee, the counselor can then illumine areas of the counselee's life that represent areas of concern and needed attention. *Yet, the counselee may still choose the path of least resistance and not follow the guidance of the counselor.*

Sources of Illumination

As I have called this approach to counseling the Genesis Model, it is therefore appropriate that I refer to a Psalm of Creation that describes God's creative and illuminating abilities. Hidden in this psalm are three sources of illumination or revelations that a counselor can draw upon when helping a person. Over the years, the Lord has given me wisdom and insight that I know was not mine. Below, the reader will find Psalm 19:

I have divided this psalm into three different sections, each representing a unique way in which God illumines darkened places in a counselee's life. Embedded in this psalm are three sources whereby God brings illumination or revelation.

Section One: General, Cosmic, or Abstract Revelation (v. 1–6; emphasis added)

> The heavens declare the glory of God;
> the skies proclaim the work of his hands.
> *Day after day they pour forth speech;*
> *night after night they reveal knowledge.*
> *They have no speech, they use no words;*
> *no sound is heard from them.*
> *Yet their voice goes out into all the earth,*
> *their words to the ends of the world.*
> In the heavens God has pitched a tent for the sun.
> It is like a bridegroom coming out of his chamber,
> like a champion rejoicing to run his course.
> It rises at one end of the heavens
> and makes its circuit to the other;
> nothing is deprived of its warmth.

The first way that God communicates to counselors and those seeking counseling is in a *general way*. God brings general revelation *first* because God knows that if we were to receive an initial laserlike, bottom–line, word of direction, we most likely would not accept it. As noted above, I have emphasized, "Day after day (creation) they pour forth speech ... (yet) *they have no speech, (and)they use no words.*" While writing and conducting research for this chapter, I came across interesting material on the subject of silence (the absence of words!). I discovered several references to St. John of the Cross,[371] who

---

[371] St. John of the Cross was a sixteenth-century Spanish mystic and Roman Catholic priest who is best remembered for his treatise on "The Dark Night of the Soul."

reportedly said, "Silence is God's primary language." It is out of darkened and shapeless silence that God said, "Let there be light." God speaks to us out of the silence. There will be godly sounds (God's hints), but no clear words in the perceived silence of our earthly lives. Admittedly, when God talks to me, *generally* it is easy for me to default into confusion as to what I think I have heard from Him. I have learned that God's silence is actually a prompting to pursue Him *more deeply*. Silence may be one of the most intimate of places in the human psyche. It is in silence that God pierces us most deeply.[372]

> *I have learned that God's silence is actually a prompting to pursue Him more deeply. Silence may be one of the most intimate of places in the human psyche. It is in silence that God pierces us most deeply.*

Section Two: Scriptural Revelation (vv. 7–10)

The law of the LORD is perfect,
refreshing the soul.
The statutes of the LORD are trustworthy,
making wise the simple.
The precepts of the LORD are right,
giving joy to the heart.
The commands of the LORD are radiant,
giving light to the eyes.
The fear of the LORD is pure,
enduring forever.
The ordinances of the LORD are firm,
and all of them are righteous.

God will speak to both counselors and counselees through scriptural revelation. *Five times* in three verses we read the words *law, statutes, precepts, commands,* and *ordinances* as concrete ways in which God speaks to us. Do you notice how the communicating process with God transitions from general exchange to a more tangible way of relating? I so love being quiet before God and being directed to a particular passage of Scripture only to discover that the Lord would have me share that same Scripture later in the day with

---

[372] I will explain later in this chapter what I mean by "God piercing us deeply."

someone who would be encouraged by it. A final exhortation about scriptural revelation: It is one thing to spend consistent time reading the Bible because one is preparing a message or a lesson. It is quite another matter to read Scripture with no other goal in mind other than to say, "Here I am, Lord."

Section Three: Personal Revelation (vv. 10–14)

> They are more precious than gold,
> than much pure gold;
> they are sweeter than honey,
> than honey from the honeycomb.
> By them *your servant* is warned;
> in keeping them there is great reward.
> But who can discern their own errors?
> Forgive my hidden faults.
> *Keep your servant* also from willful sins;
> may they not rule over me.
> Then I will be blameless,
> innocent of great transgression.
> *May these words of my mouth*
> *and this meditation of my heart*
> be pleasing in your sight,
> LORD, my Rock and my Redeemer.

After a person has become familiar with hearing God's voice in general and scriptural ways, God invites His children into what I call "deeper water." It is in deeper water that God gets our full attention. In these sovereign and secret places, there is no mistaking the presence and person of the Holy Spirit guiding one into knowing God as both rock and redeemer.

A friend of mine has remarked on more than one occasion, "Intimacy means, 'into me, see.'"[373] I do not know where

---

[373] This understanding of intimacy has been used by many contributors, most recently by Mary Pritchard in the *Huffington Post*, July 28, 2014.

Harold first learned this definition, but it makes clear sense to me. It is in a setting of intimacy that God allows us to see things about ourselves and others that we previously had not been able to ascertain. I would also remind readers that Jesus said, "Blessed are the pure in heart, for they shall see God."[374] I understand this beatitude to mean that visions of God from the heart's purity.

I stated earlier that it is in the deeper places, the more intimate encounters with God, that the Lord penetrates or pierces us *deeply*. Can you imagine if the *first revelation* you ever heard God speak to you was about the error of your ways, your "hidden faults," your "willful sins," or some "great transgression" (see vv. 12–13)? In God's patient grace, using general and scriptural stages, God begins to unplug our ears and circumcise our hearts. God woos us in general ways first and then moves into deeper and more intimate ways of communicating.

I want to conclude this section on receiving illuminating messages from God by stating three practical applications as they relate to counseling. First, if a counselor thinks that God is illuminating a truth in his or her mind about the counselee, waiting to share the message is rarely a bad thing. If God has truly given a general, scriptural, or personal word, the word will still be there for the counselor to retrieve. And if the counselor forgets, God will bring it back to remembrance—trust me on this! Again, err on the side of patience rather than impetuosity.

> *If a counselor thinks that God is illuminating a truth in his or her mind about the counselee, waiting to share the message is rarely a bad thing.*

Second, if a counselor feels led to share a deeper or personal message with a counselee, the counselor must be confident that a very

---

[374] Matthew 5:8 (NASB); I will devote the entire next chapter to being able to see the activity of God in the counseling relationship.

safe place for such a personal or penetrating word is established. The counseling principle of creating a safe place cannot be overemphasized. Counselors can always stand to be reminded that the deeper the wound a person has suffered, the longer it often takes to create a setting where trust can be assured.

> *Counselors can always stand to be reminded that the deeper the wound a person has suffered, the longer it often takes to create a setting where trust can be assured.*

And third, counselors need to see their counselees as a bank—a secure place where significant transactions occur. A counseling rule of thumb is that deeply personal words or suggested life changes made by the counselor to the counselee mandate substantial emotional or relational "deposit" (i.e., affirmations of growth, encouragement). As in a conventional bank, if a counselor neglects to make adequate deposits and proceeds to withdraw more than the balance in the account, the check will bounce. Why? Making verbal and supportive deposits (affirmations) with the counselee can ensure that an eventual withdrawal (a word of correction or challenge) will be more readily received.

Why People Do Not Change

We return to the crucial question, "Why do some people, knowing what is best for them, resist change and thereby forfeit a more productive life?" Below I identify five established reasons as to why some people will not change. I am sure there are other factors, as well.

- People do not change because of *the pain factor*. In this case, people have not lost enough or experienced enough pain to have the motivation to change. I recall speaking to a mother on one occasion whose son was being sent to a treatment facility for twelve months. The mother thought it was "just terrible" that her son had to be sent away. His incarceration was the reason for her pain. I asked the mother why her son was being court ordered to the facility, and she told me that her son and his friends had blown up her garage and set it on fire while running a methamphetamine lab. You would think the mother would have understood the court's ruling. As she revealed this, in her son's presence, he silently sat with a smile on his face, as if to say, "I don't give a Continental!" Sadly, this mother will potentially experience the pain of losing her son to death rather than for a twelve-month period of time of incarceration.

- People do not change because of the *desire factor*. Simply put, there are people who just do not want to change. Period. I have seen people who, after being challenged with truth, modify their behavior for a period of time, but after the "heat is off," they go back to their former way of living. An individual without the motivation to change will not be able to sustain the desired behavior. Be aware that one component of the desire factor has to do with the counselor. In some instances, people resist change not because they do not like the results that the change can bring; they refuse the suggested change because the counselor has not been clear enough about what is involved in the needed change. Therefore, the problem is not with the counselee, *but rather with the counselor.*

- People do not change because of the *environment factor*. This is especially important to keep in mind when counseling people who struggle with an addiction of any kind. People who have addictions in their lives often associate with other people who also have addictions. I tell my counseling students that relationships are contagious; you catch what you are around. I have counseled many former addicts who have successfully broken free from their addictions and have told me, "I had to get a whole new set of friends." This is reality!

- People do not change because of the *difficulty factor.* People want the easy out. Don't we all? This factor is about more than just laziness or not wanting to change. These people are whiners who complain about how easy other people have life. These same people do not realize that the people to whom they are comparing themselves have worked hard to get what they have.

- People do not change because of the *starting factor.* Some people do not know where to begin. They frequently come to counseling feeling overwhelmed about many things. Some people have a history of wanting to change and starting a change regimen in the past, but they have failed at sustaining healthy behavior. Due to past failures at achieving change in their lives, these people do not want to risk yet another defeat. People who need help with the starting factor are best helped by a counselor helping them to set clear goals, identify realistic expectations, and isolate a specific time for when the goal will be achieved.

Conclusion

Light was the first element of God's creation, followed by filling an empty universe and establishing order over it by those created in God's own image. In like fashion, God's counselors will illumine areas of darkness that reside in the life of a counselee. Illumination births into existence a "new creation."[375] I said at the outset that the Genesis principle of

---

[375] 2 Corinthians 5:17 (NIV)

illumination is the most difficult stage for me *personally*. I know that a life lived out from the shadows begins with an often painful illuminating process. And I know, further, that one cannot mold or shape that which cannot be seen—hence, the critical principle of illumination.

Chapter 10

The God Who Sees

I pray that the *eyes of your heart* may be enlightened in order that you may know the hope to which he has called you, the riches of his glorious inheritance in his holy people.

Ephesians 1: 18 (emphasis added)

The depth of our hunger for God will be the length of our ability to reach God.

James Goll

Genesis Model Principle 5

<u>Genesis Principle:</u> God sees what has been created.

<u>Genesis Principle Applied:</u> Counselors are to see clearly that which is before them.

Where were you when God found you? Genesis 16 is the Old Testament story of God finding a woman named Hagar. Scripture tells us that she was out in the wilderness. God often finds people in a wilderness of some kind;

I rather think the wilderness might be one of God's favorite places. Why might this be true? Only when people find themselves lost and directionless might they become desperate enough to give God a legitimate shot at helping them.

> Only when people find themselves lost and directionless might they become desperate enough to give God a legitimate shot at helping them.

The story of Hagar is an account of a woman on the run. While Hagar is running, God finds her and meets her deepest needs. In the end, Hagar grasps something very special about her God, which can be applied to the Genesis Model of counseling.

The name that Hagar gives to God is *EL-Roi,* which translates to "the God or the strong one who sees." There will come a time in a counseling setting when God will allow His counselors to see what He sees. It will be while catching a counselee "on the run," in some kind of "wilderness experience," that God will allow His counselors to see things clearly. Once a counselor comprehends what needs to be accomplished, those who are in a wilderness-like place, as was Hagar, can be redirected to what the psalmist calls a spacious place.[376]

Sarai, Hagar, and Abram

Hagar was an Egyptian slave, a maidservant of Sarai, wife of Abram. When Sarai is unable to conceive, despite God's promise of children, she decides to create a family through a culturally accepted means.[377] Sarai gives her maidservant,

---

[376] Psalm 18:19. "He brought me out into a spacious place; he rescued me because he delighted in me." Thank you, Kristen, for allowing me to be a part of your spacious place.

[377] Genesis 16:2; See James Burton Coffman, "Commentaries on the Old and New Testament." Published by Abilene Christian University.

Hagar, to her husband Abram for the purpose of providing an heir. The situation quickly deteriorates. Upon discovering that she is indeed pregnant, Hagar begins to treat Sarai with contempt.[378] The drama builds when Sarai complains to Abram about her ill treatment from Hagar by playing the blame game. Sarai says to Abram, "This is your fault!"[379] Abram is no better than the two bickering women of the story as he retorts, "Look, she is your servant girl, you deal with her."[380] Feeling emotionally abandoned by Abram and belittled by Hagar, Sarai does what any person might do under similar circumstances. "Sarai treated Hagar harshly." And the predictable result? "She (Hagar) finally ran away."[381]

While in the wilderness, sitting by a spring, an angel of the Lord[382] appeared to her and said, "Hagar, servant of Sarai, where have you come from and where are you going?"[383] The question about where Hagar has *come from* is significant. If a person refuses to acknowledge pain in the past, it is difficult to move into complete healing in the future.[384] During a time of great pain early in

> "Bill, God is not obligated to heal that which we refuse to release."

---

[378] Genesis 16:4

[379] Genesis 16:5 (NLT); Does this remind you of another "blame game" story in Genesis 3?

[380] Genesis 16:6 (NLT)

[381] Genesis 16:6 (NLT)

[382] The reference to the angel of the Lord (16:7) is sometimes described as the Lord himself (Genesis 16:10–13; Exodus 3:2–6; 23:20; Judges 6:11–18). God used this messenger to appear to humans who otherwise would not be able to see God and live (Exodus 33:20). The angel of the Lord would bring revelation, deliverance, and destruction. Many Bible scholars have speculated that the angel of the Lord was God himself—a preincarnate appearance of Christ. The language in the story of Hagar leads us to believe that the angel in this incident was, in fact, an appearance of God himself.

[383] Genesis 16:8 (ESV)

[384] Steven Arterburn in his book, *Healing Is a Choice*, spends an entire chapter on this very concept. Says Arterburn, until a person feels the pain that has trapped him or her, the person will remain in the same pain.

my ministry, I went back to seek the counsel of the pastor in my home church. Lloyd told me, "Bill, God is not obligated to heal that which we refuse to release." A painful past must always be acknowledged to be cleansed.

While Hagar does respond to the first question, she never reaches the point of answering the second question, "Where are you going?" A careful reading of the text reveals that there is no mention of a destination to which Hagar is running. It is one thing to be unwilling to acknowledge the past but equally devastating is to live life on the run, without direction.

In Hagar's encounters with the messenger of God, she tells of being badly treated, justifying her self-inflicted exodus. Running, for Hagar, is her survival plan. Yet, the angel tells Hagar, "Go *back* to your mistress and *submit* to her," while adding, "I will so increase your descendants that they will be too numerous to count."[385] "The angel of the Lord also said to her: 'You are now with child and you will have a son. You shall name him Ishmael (which means, "God hears") for the Lord has heard of your misery. He will be a wild donkey of a man; his hand will be against everyone and everyone's hand against him, and he will live in hostility toward all his brothers.'"[386]

Even though Hagar was nothing more than a simple Egyptian maidservant, God cared for her. Hagar proclaimed, "You are the God who sees me," and "I have now seen the One who sees me."[387] Hagar did go back and submit herself to Sarai. From this story, we learn that even when the circumstances of life seem unfair, we need to obey God and the authorities that God has placed in our lives.

Years passed in Abram's life before the prophetic promise of a son would be fulfilled. When Abram was ninety-nine years old, God changed his name to Abraham, saying, "Serve me

---

[385] Genesis 16:9–10 (NIV)
[386] Genesis 16:11–12 (NIV)
[387] Genesis 16:13 (NIV)

faithfully and live a blameless life."[388] The promised son, Isaac, was born to Abraham,[389] yet God never forgot Hagar and her son, Ishmael. We learn that God was with Ishmael as he grew up and that he lived in the desert and became an archer. The last we hear of him is that Hagar finds her son a wife in Egypt.[390]

God is amazing. So many situations may seem hopeless, yet God remains faithful. "The One who sees" will help us in our distress, providing direction for our circumstances. Never fear or be discouraged. God is good! In story after story, we see the faithfulness of God to fulfill His promises. God only asks that we trust, believe, and *look for* His direction.

Seeing the Activity of God: A New Testament Context

The first-century church lived in the realm of seeing the supernatural presence of God and hearing the spoken directives of the Spirit. Luke records the birth of the church as *seeing* tongues of fire that rested upon all those who gathered in the upper room.[391] Philip's steps were ordered by an angelic visitation to travel the desert road that runs from Jerusalem to Gaza.[392] Philip, obedient to God's direction, met a man from Ethiopia and ended up baptizing him.[393] Saul had his religious steps reordered by dramatically encountering a blinding light that was indeed Jesus himself. Ananias's perspective was challenged upon receiving an open vision in which the Lord gave him instructions concerning Saul.[394] Numerous

---

[388] Genesis 17:1 (NLT)
[389] Genesis 21, although the prophecy of Isaac's birth took place in Genesis 18
[390] Genesis 21:20–21
[391] Acts 2
[392] Acts 8:26a
[393] Acts 8:36–38
[394] Acts 9:10

times in Paul's life, the apostle had visions through which his travel plans were changed.[395] Peter's prejudicial thinking was transformed because of having a vision, something he saw.[396] God literally "turned on the lights" for Peter in a darkened prison cell while Peter was shackled between two prison guards. At one point, he thought he was having a dream or vision, but then he realized that the supernatural was more real than the natural bondage of prison.[397] John, the writer of Revelation testifies, "I was in the Spirit on the Lord's Day, and I heard behind me a loud voice, as of a trumpet, saying, "I am the Alpha and the Omega, the First and the Last," and "What you *see*, write in a book and send *it* to the seven churches."[398] Yes, when heaven invades earth, life and ministry change. The church today must realize that a "failure to launch" comes any time there is short-sightedness on the part of leadership. Moreover, churches that lack transforming visionary experiences like Peter's are often void of vitality.

A New Testament Case Study on Seeing: The Road to Emmaus

The gospel writer records, in Luke 24,

> Now behold, two of them were traveling that same day to a village called Emmaus, which was about seven miles from Jerusalem. And they talked together of all these things which had happened. So it was, while they conversed and reasoned, that Jesus Himself [this is the resurrected Christ] drew near and went with them. But God kept them from recognizing Him.[399] … And He said to them, "What

---

[395] Acts 9:12; 16:9; 18:9; 22:17
[396] Acts 10:9f.
[397] Acts 12:6–10
[398] Revelation 1:10–12 (NLT)
[399] Luke 24:13–16 (HCSB)

kind of conversation is this that you have with one another as you walk and are sad?" Then the one whose name was Cleopas answered and said to Him, "Are you the only stranger in Jerusalem, and have you not known the things which happened there in these days?" And He said to them, "What things?"[400]

The travelers had some experience or knowledge of Jesus, yet they did not recognize, or *see*, Him. Some *huge truths* are as follows: We see what we *expect* to see, what we *want* to see, what we *are educated* to see, and what our culture *has influenced* us to see; and our *current life situations* affect our ability to see. Most assuredly, our pasts often define what we see or think is possible. Sean Smith states, "The longer you tolerate something, the longer it dictates your experience."[401] Unless we make the effort to be discerning, to consciously think about other aspects of what we are looking at, it is very likely that we will *not see* what God intends us to see.

In what my wife calls "the dailies," a person must consciously and intentionally process everyday circumstances and invite Jesus to offer an interpretation of what he or she is seeing. Everyone has heard of the acronym on bumper stickers and other media, "WWJD" (What Would Jesus Do?). I would like to make a small adjustment to that. How about, "What Would Jesus *See*?" When we do not pause to ask Jesus the deeper meaning of the natural things of life, we merely reenact the drama of the Emmaus Road story. When we do not ask Jesus to give us a vision of our lives from heaven's perspective, we are

> *When we do not ask Jesus to give us a vision of our lives from heaven's perspective, we are no different than the men on the road. It is entirely possible to "walk with Jesus" and never see Him!*

---

[400] Luke 24:17–19 (HCSB)
[401] Sean Smith, *Prophetic Evangelism: Empowering a Generation to Seize Their Day* (Shippensburg, PA: Destiny Image Publishers, 2004), 27.

no different than the men on the road. It is entirely possible to "walk with Jesus" and never see Him!

In verse 25, Jesus calls the travelers "foolish." The word *foolish* in the original Greek text can mean "inconsiderate."[402] It can also mean "not reasoning right." Even though they had been taught, they had not deeply understood the prophesies that appeared in the Hebrew Scriptures concerning the Messiah and His resurrection. They didn't *see* the Christ who was with them because they didn't *expect* to see Him! Jesus not only calls them fools, which tells us that He expected them to be able to recognize him, Jesus calls them "slow of heart to believe in all that the prophets have spoken!"[403] There is a side of my thinking that believes their "knowledge" was really nothing more than superficial or superstitious wishing.

When the men finally *see* Jesus, they perceive who it was that was with them all along. Everything that they had experienced, including the crucifixion and resurrection, now makes sense. If you can see God working in the circumstances of your life, then life begins to take shape. If a person does not look for the hints and manifestations of God, then life will be much more difficult.

> *If you can see God working in the circumstances of your life, then life begins to take shape. If a person does not look for the hints and manifestations of God, then life will be much more difficult.*

Our Contemporary Context: From Paralysis to the Prophetic

Today we live in a culture of skepticism. The motto of the "Show-Me State," Missouri, implies that unless people see something, they will not believe it. In the economy of the Spirit, just the opposite is true—"believing leads into the realm of seeing."

---

[402] *Strong's Concordance with Hebrew and Greek Lexicon*
[403] Luke 24:25b (ESV)

The biblical origin to the contemporary reality of skepticism or suspicion is Genesis 3. Suspicion or skepticism is introduced as the incarnation of evil speaks to the woman, saying, "Did God really say …?"[404] With this very question, a culture of suspicion is malevolently introduced. I believe one of our enemy's main strategies is to get people to question the goodness of God. I think it is easy for us to default into a suspicious or questioning mentality rather than walk in a faith mentality. I would remind readers at this juncture, "without faith it is impossible to please God."[405]

Especially in contemporary culture, it is imperative that counselors be able to see presenting issues, as well as the insidious ones that lie in the life of a counselee at a much deeper level. Seeing in the Spirit is of vital importance for God's counselors. Counselors must know that if they see issues in a person's life or a word of knowledge is given to them to share with the counselee, the counselee may not receive the word that is being given to them by the Lord. The counselee who does not cooperate or accept what he or she has been told will continue to experience a life of ongoing losses and more costly disappointments. The resistant counselee will become increasingly self-centered. The hearing but not believing counselee lives life with an emphasis on empirical knowledge, predictable outcomes, and a "faith" that is void of intimacy with Father God. It would be impossible for me to overstate the level of emotional and intellectual exhaustion that comes from this approach to life and decision making.

Alongside questioning the goodness of God, a second element which creates a suspicion-based mentality, is *the removal or the threatening of values, disciplines or beliefs that provide joy.* This makes sense to be because scripture teaches that "the joy of the Lord is our strength."[406] If joy is

---

[404] Genesis 3:1 (NLT)
[405] Hebrews 11:6 (NIV)
[406] Nehemiah 8:10 (NIV)

taken from a person, then strength, endurance and desire to complete the journey is often lost.

A third common reality that can create the mental prison of suspicion is the all-consuming experience of facing what seems to be a *paralyzing fear*. Fear can be a necessary and needed response to a physical or emotional danger, but oftentimes, it is not. Brazilian author, Paulo Coehlo, has said correctly, "There is only one thing that makes a dream impossible to achieve: the fear of failure…having the possibility to achieve the dream is what makes life interesting."[407] I would remind readers at this juncture, "without faith it is impossible to please God".[408]

Seeing as Jesus Would Have Us See

Let me share a story from an impromptu gathering in my own home where I "saw" the activity of God. Two friends dropped by the house just to catch up as friends often do. One of them, in particular, shared a disappointment that they currently encountered. My sense was they just needed someone to listen, so I did. As our informal, familial conversation continued, a green-hued garment, much like a scarf or neck wrap, appeared over their head. It seemed to rest, almost floating in place. While in mid-sentence my friend asked, "What is that?" I responded, "What do you mean?" They reported experiencing a sudden saturation of peace--tremendous and yet, strange. Although their concern remained unresolved, the feeling of 'strange peace' seemed stronger than the presenting concern.

The Lord gave me a partial explanation of what had transpired and, I share it here. There will be times when the Spirit of the Lord 'appears' for no reason other than to bring peace. I told my friend that they found this experience strange

---

[407] Paulo Coehlo, *The Alchemist*. San Francisco, Harper Collins. 1994
[408] Hebrews 11:6 (NIV)

because they were unaccustomed to sensing the presence of the Lord. In the economy of God, God merely wanted my friend to know, "everything would be OK". In the days ahead, my friend returned to report that all had worked out much better for them than they could have expected. God is good.

I take time now to offer specific words of encouragement to counselors who have an increasing desire to grow in their ability to see more deeply into the lives of their counselees.

1. God gives vision to those who are receptive. As a counselor, I am always receptive to receiving visions. From the above story we can learn that people with unresolved emotional issues can also be somewhat receptive to a visionary experience.

2. God may give a vision or an impression of something but may not reveal all the details surrounding the experience or even the interpretation of what has been seen.

3. When anyone receives a vision from God, his or her first "go-to" response should be to pray. It has been my experience that while I am praying, I am often directed to Scripture.

4. Experience has taught me that there will be times when God will use a vision or an impression only for the purpose of getting my attention. Once God has my attention, it is as if God is saying, "Now a word from your sponsor. Forget what you think you have seen; I have something else I want to tell you." (This is very much like Moses' experience at the burning bush.)

5. Even with clear manifestations from God, some people will choose to not be obedient; this tragically often results in significant losses. This truth is most assuredly found in God's first prophetic warning to Cain in Genesis: "You will be accepted if you do what is right but if you do not … and refuse to do what is

right … sin is crouching at your door, eager to control you."[409]

6. <u>Bottom line</u>: Any visionary experience from God is always an open invitation to trust Him more deeply. Experiences, like the one in my home, invites a person to move beyond his or her known, quantifiable information and pray as Samuel did, "Here I am Lord…"[410]

Seeing 101: An Introduction

So, where does a person begin if he or she wants to develop the ability to actually "see" the things of God? First, it is important to know that Jesus had something to say about the direct connection between the effectiveness of His ministry and the ability to see. Jesus said, "I assure you, most solemnly I tell you, the Son is able to do nothing of Himself (of His own accord); but He is able to do only what *He sees the Father doing*, for whatever the Father does is what the Son does in the same way [in His turn]."[411]

Second, if a person wants to develop an ability to see the activity of God, that person may seek someone who has this level of faith and learn from him or her. Scripture documents that successful seers can pray for those who desire an increased ability to see. One biblical example of a spiritual leader praying for someone who needed to see the things of God is found in 2 Kings 6. Elisha prayed that the eyes of his young assistant would see heaven on earth.[412]

---

[409] Genesis 4:7 (NIV)

[410] 1 Samuel 3:4 (NIV)

[411] John 5:19 (Amplified translation)

[412] Elisha took on an apprentice prophet whose name was Gehazi (see 2 Kings 4:12a). Gehazi, like Elisha, pursued a double portion anointing. However, due to greed, he would not become Elisha's successor (see 2 Kings 5:20–27). Greed not only disqualified him but was cursed with

The servant of the man of God arose early and went outside, and there was an army, surrounding the city with horses and chariots. And his servant said to him, "Alas, my master! What shall we do?" So he answered, "Do not fear, for those who are with us are more than those who are with them." And Elisha prayed, and said, *"LORD, I pray, open his eyes that he may see."* Then the LORD opened the eyes of the young man, and he saw. And behold, the mountain *was* full of horses and chariots of fire all around Elisha.

Asking an experienced mentor to help you develop in recognizing the movement of the Spirit is a wonderful first step. Notice I said *first step.* I would stress the importance of having people in your life who have authentic[413] experiences of seeing God. Stay away from *negative and critical people* who will simply use every opportunity to discredit the deep desires of your heart.

> *Stay away from negative and critical people who will simply use every opportunity to discredit the deep desires of your heart.*

Third, seeing involves a patient waiting upon the Lord. One reason a seer sees the activity of God is that this person is trusted by God and has proven him- or herself faithful during very troublesome times. These trusted servants have often paid a price for this level of anointing, but they would assure you that they would not trade what they now hold in their hearts. In my own practical experience, I know that patient waiting is directly tied to

---

leprosy! There is a tremendous lesson here for all "want-to-be" seers. Sometime later, Elisha began to train up the anonymous person mentioned in the text above.

[413] One way of measuring prophetic authenticity is to ask the question, "Is that which is being seen resulting in a greater humility in the person's life who is sharing the visions of God?" and "Will the sharing of what has been seen advance greater intimacy with Jesus in the life of the person who is being helped?"

fasting. One specific way that I fast to better see the things of God is that I regularly fast from my car radio as I drive to work. It is in the quiet of my car that God brings parts of my day together and shows me things I will need to know.

At this juncture, I want to outline specific practical tests that can let people know that they are actually seeing and hearing from God. I am indebted to the life and ministry of James Goll, who has written much on the ability to see the activity of God.[414]

Seeing 201: Tests for Seeing Prophetically

Scripture both encourages and instructs God's people to test that which they think is a message from God.[415] Testing or evaluating communication that we receive from God is not unspiritual—quite the contrary. We can explore messages that we think are from God by way of prayer.[416] We can approve that verifying a word from God is a safeguard that keeps us from being conformed to worldly ideas.[417] We can test a word or experience that we think is from God by way of Scripture.[418] And finally, interpreting a word, vision, or experience will result in a spiritual maturity that we previously did not have.[419] Just because we sincerely think something is from God does not mean it is so. People can be very sincere

> *Just because we sincerely think something is from God does not mean it is so. People can be very sincere about what they think they have heard or seen from God but be sincerely wrong.*

---

[414] Please see James Goll, *The Seer: The Prophetic Power of Visions, Dreams and Open Heavens* (Shippensburg, PA: Destiny Image Publishers, 2004).
[415] 1 John 4:1
[416] Philippians 4:6
[417] Romans 12:2
[418] Acts 17:11
[419] Hebrews 6:1–20

about what they think they have heard or seen from God but *be sincerely wrong.*

In *The Seer*, James Goll offers practical tests that serve as safeguards against a person's flesh. Goll is right in saying, "None of us are immune to the effects of outward influences on our lives.... We can be strongly affected in our spirits and souls by such things as the circumstances of life; our physical or bodily circumstances; by Satan or his agents or, by people around us."[420] Below, please find my own adaptations of Goll's "vision tests."

The Self-Test

1. Is there evidence of the Holy Spirit's working in my life?
2. Am I regularly in His word *for devotional purposes*?
3. Am I committed to being obedient to the Spirit's leading, no matter what?
4. Am I willingly submitted and accountable to people in spiritual authority?
5. Is the word or vision I am receiving exalting me or Jesus?
6. Will what I am sharing promote more of a dependence on me or Jesus?
7. Is there a redemptive quality for the vision or word?
8. Will that which I am sharing lead the person into a closer walk with Jesus?

The Source or Origin Test[421]

1. Is the vision or word for the person with whom I am ministering or actually for me?[422]

---

[420] Goll, *The Seer*, p. 74

[421] Goll credits Mark and Patti Virkler and their book, *Communion with God*, with this test. The biblical foundation for this test is 1 John 4:1.

[422] The error of mistaking a word from the Lord that is actually for *us* rather than the person with whom we are ministering is a common mistake. A rule that I try to practice while I am counseling others is that when I get

2. Does the image, vision, or word seem more destructive than redemptive?

3. Am I receiving any distraction from my fellowship with the Spirit?

4. How much peace is in my life during and after the vision?

The Fruit Test[423]

1. Does this vision elevate me or the counselee over the person of Jesus Christ?

2. Do I find myself fearful, compulsive, anxious, or confused?

3. Do I find myself sensing an inflated ego because of the vision?

4. Do I sense a quickened faith, power, peace, "sweet fruit,"[424] enlightenment, knowledge, or humility?

5. Will the word or vision help the person live more independently with Jesus, rather than me?

6. As I counsel the person, do I find the spiritual fruit of self-control more and more evident in my life (see Galatians 5:22)?

The Scripture or Jesus Test

1. Is the word or vision in agreement with Scripture (2 Timothy 3:16)?

2. Is Jesus being exalted?

3. Can I sense that what I am seeing or hearing will bear near immediate fruit?

---

a word from the Lord, I try to intercede immediately and ask the Father, "Is this for me or for the person I am counseling?"

[423] Goll actually lists this in another area, but I felt as though "fruit test" was clearer.

[424] See Galatians 5:22f.

4. Will the prophetic word turn the person toward God?

5. Does the word or image promote spiritual elitism or schism?

Seeing 301: Seeing and the Place of Brokenness

At the outset of this chapter, your eyes might have sailed right past this important truth: "The depth of our hunger *for God* will be the length of our ability to *reach God*."[425] A person with an unusually deep hunger for God nearly always experiences a corresponding breaking or turning point to the yearning or pursuit, encouraging *cooperation with* the activity of God. My understanding and orientation to breaking is not to be seen as an expression of judgment or discipline, although I know that Scripture clearly communicates this reality as well.[426]

Breaking, for our purposes here, is understood to mean an activity or experience that is redemptive in nature and, at times, even sought after. God's breaking or redemptive fashioning can lead to an increased ability to see the activity of God,[427] greater faith, and deeper levels of demonstrated mercy and grace that are extended to others. My heart is aligned with the heart of Isaiah, who writes, "A crushed reed he *will not break*, a dim wick he will not extinguish; he will faithfully make just decrees."[428]

In John 12, Jesus is anointed by Mary, who breaks a pint of costly nard over his head.[429] Smith writes that "brokenness releases the treasure"[430] that God has placed within the servant of God. If a container is not broken, similar to Mary's

---

[425] James Goll

[426] Psalm 2:9; 72:4; Job 34:2–3; Isaiah 30:14; Jeremiah 19:11

[427] Matthew 5:8. Jesus states that purity is a prerequisite for seeing God.

[428] Isaiah 42:3 (NET)

[429] Mark 14:3; Luke 7:37; John 12:3

[430] Sean Smith, *Prophetic Evangelism*, p. 109.

breaking of the alabaster jar, the contents within the vessel cannot be released. The apostle Paul writes of the release of the hidden treasures that lie waiting within God's servants when he says, "We now have this light shining in our hearts, but we ourselves are like fragile clay jars containing this great treasure. This makes it clear that our great power is from God, not from ourselves."[431]

An elevated level of spiritual discernment[432] is the second result of the breaking process. When God's people see the activity of the kingdom and testify to its reality, anticipated criticism from others is a predictable outcome.[433] John's account of the anointing story identifies Judas as Mary's chief critic. Judas is quoted as saying, "That perfume was worth a year's wages. It should have been sold and the money given to the poor."[434] John goes on to tell us that Judas's criticism of the breaking of the jar and perceived wastefulness of the costly nard was due to his role as the "Chief Financial Officer," which allowed him easy access to frequently steal from the offering.[435]

Judas's criticism of Mary is rooted in the fact that he was a thief; he lived a life "in the shadows," believing that no one would ever find him out. For us there is a contemporary application: much criticism is rooted in ungodliness. Bill Johnson has said, "Criticism in the form of a question is not a question." Today, Christians who see and testify to the activity of God's Holy Spirit will hear criticism, particularly from sectors of the religious community who are highly suspicious that God still

---

[431] 2 Corinthians 4:7–8 (NLT)

[432] First Thessalonians 5:21–22 teaches that it is the responsibility of every Christian to be discerning: "But examine everything carefully; hold fast to that which is good; abstain from every form of evil." The apostle John issues a similar warning, "Do not believe every spirit, but test the spirits to see whether they are from God; because many false prophets have gone out into the world" (1 John 4:1). According to the New Testament, discernment is not optional for the believer—it is very necessary essential.

[433] John 12:4–5

[434] Ibid.

[435] John 12:6

moves in this way. Further, mature Christians must not take offense or respond with any expression of retaliatory behavior when their spiritual giftedness is questioned.

A third principle in this anointing story is when *Jesus sees* and acknowledges Mary's heartfelt desire. Christian seers today, in similar fashion, can be assured that God sees the motivations of their hearts as they seek to advance the cause of Christ and his kingdom. Jesus speaks in reference to the Father's recognition of ministry: "When you do a charitable deed, do not let your left hand know what your right hand is doing, that your charitable deed may be in secret; and your Father who sees in secret **will** Himself **reward** you openly."[436]

John's story illustrates that the breaking of the jar releases not only the criticism of others (12:4) and the affirmation of Jesus (12:7), but moreover the breaking of the jar creates a stir in the community (12:9). When God's sincere and faithful servants move in a sacrificial or unexpected way, as Mary, they will draw a crowd. John records that "curiosity seekers" came to see what was transpiring at Lazarus's home.[437] When God's servants are willing to have their vessels (hearts) break over the things that break the heart of God, people will be drawn, the net will be cast, the invitation to enter the kingdom will be made, and the result will be a bountiful harvest.

I offer final summary thoughts here about brokenness and the increased ability to see in the Spirit. Today there are people who, like Lazarus, "host the presence" of the Lord (12:1). These people naturally and regularly welcome Jesus into their lives, jobs, homes, and everyday activities. These mature disciples no longer have the personal need to pontificate about glowing successes from ten years ago as if

---

[436] See Matthew 6:1–4. Matthew 6 actually identifies three spiritual disciplines that are to be done "in secret," with no fanfare. Jesus identifies the first, giving (6:1–4), followed by prayer that does not bring attention to the one who is praying (6:5–6), and finally, fasting (6:16–18).
[437] John 12:9

they only happened yesterday. The broken person "hosts the presence" of the Lord because he or she has learned to strive less, be more in tune with the economy of the Spirit of God, recognize the unique ways and patterns in which God speaks to him or her, and integrate the economy of the Spirit into the counseling environment.

There are others who, like Judas, are critical of the ministry of the Lord (12:4); those who represent the crowds and are merely *curious* (12:9). I refer to these people as spiritual rubberneckers (like people who slow down to gawk at a traffic accident). And there are those equivalents of the religious leaders of Jesus' day who want to destroy the ministry of Jesus and the testimony of Lazarus (12:10).

Seeing 401: 20/20 Insight

I offer two concluding ideas on the development of seeing in a counseling relationship and one practical word for pastors who have seers in their churches.

First, the seasoned counselor or seer will be well acquainted with what I refer to as the portal of desperation. While writing, it occurred to me that desperation comes to those who have submitted to God and have been broken in the right places. While teaching on the first day of my first class as a part-time university instructor, my world got rocked. The class was called The Church and Social Problems. I told the class that I had just moved from California, where I had been a pastor for eighteen years and had been an intake counselor at a residential facility for drug and alcohol residents. A student we refer to as a nontraditional student (not eighteen to twenty-four years of age) came forward after class and told me that he was giving college a second try. This student briefly shared his own story, which included his own struggle with the very things I had talked about.

At the end of our conversation, he said, "You are a chaser!" I asked, "What's that? Is this a Southern term?" I didn't know. He went on to tell me about a book titled *The God Chasers* by Tommy Tenney. The next day in class, he loaned me his copy. I read it over the weekend—it was my story! That next week, I was looking forward to talking with my new friend. He wasn't in that class or the class after that. A week passed. I went to the registrar's office so I could find out how to get in touch with the missing student. After about ten minutes, our campus registrar came back and said these words, "Bill, I know you are concerned about this student and what I am going to tell you will frustrate you, but we have never had a student on this campus with this name." My story of the student and "portal of desperation" go together. I believe that one reason God had our family move from California to Tennessee was to tell me who I would become. People who see in the Spirit are desperate for the things of God and will go to any length to enter into God's presence. I have also learned that a heart desperate for the things of God stands a much greater chance of experiencing the incomprehensible mysteries of God.

> *I have also learned that a heart desperate for the things of God stands a much greater chance of experiencing the incomprehensible mysteries of God.*

Second, in addition to desperation, the seasoned counselor seeking the gifting to see under the guidance of the Holy Spirit will exhibit *increased levels of discipline* in his or her life. I know this may sound so very basic, but this is so very is important if a person is to have heightened vision for their life and ministry. I have already mentioned my fasting from my car radio as I drive into work. It is during these times that my mind "sees" the day that is ahead of me. In that seeing, God often talks to me about students, decisions, and people I will encounter during the day; in every sense, I am being prepared for my day in the Spirit.

The third idea I want to share is specifically for pastors who have people in their churches who have a seeing ability. If I were pastoring today and had a person with an extraordinary ability of seeing in the Spirit, I would want this person right at my elbow. Here is why: seers see *before* anyone else sees and see *more* than anyone else sees, so it makes logical sense that as the shepherd/leader of a church, you would want access to that same information; and I also know from experience that seers are a different breed of person, and I say this respectfully.[438] Having studied the subject of seeing, and being with people who do see, I know that seers can have a depressive personality orientation (much like Elijah), are prone to isolate (again, like Elijah), and can overact to situations. For these reasons, pastors should keep these gifted servants "closer than a brother."

I close this chapter with my favorite reference to seeing. In a highly honest and personal way, the Apostle Paul offers his own testimony on seeing.

> When I was a child, I spoke as a child, I understood as a child, I thought as a child; but when I became a man, I put away childish things. For now we see in a mirror, dimly, but then face to face. Now I know in part, but then I shall know just as I also am known.[439]

---

[438] This could turn into an extended teaching, but for brevity's sake, a study in the life of Elijah provides one overview as to the personality and emotional make-up of a seer. There has been a lot of material developed on this subject that is easily accessible if a person is a disciplined researcher and student.

[439] 1 Corinthians 13:11–12 (KJV)

Chapter 11

The God Who Separates

"… then God separated the light from the darkness."
Genesis 1:4

Genesis Principle 6

<u>Genesis Principle:</u> After creating light and declaring it "good," God then separates the light from the darkness.

<u>Genesis Principle Applied:</u> Counselors are to aid counselees in freeing themselves from the mental, emotional, and existential darkness that plagues them.

Michelangelo Buonarroti has been described as one of the greatest artistic geniuses of all time.[440] His crowning achievement is the vaulted frescoed ceiling of the Sistine Chapel.[441] Starting from the chapel's entrance, which depicts scenes of fallen humanity, and proceeding from east to west,

---

[440] *ArtWolf,* an online art publication, lists Michelangelo at number fourteen out of the top one hundred greatest artists of all time. Michelangelo, first and foremost, identified himself as a sculptor.
[441] Rome, Italy

Michelangelo's soaring masterpiece culminates above the altar area with his interpretation of God's separating light from darkness. Clearly, for both artist and onlooker, the theme of separation is readily apparent. In similar fashion, the literary and theological theme of separation is just as apparent in the story of creation found in Genesis 1 and 2.

In Genesis 1:2, we read, "The earth was formless and empty, and darkness covered the deep waters." The words *formless, empty,* and *dark* offer a lucid description of anyone living apart from the Creator. While darkness covered creation,[442] "God said, 'Let there be light' and there was light,"[443] and "God saw the light was good." *Then,* "God separated the light from the darkness."[444]

> *The concept of separation is dynamic, causative, and definite. The word denotes nothing passive, casual, or pedestrian in nature.*

Genesis 1:4 is the first occurrence in Scripture that conveys the idea of separation.[445] The English word *separated* is the Hebrew word *badal*[446] and is best understood to mean "to divide, separate, or sever."[447] The concept of separation is dynamic, causative, and definite. The word denotes nothing passive, casual, or pedestrian in nature.

It was not God's intent that everything in creation be dichotomous—either dark or light; rather, light and darkness coexist. The two must be exclusively unique and each

---

[442] And in similar fashion, "gloominess or dimness or despair" covers or enters a counselee's life.

[443] Genesis 1:3 (NIV)

[444] Genesis 1:4 (NASB)

[445] I will return to this idea of separation in Scripture later in this chapter. This concept of separation is significant in the Bible and for many different reasons.

[446] *The New American Standard Old Testament Hebrew Lexicon* is Brown, Driver, Briggs, Gesenius Lexicon, which is keyed to the "Theological Word Book of the Old Testament." These files are public domain.

[447] Ibid.

within their own separate domain. God's separating light from darkness also provides invaluable information about His character, revealing not only *what* God does but also *how* God accomplishes a desired result. God's approach to His creational design is etched intentionally; it is neither haphazard nor cavalier. Next to God's unconditional love and extravagant grace, the element of intentionality is centermost to God's character.

From a counseling perspective, intentional separation (severing unhealthy behavior from a healthy disposition) is to be considered a culminating goal for any counselor or caregiver. Separating a person from undesirable or painful realities is what a counselor works toward.[448] A counselor who assists a counselee to see reality more clearly will share insights, interpret circumstances, and bring greater perspective to a given situation. Due to greater clarity, a counselee will then need to make a decision that will involve choosing to separate from less desirable ways of living and move toward more productive ways. Again, intentional separation is a *key takeaway principle* for anyone trying to help a person in pain.

Genesis 1:5–14 contains a more detailed or explicit description of separation. Verse 5 reads, "And God called the light day, and the darkness He called night."[449] The theme of separation continues to permeate the Genesis story. God not only separates light from darkness on the first day, but God also separates the waters of the earth from the waters of the heavens[450] and the waters from dry ground.[451] A final description of the separating process emerges on the fourth day of creation when God distinguishes a tangible difference

---

[448] I will describe specific intentional separation principles in the counseling process later in this chapter.
[449] Genesis 1:5 (NIV)
[450] Genesis 1:6a
[451] Genesis 1:6b

between greater and lesser lights.[452] I so appreciate John Wesley's lyrical[453] summary of the separating process in the creation story.

> That God divided the light from the darkness—So put them asunder as they could never be joined together: and yet he divided time between them, the day for light, and the night for darkness, in a constant succession. Tho' the darkness was now scattered by the light, yet it has its place, because it has its use; for as the light of the morning befriends the business of the day, so the shadows of the evening befriend the repose of the night. God has thus divided between light and darkness, because he would daily mind us that this is a world of mixtures and changes. In heaven there is perpetual light, and no darkness; in hell utter darkness, and no light: but in this world they are counter-changed, and we pass daily from one to another; that we may learn to expect the like vicissitudes in the providence of God.
>
> That God divided them from each other by distinguishing names. He called the light Day, and the darkness he called night—He gave them names as Lord of both. He is the Lord of time, and will be so 'till day and night shall come to an end, and the stream of time be swallowed up in the ocean of eternity.
>
> That this was the first day's work, The evening and the morning were the first day—The darkness of the evening was before the light of the morning, that it might set it off, and make it shine the brighter.[454]

---

[452] Genesis 1:14

[453] I can only wonder if Wesley's hymn-writing brother, Charles, had any influence on this particular piece of writing.

[454] John Wesley, *Explanatory Notes.* Bible Study Tools; www.christnotes.org.

Types of Separation in Scripture

The theme of separation as documented in Scripture plays a significant role in the biblical narrative. Samuel Balentine, commenting on the "structuring or dividing process" as depicted in the story of creation comments, "The structuring process of the creation narrative emphasizes a central idea of symmetry and perfection.... *Divisions and boundaries* of each day are essential to observe and maintain if created order is to continue as God intends."[455]

At the outset of creation, Adam and Eve are directed by God to live apart from the Tree of Life and to not eat from it.[456] Through their disobedience,[457] Adam and Eve are separated from God and banished from the garden[458]—an *eternal* separation. Cain, Adam and Eve's firstborn son, is told to separate himself from that which is seeking to devour him.[459] Because of Cain's disobedience, he is separated from God's presence as were his parents before him.[460] Noah and his family are separated from sinful humanity and are spared from the onslaught of the flood.[461]

The original law given to Moses on Mount Sinai[462] and all other corresponding laws[463] are provided for the nomadic

---

[455] Samuel Balentine, *The Torah's Vision of Worship* (Minneapolis, MN: Augsburg Fortress Press, 1999), pp. 84, 86 (emphasis added).

[456] Genesis 2:16–17

[457] Certainly another separation takes place because of sin. Perfection is separated by brokenness, and a life of purity and confidence will be replaced with hiding and fear (see Genesis 3:10).

[458] Genesis 3:23

[459] Genesis 4:7

[460] Genesis 4:16

[461] Genesis 6: 9f.f

[462] Exodus 20

[463] Many people do not realize that God gave, in addition to the original Ten Commandments, 613 additional "laws of the land." These laws were given by God, motivated out of love, so that God's people would know very practical things concerning prayer, how to treat Gentiles, forbidden sexual relations, treatment of the poor, and even how life is to be lived

Israelites by God. The chosen children of Israel were given instructions as to how they should live and what they should avoid. This would be another example of the separation motif based upon God's spoken and written directives. The temple is a clear architectural representation of the dwelling of God that is configured into sections or rooms.[464] And finally, "On the day of judgment ... the wicked will be burned up like straw. They will be consumed—roots, branches, and all,"[465] forever separated from the presence of God.

Scripture instructs God's people to separate themselves from at least three major sources of potential misfortune. First, they are to separate themselves from sin[466] and sin's counterpart, worldliness.[467] This is an example of *personal separation*. James states that "pure religion" includes keeping "oneself unspotted from the world,"[468] and that "whosoever will be the friend of this world is the enemy of God."[469] A second instruction concerns false teachers.[470] This principle of *doctrinal separation* is perhaps the Apostle Paul's strongest directive to the young pastors, Timothy and Titus.[471] A third type of separation found in Scripture is that God's people are to be separated from those who say they are followers of Christ but are not.[472] This is an example of *ecclesiological separation*. Jesus says, "Moreover if thy brother shall trespass against thee, go and tell him his fault between thee and him

---

in particular times and seasons. The bulk of this instruction is found in Leviticus and Deuteronomy.

[464] 1 Kings 6

[465] Malachi 4:1 (NLT)

[466] Isaiah 59:2; Romans 12:1; 1 John 2:15–17

[467] Galatians 5:19f; Ephesians 5:15f.; 1 Thessalonians 4:3f.; 2 Timothy 3:1–9

[468] James 1:27 (KJV)

[469] James 4:4 (KJV); John 15:18–21

[470] 2 Corinthians 6:14; Ephesians 5:11; 1 Timothy 6:35; 2 Timothy 3:5

[471] Titus 2:1,2

[472] 2 Thessalonians 3:6; 2 Corinthians 6:14–15; 2 Timothy 2:15–22; 3:6, 14–15; Titus 3:10

alone: if he shall hear thee, thou hast gained thy brother. But if he will not hear [thee, then] take with thee one or two more, that in the mouth of two or three witnesses every word may be established. And if he shall neglect to hear them, tell [it] unto the church: but if he neglect to hear the church, let him be unto thee as a heathen man and a publican."[473]

Jesus and Separation

Separation is a common theme seen in Jesus' earthly life and teachings. Jesus practiced all three previously mentioned examples of separation (personal, doctrinal, and ecclesiastical) as demonstrated in Scripture. He separated himself from the world so as to be completely without sin,[474] repeatedly drawing a dividing line between himself and the hypocritical teachers of the law. Jesus levied heavy indictments against the religious teachers of his day and was seemingly harder on the hypocrisy of religious people than on those caught up in the most grievous expressions of sin.[475] It should be observed here that it was religious people who crucified Jesus. Sadly, times have not changed.

Parabolic teaching about separation is unmistakably illustrated by Jesus' instruction in the following: the wheat from the tares,[476] sheep from goats,[477] good fish from bad fish,[478] and fruit-bearing trees from non–fruit-bearing trees.[479] Another example of separation in the teaching of Jesus is found when he tells his disciples that they are to be in the

---

[473] Matthew 18:15–17 (KJV)
[474] Hebrews 4:15
[475] Matthew 23 is an entire chapter where Jesus rails against the Pharisees as they do not practice what they teach. Compare Jesus' attitude towards the Pharisees and the woman caught in adultery (John 8:1f).
[476] Matthew 13:30
[477] Matthew 25:31–32
[478] Matthew 13:47–50;
[479] Mark 11:12–14; Matthew 21:18–22

world but not of the world.[480] At the end of his public ministry, Jesus offers an eschatological teaching about those who are prepared to meet the anticipated Bridegroom and those who are not. Those unprepared for the Bridegroom's coming will be separated from the presence of God on the final day of judgment.[481]

The most significant aspect of separation in the life of Jesus that personally impacts me is found at the end of his earthly life. Jesus knows he will be betrayed by one of his chosen disciples,[482] and the eleven who remain will also forsake him[483].This is an unblemished example of *relational separation*. Ultimately, Jesus concludes his life and ministry with two final separation sayings. "My God, My God, why have you forsaken me?"[484] evokes an excruciating *emotional separation*. Jesus' final three words, "It is finished,"[485] are a reference to a *separation from earthly life* unto death.

Separation and Pastoral Counseling

When someone is walking in darkness, shining a light does not remove or separate the person from the proximity of their darkness. God's illuminating presence only provides information that allows a person to more clearly see their surroundings. That is what Jesus is to us—the light by which we see our circumstances. Likewise, one of the roles of the Christian counselor is that of luminary.[486] Counselors shed light on a situation, belief system, or not-so-distant experience

---

[480] John 15:18f.
[481] Matthew 25:1f.
[482] Matthew 26:21
[483] Matthew 26:36f.
[484] Matthew 27:46 (NIV)
[485] John 19:30 (NIV)
[486] I would remind the reader that Jesus said to his friends that they were to be "the light of the world." See Matthew 5:14.

in the life of the counselee and then "hit pause" to see what the counselee will do with the illumined information.

The Genesis story tells us that "God saw that the light was good"[487] and then "separated the light from the darkness."[488] As with the role of luminary, the subsequent role of separator is modeled by God. *Separation* is the sixth element in the Genesis Model of counseling. God's counselors introduce or utilize the concept of separation anytime they offer healthy alternatives to living as compared to destructive behaviors. After other ideas or options are identified by the counselor, the person seeking counsel will need time to process the possibilities for change that have been presented.

A hard counseling reality is that many people expect Jesus (or the counselor) to eliminate their painful circumstances for them and are disappointed when God merely sheds light on a situation. People are stunned that God does not mysteriously remove the consequences that *they* have created for themselves![489] It grieves me to say that some people appear to work harder at getting themselves *into* trouble and then make only superficial attempts at extricating themselves *from* trouble. A strong word of caution here to counselors: never, ever work harder than the counselee in the counseling relationship. It is imperative that the counselor determine whether the counselee is only physically present or is *emotionally, mentally, and*

> *It grieves me to say that some people appear to work harder at getting themselves into trouble and then make only superficial attempts at extricating themselves from trouble.*

---

[487] Genesis 1:4a (NIV)

[488] Genesis 1:4b (NIV)

[489] People wrongly interpret the passage, "Ask whatever you will in my name …" (John 13:14a), failing to cite the remainder of the verse, "*so that* my father would be glorified" (John 13:14b, emphasis added). Many personal prayer requests are not for the Father's glory but rather, merely a plea to avoid an embarrassing situation.

deeply invested in the counseling process.[490] On one occasion, I recall saying to a person after only ten minutes into a counseling session, "We are done today." He, of course, asked, "Why?" I then told him, "Because it is clear to me that you really do not want to be here today."

The platform of separation is the launching pad from a counselee's shadows into a renewed life. It is here the counselee is offered the choice to detach him- or herself from former expressions of nonproductive living. Although stated previously, I emphasize again the importance of people separating from destructive or unhealthy relationships. Relationships are contagious; people "catch" or get "infected by" unhealthy elements found in others. I have routinely heard from former counselees who successfully broke free from varying addictions, "It was the company I was keeping that kept me(in addiction)." Further, to make my point even clearer, I have heard, "I needed to find a whole new set of friends."

The fragile stage of separation is a counselor's and counselee's "perfect storm." A *perfect storm* is a meteorological term used to describe a unique set of extreme circumstances that create an unusual environment of dramatic proportion— this is not an uncommon description of a counseling environment. The invitation offered by the counselor to the counselee to remove pain-producing elements from his or her life can result in an emotional (feeling) or intellectual (reasoning) "storm" of some kind.[491]

---

[490] Kollar makes the distinction in his book *Solution Focused Pastoral Counseling* that three roles or attitudes can be seen in those seeking counseling. They are the willing counselee who desires change, the resistant counselee who does not want change, and the attending counselee who is physically present but does not invest him- or herself in the counseling process.

[491] This will be further explained along with the subject of resistance in counseling.

In his book *Experiencing God*, Henry Blackaby says that having a "crisis of faith" is one predictable outcome and quite *normative* when a person is seeking God. This truth also holds for a person in the separation stage of pastoral counseling. Counselors will hear comments such as, "I can't do that" or "That is impossible." When a counselor hears this, there is valid cause to revisit the desired outcomes that the counselee has earlier identified. A counselor attempts to reestablish momentum by asking questions like, "Let me be clear as to what you said earlier. Do you still want to make a decision by the end of the week?" and "Do you still want your children to know that (blank)?"

It was best-selling author Steven Covey who first posited the concept, "Begin with the end in mind."[492] To help a counselee see the end result before taking action is a very powerful and energizing weapon in the counselor's arsenal. Being able to visualize the final result or a desired outcome allows people to formulate plans and gain necessary emotional traction[493] so that they can transcend that which appears to be so daunting. "Beginning with the end in mind" is particularly effective when there is a seeming impasse facing the counselee. It is important for counselors to know that the concept of successful separation is commonly threatened because of a lack of preparation *on the part of the counselor*. A counselor must prepare a person for separation before any life change is ever considered. Below I address the

> *Being able to visualize the final result or a desired outcome allows people to formulate plans and gain necessary emotional traction so that they can transcend that which appears to be so daunting.*

---

[492] Covey, *7 Habits of Highly Effective People*.

[493] *Emotional traction* is a phrase I use to describe the counselee's difficult but necessary movement forward in the counseling process; this activity is most often "uphill." See Glossary of Terms in Appendix B for further information.

principle of pre-separation for counselors. The ideas associated with it describe specific dynamics for counselors who are trying to help people separate from damaging realities. These concepts must not be overlooked.

Pre-separation[494]

Before one can address how the process of separation begins, it is critical that counselors and caregivers understand the underlying hidden dynamics that are very much in play in the counselee's life *before* separation ever occurs. Anyone who desires to help another person bring any type of change to his or her life must not forget the following:

1. Separation or change of any kind is often an emotional experience.
2. People can handle just so much change.
3. Nearly all change requires a loss or a giving up of something.
4. Change will involve careful planning and prioritizing of details by both counselor and counselee.
5. Separation is an essential nonnegotiable for creating anything new.
6. People change only when future possibilities outweigh present difficulties.
7. There will be some times where all a counselor can do is listen.

Resistance is part of the pre-separation phase of counseling. When the person who is asking for help resists or rejects the overtures made by a friend or counselor, the one doing the

---

[494] *Pre-separation* is a term I have applied and further developed and that describes a "hidden" and therefore often unseen dynamic in the counseling process. See Glossary of Terms in Appendix B for further information.

caregiving must reject rejection. It is natural for people to resist change. If I were to give a presentation called "Resistance 101," I would include the following four portraits of resistance.

The Historical Resister

Historical resisters challenge and subtly reject (often through debate or argumentation) change because they have tried something in the past similar to what is being recommended and were not successful; therefore, they are less apt to buy into change. These counselees use this shield as a means to control others and their own unresolved feelings of disillusionment. They often say, "I tried something very close to that before, so I know it won't work this time either." John Maxwell coined the phrase "failing forward" to explain how to help people move through past disappointments. Maxwell says of *achievers*, "Achievers reject rejection, ... see failure as temporary, ... focus on their strengths, ... and have the ability to bounce back."[495]

The Intellectual Resister

The intellectual resister struggles with unfamiliar new ideas because they say they do not understand what is entailed in the proposed change. Like historical resisters, the need to control a situation is evident. These counselees often speculate that what they are being told may not be accurate and therefore decline the proposed change, revealing unresolved trust issues with people in authority. The best intervention for a counselor who is working with an intellectual resister is to play into their hand—actually, *their mind*. A counselor who is successful with an intellectual

---

[495] John Maxwell, *Failing Forward* (Nashville: Thomas Nelson, 2000).

resister will learn to ask clarifying questions such as, "What is an obstacle that you see with this idea?" The astute counselor will allow the intellectual resister to remove the obstacles with their own words!

The Emotional Resister

Emotional resisters fear change because they do not want to run the risk of looking bad. They will go to great lengths to distance themselves from painful past feelings. In his book *Healing Is a Choice*,[496] Steven Arterburn makes a specific argument for the absolute necessity of a person's facing the pain of the past so that the future may be fully lived.

The possibility of experiencing failure or being threatened in any way leads to a tremendous internal emotional conflict. Resistant males often display signs of visible anger. Females customarily show their emotions either through tears or by emotionally removing themselves from the situation. An example of the emotional resister would be a person who declines an invitation to run a 5K with good friends because she knows that she cannot compete at that level. The emotional resister declines new opportunities because giving the appearance of looking good is more important than the reality of looking bad. These resisters cannot tolerate a situation in which they are unable to maintain their "I've got it all together" facade.

The Chronic Resister

Similar to what I call the counseling junkie, the chronic resister will sincerely ask for help, make multiple appointments, and make a seemingly good start, but in the end he or she has firmly

---

[496] Steven Arterburn, *Healing Is a Choice* (Nashville: Thomas Nelson. 2005, 2011), see Chapter Two, "The Choice to Feel Your Life."

established reasons that change is impossible. Counselors need to be able to make a judgment *early on* when it comes to the chronic resister. This resister is a time bandit and a major emotional rip-off artist for unsuspecting counselors. Is there any hope for the chronic counselee? Of course there is, but the counselor must practice fierce boundary making, establish clear accountability, and identify specific and measurable goals. I will be honest—I have had little success with chronic resisters and have learned to pull the plug early so that I can move on to other people who are willing to move forward with their lives and work with diligence on their equally serious issues.

What about the Brain?

A final element in the pre-separation phase in this sixth stage of the Genesis Model involves a counselee's thinking. The more time I spend with counselees, the more I find that it is a person's thinking that frequently undermines possibilities for personal growth, professional development, or long-term relational happiness. Dr. Caroline Leaf, in her book *Who Switched Off My Brain?*,[497] states that the average person has more than 30,000 thoughts a day and that more than 1,400 are fully capable of causing physical and chemical chaos in one's life! A Christian cannot reflect on the subject of the mind for very long without considering Paul's watershed text on thinking. The Apostle Paul wrote, "Do not be conformed to the world but be transformed by the renewing of your mind."[498]

Several years ago Dr. David Burns, in his book *Feeling Good*,[499] identified "mental distortions" commonly found in people from all walks of life. Unhealthy, unrealistic, or groundless thinking is an "equal opportunity employer."

---

[497] Leaf, Caroline, Who *Switched Off My Brain?* (Nashville: Thomas Nelson, 2009).
[498] Romans 12:1–2 (NASB)
[499] David Burns, *Feeling Good* (New York: Harper Collins Publishers, 1980).

Toxic thoughts breach what was thought to be a competent and effective mental filter. I will not reiterate all of Burns's observations on mental distortions or negative beliefs, but I do want to identify five that I have routinely seen. Each of these expressions of errant thinking sabotages a person who wants to separate him- or herself from unhealthy and unproductive ways of living. I have added my own healthy "mental counterattack" to Burns's toxic ways of thinking.

Unhealthy Thinking	Mental Counter Attack
1. Dichotomous thinking (i.e., either/or rational)	Healthy people think in terms of spectrums.
2. Overgeneralizing (e.g., everyone; no one)	Healthy people think thoroughly and specifically.
3. Negative mental filter (e.g., glass half empty)	God is always at work in the process.
4. Catastrophizing (an overly negative spin on a situation)	The healthy person has learned to put things into perspective and seeks the help of others.
5. Personalizing (making the situation unique to the person)	The healthy person takes life's circumstances in stride and has the ability to move on.

Separation

There are many characteristics commonly found in people who say they want to separate themselves from unpleasant or distasteful realities. These daunting obstacles can represent a Herculean-size challenge for the person who desires change. Examples of separation challenges can include, but are not limited to, the following:

- An alleged inability to separate from a relationship (relational choices)
- Long-standing or well-entrenched habit patterns (destructive behaviors)
- An inability to be disciplined (a wide-ranging difficulty)
- The absence of a successful role model or advocate in this person's life (not having an example of success)
- An orientation to life that has flawed mental images (inaccurate self-perception)

I have developed "The Readiness Profile" for those seeking counseling, a straightforward twenty-question inventory (a ten-minute exercise) that is self-scored. After the sum is tabulated by an individual, I then interpret the profile. People taking the inventory will be able to identify four common blocks that impede them from moving forward in life. Appendix A contains the Readiness Profile along with instructions for administrating it. When these obstacles are identified and then removed, a person will gain both initial forward movement, and traction (ongoing forward momentum).

Readiness Profile

Circle the number for each statement according to
how true each statement is of you. Total your score.
Scale: 5 (always), 4 (often), 3 (sometimes),
2 (rarely), 1 (never)

1. I look carefully at all my options before making a decision.   1 2 3 4 5

2. I feel passionate about a number of things.   1 2 3 4 5

3. I would rather work with people than work alone.   1 2 3 4 5

4. I work to make the best out of any situation.   1 2 3 4 5

5. I am more likely to choose the "back roads" than the wide open highway.   1 2 3 4 5

6. I second-guess myself.   1 2 3 4 5

7. I adapt to new situations easily.   1 2 3 4 5

8. When people need help, it is not uncommon that they call on me.   1 2 3 4 5

9. Being told that I might be wrong is hard for me to hear.   1 2 3 4 5

10. I am very comfortable about asking others for the help I need.   1 2 3 4 5

11. I am good at getting around obstacles.   1 2 3 4 5

12. My emotions can get the best of me.   1 2 3 4 5

13. If there is no door, I will make one.   1 2 3 4 5

14. I think I may need to make some changes in my life.   1 2 3 4 5

15. I will consider change even though it is inconvenient.   1 2 3 4 5

16. I generally think things will work out   1 2 3 4 5
    for me.

17. I believe in not getting my hopes too high.   1 2 3 4 5

18. I am easily frustrated when things don't go   1 2 3 4 5
    my way.

19. I am inclined to improvise rather than do   1 2 3 4 5
    the "same old, same old."

20. I am mostly a very positive person.   1 2 3 4 5

Total: _____

Readiness Indicators

_____ :	_____	_____ =	_____
_____ :	_____	_____ =	_____
_____ :	_____	_____ =	_____
_____ :	_____	_____ =	_____

Conclusion: Separation and the Unknown

In concluding this chapter on separation, I draw on the experience of psychiatrist Louis McBurney of Marble Retreat Center.[500] Dr. McBurney has identified four common fears that are operative in the lives of people who seek to make changes. These fears can electrify and fortify a person's ability to successfully implement change. McBurney's research confirms that people fear rejection, embarrassment, loss of control, and facing negative feelings. In the course of this chapter, I have touched on each of these and now bring them back to the reader's attention as a reminder. When these fears are active in a person's life at any level, the ability to separate oneself from identifiable issues is greatly diminished.

---

[500] McBurney, Louis. From *Leadership*, Summer 1996.

People approach the concept of separation in many different ways. Some people choose separation only *partially* (there is perceived safety in the familiar), others will separate when they have a *vision* for their future that is more attractive than their present (seeing a reason for change), and there are those who *actively choose separation* when they know change will produce lasting results (change will bring sustained results). The following piece of writing from many years ago is a fitting conclusion.

Success[501]

The road to success is not straight.
There is a detour called failure,
a road block called confusion,
speed bumps called friends,
caution lights called family,
and flats we know as job lay-offs.
But…if you have a spare called determination,
an engine called perseverance, insurance called faith,
and a driver named Jesus
you will make it to a place called success.

---

[501] Original authorship of this piece of writing is unknown; however, it can be found on http://www.verybestquotes.com.

Chapter 12

The God Who Blesses

Then God *blessed* them and said, "Be fruitful and multiply. Fill the earth and govern it."
Genesis 1:28

Genesis Principle 7

Genesis Principle: Scripture records that on the seventh day God blessed the work of His hands.

Genesis Principle Applied: Counselors need to speak appropriate words of blessing over the newly created person.

Unlikely Champion: The Recipient of Blessing

Seabiscuit was the Depression-era racehorse that was regarded as physically too small, ridden by a jockey seemingly too big, and handled by a trainer reportedly too old. When scrutinizing the horse's running ability, Seabiscuit's trainer, Sunny Fitzsimmons, reportedly said, "The horse is so beat up on the inside it has forgotten how to be a horse." To this, Seabiscuit's owner observed, "Sure runs fast, though." "Yes," countered

Fitzsimmons, "in all directions." In short, the horse badly needed to receive encouragement that it had never known.

As previously referenced within the Genesis Model, there are two critical times for counselees that are identified as break points. The first break point occurs when a counselee is illuminated with the truth in regard to his or her surroundings.[502] The counselee *sees*, perhaps for the first time, why things are the way they are. Break point two follows on the heels of break point one. At this crossroad, the counselee must decide, after seeing reality, whether or not he or she will separate from former and less productive ways of "doing life."[503] Like the horse Seabiscuit, a person who sees reality *and* decides to no longer run "in all directions" stands in great need of encouragement or blessing.

Introducing the Principle of Blessing

A careful reading of the Genesis account reveals that after the creation of both man and woman, God "blesses them."[504] Then, God commissions both the man and the woman immediately to fill the land[505] and establish order.[506] Why do most churches today not follow God's Genesis design of immediate deployment? I am not advocating that the training up or mentoring of new believers be eliminated; however, in some form or fashion, the church has missed out by not using the contagious excitement that is often seen in a person who has been newly minted by the hand of God.

I recall talking in an airport with a well-known pastor. We, of course, "talked shop." I asked him, "What is your biggest leadership challenge?" His response was that his leaders could

---

[502] This is Genesis Principle number four; see Chapter Seven.
[503] This is Genesis Principle number six; refer to Chapter Ten.
[504] Genesis 1:28 (NIV)
[505] Genesis 1:28a
[506] Genesis 1:28b

not get enough people to fill the needed number of Sunday school teaching slots and that qualified deacons were at a premium. He also reported an increased turnover rate on his elder board. I asked, "Can you tell me about your training program for leaders?" He was noticeably pleased with the question as he described a highly elaborate, eighteen-week leadership orientation that *precluded* service in any formal church capacity.[507]

I told him that Jesus was an arsonist, essentially instructing his disciples to keep the ministry fires going. I noted at some point in church history the church began to douse the flames of faith with the over administration of details, erecting ridiculous hoops to jump over, creating fear-based procedures to follow, and the mandating of pointless prohibitions that 'will not be questioned'. All of the above, as well intentioned as they may be, are actual impediments to the hastening and advancing blaze of the Holy Spirit. The last conviction I shared was that young Christians today want to get involved in ministry now, *not* eighteen weeks down the line.

In a similar vein, consider this contemporary reality. College students stand in great need of affirmation and acknowledgement. During the past fourteen years, I have observed many young adults in the classroom and in my office who profess to be followers of Jesus Christ, yet they are fairly banged up due to wounds of the past and unreconciled histories that would make the strongest of people blush. Wasting away, they are starving to experience words of blessing and commission.

The Barna Research Group,[508] gathering data over the last four years, provides compelling documentation. Partnering

---

[507] I do not want to go into any detail here, but suffice it to say that this church's training program was long on the church's history, theology, and church structure, but the practical "how to" of ministry was *never* mentioned.

[508] Barna Research Group is located in Ventura, California, and has been in existence since 1984. George Barna has been a leading Christian researcher, delving deeply into many facets of both church and culture.

with various authors and researchers to better understand and subsequently explain the spiritual decay of college-aged people, the group has produced findings that empirically demonstrate that people under the age of thirty are not only leaving the church but, more shockingly, *avow that they are now either agnostic or atheist.*[509] The younger demographic cites two reasons for staying away; both criticisms could easily be silenced if the church would consistently offer words of encouragement. The two complaints are as follows: the church today defines itself more on the grounds of what it is *against* rather than what it is *for*, and the younger demographic sees how older and established so-called Christians treat one another and this behavior frightens them. In short, the eighteen- to thirty-year-old segment of culture thinks that Christians are unsafe people to be around. If this statement does not bother you at some level, check your pulse.

The Counselor

When I think of a counselor, my mind transitions to the person, work, and ministry of the Holy Spirit. Isaiah prophesied nearly eight hundred years before the birth of Jesus that a "Wonderful Counselor"[510] would be provided as a comfort for all humanity. The Greek New Testament word for this promise is *parakletos*. This word is frequently translated as "to encourage"[511] and also carries with it legal imagery that describes an attorney in the Greek courts of law assisting another who is in need.

---

[509] For more information on this established trend, and it is established, see Gary Kinnaman's book, *You Lost Me* or its previously released companion text, *UnChristian* (Grand Rapids, MI: Baker Books, 2011). Gabe Lyons, a writing partner with Kinnanman, has also released *The Next Christians* (Multnomah Books, 2012).

[510] Isaiah 9:6 (NIV)

[511] See Kenneth Wuest, *Word Studies in the Greek New Testament*. William B. Eerdmans Publishing, 1961.

A clear New Testament case study of one who both encourages and defends would be the early church leader Barnabas. In Acts 9, following the conversion of a former church persecutor, Saul, Barnabas does what no one else will do—he stands up and vouches for the authenticity of Saul. Barnabas testifies to the authenticity of Saul's conversion. He offers us several lessons on how to be an encourager and bring words of encouragement and blessing to others. Barnabas *initiated* his strong defense of Paul. True encouragers do not wait to encourage. When Paul was brought to the other apostles,[512] Barnabas offered *clear and specific testimony* as to Paul's changed character.[513] Authentic encouragers step up and demonstrate faithfulness. I am reminded of the text, "A true friend stays closer than a brother."[514]

Barnabas not only took an interest in individuals, like Paul, he also had the unique ability to *encourage entire groups of people*. On one occasion, Luke records, "News of this reached the church in Jerusalem, and they sent Barnabas to Antioch. When he arrived and saw what the grace of God had accomplished, he was glad and *encouraged them all* to remain true to the Lord with all their hearts. He was a good man, full of the Holy Spirit and faith, and a great number of people were brought to the Lord."[515] I think a case can be made that Barnabas not only had a reputation for being an encourager, but of greater significance, he was a man *full of the Holy Spirit and faith*. These attributes, once unified, produced a powerful evangelistic ministry.

Luke documents two additional facts about Barnabas in Acts 11 that fit the profile of an encourager: "So the believers in Antioch decided to send relief to the brothers and sisters in Judea, everyone giving as much as they could. This they

---

[512] Acts 9:27a
[513] Acts 9:27b
[514] Proverbs 18:24 (NLT)
[515] Acts 11:22–24 (NIV)

did, entrusting their gifts to Barnabas and Saul to take to the elders of the church in Jerusalem."[516] The above two verses tell us that an encourager is responsible, trustworthy, strong, and passionate, while being simultaneously focused and task oriented.

The Crucible of Encouragement

David Seamands wrote in *Healing for Damaged Emotions*, "Many Christians find themselves defeated by the most psychological weapon that Satan uses against them. The weapon has the effectiveness of a deadly missile. Its name: low self-esteem. … [These people] are tied up in knots, bound by a terrible feeling of inferiority, and chained to a deep sense of worthlessness."[517] This description is a portrait of a person who sees him- or herself as "less than." You might imagine how difficult it is for this person to hear words of affirmation or receive genuine gestures of unconditional love. I include Seamands's professional evaluation of contemporary society because Genesis Principle 7 emphasizes the dynamic of affirmation in counseling.

At this stage in the Genesis Model of biblical counseling, there is still a very real chance that the reception of words of blessing and encouragement offered by the counselor may be totally missed

At this stage in the Genesis Model of biblical counseling, there is still a very real chance that the reception of words of blessing and encouragement offered by the counselor may be totally missed—hard to imagine, but true. One thing I know about the counselor as a dispenser of encouragement is that if a counselor has not learned to receive words of

---

[516] Acts 11:29–30 (NLT)

[517] David Seamands, *Healing for Damaged Emotions*. (Wheaton, IL: Victor Books, 1981.), 49.

encouragement within his or her very core, it will be difficult to practice this needed counseling principle.

I refer to this stage in the Genesis Model as a crucible. A crucible is a severe test or trial that causes lasting or permanent change. While caught in the vice grips of the "crucible of encouragement," the counselee often discovers that which has threatened his or her ongoing personal growth. This pivotal point will promote a deeper level of self-actualization and intimacy with Christ.

For the counselee, a faith based solely on knowledge is not likely to result in an intimate relationship with God. The "crucible of encouragement" or, the "incubator of intimacy," is the place where the heart is emotionally circumcised and the deep-core recesses of a person's true identity will be exposed. At this place of blessing and supreme intimacy, a person can experience a depth of healing that was not realized in previous stages of the Genesis Model.

The Apostle Paul knew this same reality as he wrote, "In becoming weak, I am made strong."[518] Even secular playwright Ernest Hemingway aptly described in literary fashion the heat of the crucible when he wrote, "The world breaks everyone and afterwards many are strong at the broken places."[519] I say to counselees at the crucible of encouragement, the magnificent place of blessing, "This is your time, only your time, to receive all that the Father has for you."

Five Expressions of Blessing for the Counselee

Over twenty-five years ago Gary Smalley and John Trent wrote the book *The Blessing*.[520] In it, they define biblical blessing as a *demonstrative act* whereby unconditional acceptance of

---

[518] Paraphrased from 2 Corinthians 12:10
[519] Original source unknown
[520] Smalley, Gary & John Trent. *The Blessing* (Nashville: Thomas Nelson Publishers, 1986).

a person is given. A "successful blessing" occurs when the recipient has a sense of well-being and is further encouraged to pursue the future. Blessing seeks to accomplish one primary goal—to help people dream again. It is in a person's home, under the canopy of their parents' love and nurturing, that children have the first opportunity to experience blessing—or, sadly, not.[521] "A study of the subject of blessing always begins in the context of parental acceptance," write Smalley and Trent. "We find the same principles can be used in any intimate relationship."[522]

In their text, the authors identify and explain with great clarity five aspects of blessing commonly found in Old Testament homes.[523] Smalley and Trent's five aspects of blessing can be applied to the relationship between a Christian counselor and the counselee. Applied to the counseling setting, a counselor appropriates these ideas of blessing to a counseling setting in the following way: the use of meaningful (appropriate) touch, verbal clarity, personal self-worth, the offering of a prophetic word or picture, and the promise of ongoing investment on the part of the counselor in the life of the counselee.

Blessing as Meaningful (Appropriate) Touch

Of the five elements of scriptural blessing, the facet of physical touch when applied in a counseling setting deserves great intentionality, judiciousness, and wisdom. We know that

---

[521] Smalley and Trent discuss the ramifications of what happens either when blessing is (intentionally) withheld or when parents simply do not know how to "bless" their children. I will not address this material, although it is significant. But suffice it to say that when a child at an early age does not receive this unconditional positive regard, the emotional ramifications are vast and long lasting.

[522] Ibid. p. 21

[523] A clear biblical example of a blessing being passed down is in the story of Esau, found in Genesis 25.

physical touch "communicates warmth, personal acceptance, and affirmation."[524] Research shows that hemoglobin levels increase with physical touch as oxygen is released, which in turn energizes the regenerative process.[525] Mental health practitioners report that one result of a lack of physical touch or meaningful physical attention or activity is referred to as "failure to thrive"[526] syndrome. The misuse or abuse of physical touch is an all-too-common reality in our day.

Jacob's blessing of Esau included an embrace.[527] "In the Old Testament," write Smalley and Trent, " ... the symbolic picture of the laying on of hands was important.... It was the graphic picture of the transfer of power."[528] We read in the story of creation that God formed Adam first from the dust of the ground.[529] Ancient historian Josephus seems to convey the idea that the dry dust was mixed with water and that a clay-like substance evolved. Hence, the word *formed* is used, much as it would be in reference to a potter who fashions clay into whatever shape is desired.[530] The aspect of touch is addressed in greater detail as we read, "He breathed the breath of life into the man's nostrils and the man became a living person."[531] John Wesley in his commentary on Genesis observes,

> Of the other creatures it is said, they were created and made; but of man, that he was *formed*, which notes a gradual process in the work with great accuracy and exactness. To express the creation of this new thing, he takes a new word: a word

---

[524] Ibid., p. 24

[525] Ibid., p. 40

[526] *Failure to thrive* is a term used by health professionals that stems from neglect, abuse, or failure to sustain an emotional bond with a child; maternal deprivation is particularly emphasized in mental health literature.

[527] Genesis 27:26

[528] Smalley & Trent. *The Blessing*, p. 38

[529] Genesis 2:7a

[530] Josephus, I. 1. C. 1.

[531] Genesis 2:7b (NLT)

(some think) borrowed from the potter's forming his vessel upon the wheel. The body of man is curiously wrought.[532]

Clearly, the inclusion of the element of physical touch is found in the creation story as we read, "So the Lord caused the man to fall into a deep sleep. While the man slept, the Lord God took out one of the man's ribs and closed up the opening."[533]

A final observation I make in regard to the practice of physical touch and the place it has in the counseling relationship comes from linguistic research. The Hebrew word *ruwach*, sometimes translated as "spirit" and sometimes as "breath," seems to denote *invisible* (as compared to physical) power. There will be times when the activity of God is quite unseen, like the moving of God's Spirit; there will be other instances when the blessing of physical touch will be displayed. In a setting where a counselor believes he or she is led of God to practice the blessing of physical touch, it will be incumbent on the counselor to be keenly aware of the context (possible issues surrounding the counselee's life; sensitivity to gender differentiation), to pray, and to instruct the person being counseled as to the biblical precedent for this expression of blessing (Jacob/Esau story). Physical touch is never to be practiced as prolonged contact of any sort.

The Blessing of Spoken Words

I already addressed in Chapter Eight that God "spoke" all of created order into existence. One could not exaggerate the significance of spoken words. Much could be said here in relation to both the choice and number of words that

---

[532] John Wesley's Explanatory Notes, Genesis 2
[533] Genesis 2:21 (NLT)

counselors speak in a counseling session. Here is a sampling of practical information as it relates to a counseling setting.

As far as gender is concerned, some studies show that women have more words in their verbal arsenal than men.[534] "On average women say 7,000 words per day. Men manage just over 2,000," wrote Hara Estroff Marano in 2004 in *Psychology Today*.[535]

From a biblical vantage point, we know that Scripture has much to say about the power of words. Scripture compares our speech to the bit in the mouth of a horse,[536] the rudder on a ship that determines direction,[537] a power source for death and life, and[538] a source of gentleness.[539] These and many other references can be made about the power of our speech. Bottom line—*our words matter.*

The Blessing of Expressing High Value

When a counselee has successfully accomplished an identified goal, a counselor should practice the blessing of "declaring high value" by saying something like, "That was a good job." This is a concrete example of validating a person's hard work. Particularly for the person who needs to make that first small but huge step in changed behavior, valuing *any* progress is critical on the side of the counselor. Allow me to make a gender-specific observation here; men, in particular, highly value a *more-than-occasional* "Atta boy!" This spoken blessing may be given in words, pictures, or parables. An

---

[534] There are many studies on the number of words that are reportedly spoken by both men and women. As one might think, these studies vary widely and are in no way conclusive.

[535] Originally printed July 2004 edition and reviewed again in March 2013

[536] James 3:3

[537] James 3:4

[538] Proverbs 18:21

[539] Proverbs 15:4

example might be, "Tom, the way you are disciplining your eating right now, by the end of the month I can *see* that you ..." This is a statement of articulated *vision*. A counselor must see and articulate that which the counselee cannot see. If you were to come to my office, you would notice several pieces of artwork—some photographs, some oil paintings, and one object fashioned of stone by my daughter, Emily. In high school, she carved what resembles a person with his arms wrapped around himself. Em told me that this is how she understood (actually *saw*) what I accomplish with people in counseling. Emily said, "Daddy, you help people let go of themselves."

Another expression of the "high value blessing" is what I call *positive comparative*—for example, "You know, Gina, if you had been given the choice last month to go out with that same group of friends, I'm not sure you would have turned down their offer, but last week when you did just that, you showed remarkable restraint, and that restraint marks growth and personal victory!" As Gina's counselor, I was comparing her old behavior with her new behavior. Counselors are needed to practice offering words of affirmation because it is not uncommon for counselees to not recognize their own progress or growth.

The Blessing of Picturing a Special Future

I cannot think of this aspect of a counselor's blessing without thinking about the ministry of the prophetic. Scripture, both Old Testament and New Testament, is ladened with examples of God's speaking words of promise and hope, especially for Israel's future. Biblical examples of picturing a special future include the following:

> **2 Chronicles 7:14:** "If My people who are called by
> My Name will humble themselves, and pray and

seek My face, and turn from their wicked ways, then I will hear from heaven, and will forgive their sin and heal their land."

Isaiah 62:3–4: "You shall be a crown of glory in the hand of the Lord, And a royal diadem in the hand of your God. You shall no longer be termed "forsaken," nor shall your land any more be termed desolate; But you shall be called Hephzibah and your land Beulah; for the Lord delights in you …

1 Corinthians 13:9–12: For we know in part, and we prophesy in part; but when the perfect comes, the partial will be done away. For now we see in a mirror dimly, but then face to face; now I know in part, but then I shall know fully just as I also have been fully known.

Philippians 4:19: But my God shall supply all your need according to his riches in glory by Christ Jesus.

Acts 2:17–18: And it shall come to pass in the last days, says the Lord, I will pour out of my Spirit upon all flesh: and your sons and your daughters shall prophesy, and your young men shall see visions, and your old men shall dream dreams: And on my servants and on my handmaidens I will pour out in those days of my Spirit; and they shall prophesy.

Ministering to people through seeing a special future entails several key ideas. Doug Addison[540] has written a very readable text on how to grow in the area of setting prisoners free. Addison identifies six key ideas for how God shatters a

---

[540] Doug Addison. *Prophecy, Dreams and Evangelism* (North Sutton, NH: Streams Publishing House, 2005).

ceiling of brass and begins to showcase prophetic images as seen in everyday life:

- Believe that God wants to talk to you (Job 33:14)
- Seek out intentional times of silence; more times of silence = a greater possibility of God speaking to you (Luke 5:16)
- Know that strategically divine appointments are part of God's will in prophetic ministry—there are no coincidences (Acts 8: 26f)
- Ask God to show you who he is drawing toward you (John 6:65)
- All it takes is just a "little faith" and God will move (Matt. 17:20)
- Picturing a special future for a person, especially at the early stages of a relationship, nearly always is for the purpose of strengthening or building up (1 Cor. 14:3).

The Blessing of an Active Commitment

Expressing an active commitment to a counselee is the fifth and final expression of biblical blessing. Frequently, the final words out of my mouth before a person leaves my office are, "We are going to get through this." Why do I say *we*? I want the person to know that he or she is not in the situation alone. My affirmation demonstrates active commitment to the counselee. I am also trying to practice Blessing Principle 4: picturing a brighter future for them. Intentionally and deliberately, I strive to portray a future for the counselee that he or she often does not see for him- or herself.

Practicing active commitment is critical for Christian counselors because we live in a disposable culture—an orientation to life that is marked by hollow promises and short-lived commitments. Let me illustrate. One time I paid extra to have a package express mailed to my elderly mother in California. A week passed; there was no package. I talked with the owner of the local franchise. I pointed to the company's guaranteed three-day delivery policy, which was in full view for customers to see. I reminded the owner that I had paid additional money for this service. His response was, "Our policy is only an approximation. We can't guarantee delivery." Connect the dots? Are you beginning to see the importance of communicating an active commitment to the people we counsel?

Practicing an active commitment can also mean holding to and maintaining biblical beliefs. Active commitment has staying power regardless of the pressure that one may face. When theology conforms to cultural dictates, that theology can be described as being the "white washed sepulchers" of which Jesus spoke in Matthew's gospel.[541] Back in my early days of ministry, the word *relevant* was used to describe a person or organization that was seeking to keep pace with culture. In the last twenty years, at least three new words have replaced the word *relevant*. There was a day when *tolerant* was used to express a seeming open-mindedness to developing cultural norms. Later, and I don't know when, the word *tolerant* received a makeover and was replaced with the word *inclusive*. But *inclusive* did not stay around for very long. Today the words *relevant, tolerant,* and *inclusive* have received another makeover. Today's word for all three is *diversity*. Like its former sister phrases, being diverse or practicing diversity is tantamount to the indictment against the church of Laodicea, whom the Lord calls "lukewarm."[542] When a person uses the word *relevant, tolerant, inclusive,* or *diverse,* this "Christian caregiver" has moved from hot to cold

---

[541] Matthew 23:27
[542] Revelation 3:16a (NLT)

in God's economy. To this person, God says, "I will spit you out of my mouth."[543]

Scripture is clear that God has an active commitment to his people, even when they have done stupid things. God was actively committed to recommissioning Saul, who was a learned Hebrew scholar, a pure-blooded citizen of Israel, a member of the tribe of Benjamin, and zealous—a real Hebrew if there ever was one![544] But Saul was missing the blessing of God. In every way possible, Saul needed to be blessed, or touched by God. It was Saul's eyes that were touched, resulting in a vision *for Gentiles*! Paul would testify often that his apostleship did not come from man but rather from the Lord Jesus himself. Because of this unique calling, it is safe to say that Saul placed a high value on the work with which he had been entrusted. As far as Paul's understanding of a special future for himself, I think Paul would say again, "I consider everything in the past but refuse in comparison to knowing Christ."[545] Even now, Paul would be actively committed to any door that his Lord would open. Of this, I am convinced.

---

[543] Revelation 3:16b (NLT)
[544] Philippians 3:5f.
[545] Philippians 3:7

Chapter 13

The God Who Rests

Thus the heavens and the earth, and all the host of
them, were finished. And on the seventh day God
ended His work which He had done, and He *rested*
on the seventh day from all His work which He
had done. Then God blessed the seventh day and
sanctified it, because in it He *rested* from all His
work which God had created and made.

Genesis 2:1–4

Thus says the Lord, "Stand by the ways and see
and ask for the ancient paths, Where the good way
is, and walk in it; and you shall find *rest* for your
souls."

Jeremiah 6:16

Genesis Principle 8

<u>Genesis Principle</u>: Scripture declares that after Creator God's
work was "complete," God "rested."

<u>Genesis Principle Applied</u>: God's counselors, at the end of
their work, are to "rest."

207

Counselors and counselees share one mutual objective—they both want rest. It is not uncommon for a counselee to ask, "How long will I be in counseling?" or "How many sessions will I be seeing you?" These are fair and legitimate questions. In this chapter, I will address the concept of rest as it pertains to the counselee while investing equal emphasis and attention to the concept of rest as it pertains to *the counselor*.[546] Before fully delving into biblical material concerning rest and counseling operatives, it is important to understand how our bodies are chemically constructed.

The Anatomy of Rest: An Electrochemical Understanding

In Chapter 11, concerning separation, I introduced research by Dr. Caroline Leaf. Dr. Leaf has examined the relationship between brain activity and a person's ability to separate themselves from destructive behavior. I want to come back to the subject of brain activity/chemistry now and, how this relates to the subject of, "rest". Leaf, a cognitive neuroscientist with a PhD in Communication Pathology, reports the following in her best-selling book *Who Switched Off My Brain?*[547]

> Behavior starts with a thought. Thoughts stimulate emotions which then result in attitude[548] and finally produce behavior. This symphony of electrochemical reactions in the body affects the

---

[546] In one respect, this chapter on rest is meant to be seen as a companion chapter to Chapter Four, "When the Counselor Needs Counsel." Counselors will be only as effective with their counselees as they are emotionally and physically healthy themselves.

[547] Leaf, Caroline. *Who Switched Off My Brain?* (Southlake, TX: Thomas Nelson, 2007).

[548] "Attitude is a state of mind that produces a reaction in the body and a resultant behavior," p. 20.

way we think and feel physically. Therefore, toxic thoughts produce toxic emotions.[549]

She later discloses, "Research shows that around 87% of illnesses can be attributed to our thought life, and approximately 13% to diet, genetics and environment. Studies conclusively link more chronic diseases (also known as lifestyle diseases) to an epidemic of toxic emotions in our culture."[550] Leaf's research strongly indicates that humanity works with a distinct disadvantage when there has been an improper processing of information due in part to brain chemistry. Leaf states, "Thoughts that you don't deal with properly become suppressed and can cause emotional and physical harm."[551]

It is worthy to note that researchers of the brain and brain activity inform us that brain movement and activity are established in utero. At birth, a newborn has about 50 percent of the neurological connections found in a fully functioning adult. The capacity for needed further development must be established by constant connection with people if the brain's standard physical growth is to be attained. Should human connection be lacking to any measureable extent during the infant's early months and years, its brain development will likely be curtailed, causing a variety of serious repercussions. Research further shows that increased amounts of stress, attributed in part to an absence of people, creates a toxic brain hormone called cortisol. If high cortisol levels are maintained in the brain over an extended period, the brain's frontal lobes develop a decreased ability to control aggression and filter negative thoughts and feelings.[552]

---

[549] Ibid., p. 29. Leaf states later in her text that one way to detoxify your brain is to not respond immediately to an emotion that you feel strongly.
[550] Ibid., p. 5, emphasis added.
[551] Leaf, p. 34.
[552] Paul Martin, *The Healing Mind: The Vital Links Between Brain & Behavior, Immunity and Disease.* New York: St. Martin's Press, 1997

Summarily, a person's brain is considered "chemically at risk" when there are mental toxins running rampant, potentially sabotaging healthy decision making. Leaf offers a serious caution when she says, "Mental toxic waste left unchecked creates an emotional black hole and moves the body slowly but surely towards ill health at best and premature death at worst."[553] We know that Scripture teaches a spiritual remedy for cognitive chemical dysfunction is to "take every thought captive." [554] However, when there has been a history of neglect and abuse in an infant's life and the increased levels of cortisol become established, the choice to actively police one's thoughts is nearly impossible to achieve.

The most practical and concrete guidance I can offer when addressing the very serious electrochemical reality of faulty human brain activity or an incomplete processing of information is to incorporate what I call the principle of sustainability. The implementation of this principle recognizes that a decision made on a given day can be "sustained" or maintained over an extended period of time. *If a certain behavior cannot be maintained,* then the choice that is being considered is most likely not a healthy option.

Hebrews 4: The Magna Carta of Rest

Scripture offers very practical instruction concerning the ways to enter "God's rest." Hebrews 4 teaches that rest is promised,[555] something into which we enter, [556] yet sadly a blessing some will not achieve.[557] Prepared by God [558] and

---

[553] Ibid., pp. 47–48.
[554] 2 Corinthians 10:5 (ESV)
[555] Hebrews 4:1a
[556] Hebrews 4:1b
[557] Hebrews 4:1b
[558] Hebrews 4:2

accessible since the creation of the world,[559] the mandate is given for God's people to enter into this rest *today*.[560] Genesis states that God rested on the seventh day[561] having completed all that was intended. God is still in His rest, and He invites all of created order to join Him in this place of peace, solitude, and celebration.

The author of Hebrews observes, "There remains, then, a Sabbath-rest for the people of God."[562] What does this mean? Certainly a case can be made for acknowledging the Sabbath and keeping it holy.[563] However, the author's focus is not in limiting his understanding of rest as merely keeping a day free from common concerns and the responsibilities of life. Rest is to be seen as *a quality of life*. God's rest is not simply about a day but rather an entire way of modeling life to which others would be drawn. When a counselee can see that his or her counselor lives and functions from a place of rest, the counselee is often motivated to adopt these same behavioral realities in life. Rest in the life of a person signals that God's Spirit has been at work transforming the inner and outer life of an individual. As God rested from his creative work, so too are His children to rest.

> *Rest is to be seen as a quality of life. God's rest is not simply about a day but rather an entire way of modeling life to which others would be drawn.*

My clarion call to counselors is this: "Give it a rest." "From what?" you ask. I will identify in Hebrews 4 three expressions of work that unconsciously catapult a person into unhealthy behaviors. If these behaviors

> *Rest in the life of a person signals that God's Spirit has been at work transforming the inner and outer life of an individual.*

---

559 Hebrews 4:3
560 Hebrews 4:6–7
561 Genesis 2:2
562 Hebrews 4:9 (NIV)
563 Exodus 20:8–11

are not acknowledged and eradicated, rest is sacrificed. Below I identify three behaviors that counselors are to actively resist so that rest can be actualized.

Counselors Need Rest

<u>Works Orientation</u>: "On the seventh day God *rested* from all his *work*."[564]

Counselors are to rest from the work of counseling.

I have a counselor friend who says, "I know I am a fixer … and I need that fixed!" Yes, counselors in particular need to regularly take stock of their own lives and learn to rest from a works orientation to life. Years ago, Chuck Swindoll said, "Christians worship their work; work at their play and play at their worship." Times have not changed.

One fundamental human need that coincides with a works orientation to life is the need to accomplish. In and of itself, the desire to achieve is not wrong. I think it would be unhealthy if a person did not want to be successful.

> *When the basic human need for accomplishment supersedes everything else in an individual's life, then we are talking trouble.*

However, when the basic human need for accomplishment supersedes everything else in an individual's life, *then we are talking trouble.* With an inordinate need to accomplish a certain goal, a person will feel devalued and worthless when success is not attained. Again, accomplishing an identified goal is not necessarily a bad thing; however, accomplishment does not validate a person.

Because of Jesus' death on the cross, true believers can rest from trying to earn their salvation or qualify for the kingdom. When we look to Jesus for our salvation,

---

[564] Hebrews 4:4 (NIV), emphasis added.

we quit looking to ourselves. Brennan Manning reflects on his own personal tyranny of performance in his book *Abba's Child* when he states, "It used to be that I never felt safe with myself unless I was performing flawlessly. My desire to be perfect had transcended my desire for God.... To feel safe is to stop living in my head and sink down into my heart and feel liked and accepted."[565] Manning then quotes Thomas Merton, who offers the following guidance to freedom from a works orientation: "Quit keeping score altogether and surrender all your sinfulness to the God who sees neither the score nor the scorekeeper but only His child redeemed by Christ."[566] I have a distant memory of sitting in an elder board meeting one night; it was at the end of the year. One elder announced, quite matter-of-factly, "I have attended X number of committee meetings this year (I do not recall the exact number) and that is equivalent to X hours (I do not recall this number either) of my service to the church." I looked over at a dear elder friend of mine. Neither of us knew if we should laugh or cry.

Henri Nouwen, a significant and influential shaper of my own spirituality, offers this prayer for those who desire rest over the companionship of demons that demand, "Work harder!"

> Dear God,
> I am so afraid to open my clenched fists!
> Who will I be when I have nothing left to hold on to?
> Who will I be when I stand before you with empty hands?
> Please help me to gradually open my hands
> and to discover that I am not what I own,
> but what you want to give me.[567]

---

[565] Brennan Manning, *Abba's Child*. Colorado Springs: NavPress, 2002, p. 27.
[566] Ibid.
[567] Nouwen, Henri, *The Only Necessary Thing: Living the Prayerful Life.* Crossroad Publishing Company. 1999

Resting from a works orientation is critical for counselors. It is easy for counselors to fall into the "Messiah trap" and want to rescue or "fix" everybody. When a counselor is consumed or driven by the need to help others, it is nearly impossible to rest. My wife has been instrumental in helping me get a handle on my life by asking, "Why do you want to do this?" or "What drives you with such energy to accomplish this?" One must realize that resting from a works orientation applies to everyone. Whether a person is a counselor or an educator, technician or handyman, housewife or contractor, resting from a works-oriented life is an important spiritual discipline for everyone to appropriate.

<u>Words orientation</u>: "For the word of God is alive and powerful. It is sharper than the sharpest two-edged sword, cutting between soul and spirit, between joint and marrow. It judges the thoughts and attitudes of the heart."[568]

Counselors are to become more mindful of the words they speak and give their words a rest.

A contemporary interpretation of this text might be that if the word of God is sharper than a two-edged sword, then both the world and the church have substituted it with the dulled clichés of academics, pastors, and counselors. When this substitution is allowed to continue, God's rest is sacrificed. In the Gospel of John, we read, "In the beginning was the Word, and the Word was with God, and the Word was God."[569] Sadly, today, many churches do not hear the word of God preached but rather hear words *about* the Word. These "words" are ones that pastors find in commentaries and are delivered with polished eloquence, giving the appearance of high intelligence. We also have words about the words; these "words" are pithy points

---

[568] Hebrews 4:12 (NLT)
[569] John 1:1 (NIV)

extracted from self-help books and make the pastor sound so very interesting. And then there are the words about the words about the words; these "words" are the pirated sermons from Internet sources that pastors pass off as their own carefully crafted sermons. These messages give the impression that hours upon hours of hard work have gone into the preparation. My point here is that churches are so far removed from hearing the living word that Christians are starving to death. Why? Because they are no longer being served the Bread of Life!

In exploring the words *joint* and *marrow* as found in Hebrews 4, I discovered that joints are the hard outer part of the bone, whereas marrow is the softer and more tender parts of the bone. According to the *International Bible Encyclopedia*, "Marrow is the nourisher and strengthener of the bones; it is said to moisten the bones: 'The marrow (moach) of his bones is moistened' (Job 21:24); 'My soul shall be satisfied as with marrow (chelebh, "fat") and fatness' (Ps. 63:5)."[570] In either case, whether the harder or softer part of our "bones," the Word of God sets us free from anything that would prevent us from entering into God's rest.

Counselors are to rest from a words orientation to life and ministry. I strongly challenge counselors to identify and dedicate one day during the week to lay aside all secular reading and researched literature and dedicate that one day to reading and reflecting only on the Word of God. A biblical *and* counseling resource that I have utilized and found quite helpful is *Quick Scripture Reference for Counseling*[571] by John G. Kruis. This book allows counselors to not only spend time in the Scriptures but also access clear biblical applications and interpretations for cases in which they are currently involved.

---

[570] Orr, James, M.A., D.D. General Editor. "Definition for 'MARROW'". "International Standard Bible Encyclopedia". bible-history.com - ISBE; 1915.

[571] Kruis, John G., *Quick Scripture Reference for Counseling*. *Grand Rapids: Baker Books. 2000*

<u>False Projection Orientation</u>: "We have a great High Priest ... who understands our weaknesses, for he faced all the same testings we do, yet he did not sin. So let us, come boldly to the throne of our gracious God."[572]

Counselors are to develop a heightened awareness of the image that they seek to project to others.

I have observed that Hebrews 4 instructs God's people to rest from "works" and "words." Hebrews 4:11 specifically exhorts a third behavior that God's counselors are to cease practicing. Knowing that our great High Priest has "faced the same testings we do," we then can "come boldly to the throne of our glorious God." Only those who are free from seeking the approval of others can come boldly before Almighty God.

The need for approval is a common one. However, at what cost do we seek it? Someone once said that codependence is listlessly saying "Yes" on the outside and screaming "No!" on the inside. Anytime a person falsely portrays him- or herself, it will eventually become too difficult to "do life," or approach the throne of God boldly. Taken a step further, when a person is living with shadows in his or her life (some measure of sin or any expression of inauthenticity), it is virtually impossible to boldly approach the throne of our gracious God. James cautions us, "Don't you realize that friendship with the world makes you an enemy of God? I say it again: If you want to be a friend of the world, you make yourself an enemy of God."[573]

The person who is driven by the need for approval will do virtually anything to achieve it. Manning describes the approval-saturated life as a life led by "The Imposter." "The imposter," writes Manning,

---

[572] Hebrews 4:14-16 (NLT). Italics added for my emphasis.
[573] James 4:4 (NLT)

is preoccupied with acceptance and approval. Because of their suffocating need to please others, they cannot say no with the same confidence with which they say yes.... To gain acceptance and approval, the false self suppresses or camouflages feelings, making emotional honesty impossible. Living out of the false self creates a compulsive desire to present a perfect image to the public so that everyone will admire them. The imposter's life becomes a perpetual roller coaster ride of elation and depression.[574]

How easy do you think it is to achieve "God's rest" while living the life of an imposter? Not easy at all. Counselors need to be on guard against the urge to meet a need or go into another counseling session all the while looking for the imposter's "still, small voice" that whispers, "They love you. They want you. And you love the feeling you get when you receive that kind of attention." The chart below illustrates the three types of life orientations described in Hebrews 4 that correspond to basic human needs, unhealthy need fulfillment, and finally, a resulting emotion over unmet needs.

Life Orientation	Basic Human Need	Unhealthy Need Fulfillment	*Failure* to Achieve Goals *Results In*
1. Works Orientation	To Accomplish	Results-Oriented Person	Devalued
2. Words Orientation	Be Recognized	Self-Oriented Person	Ignored
3. False-Projection Orientation	Receive Approval	Dishonesty-Oriented Person	Rejected

---

[574] Manning, *Abba's Child,* Colorado Springs: NAVPRESS. 1994. p. 34.

Rest and the Children of Israel

While it is true that "rest is a cessation of labor, the notion of rest is much richer than that. God's rest expresses the completion and goal of His promises and the enjoyment of the perfection and harmony of creation."[575] A study of the "rest of God" motif in the Old Testament seems to include the element of refreshment. Exodus 31:17 states that God not only rested on the seventh day but also "was refreshed." [576] One would not say that God needed a rest after all had been created, for this would threaten the theological tenet of the immutability of God.[577] Jürgen Moltmann, in his work *God in Creation: A New Theology of Creation and the Spirit of God*,[578] states "After God's rest, he drew a breath of relief. What a strange way of completing work..."[579] Moltmann describes or further explains God's "taking a breath" in the following way:

> God allows his creation to draw near to him.... God "feels" the world; he allows himself to be affected and touched by each of his creatures. He adopts the community of creation as his own milieu. In his rest he is close to them all.... This does not neutralize [however] the tensions of creation nor

---

[575] Alexander, T. Desmond & David W. Baker (eds.), *Dictionary of the Old Testament: Pentateuch*, s.v. "Rest, Peace" (Downer's Grove, IL: InterVarsity Press, 2003).

[576] Louw, J. P., & E. A. Nida. (Vol. 1). (1996, c1989). *Greek-English Lexicon of the New Testament: Based on Semantic Domains* (electronic ed. of the 2nd edition.). New York: United Bible Societies, 1996, c1989), 259–260.

[577] Pink, A.W., God is perpetually the same, subject to no change in His being, attributes, or determinations. Therefore, God is compared to a rock (Deuteronomy 32:4f) that remains immovable when the entire ocean surrounding it is continually in a fluctuating state. Even so, though all creatures are subject to change, God is immutable. (Providence Baptist Ministries, online resources)

[578] Moltmann, Jürgen, *God in Creation: A New Theology of God and Creation and the Spirit of God*. Minneapolis: Fortress Press, 1993).

[579] Ibid., p. 278

does it disallow possible opposition of created things to the Creator.[580]

What is the correlation between rest and refreshment? Moltmann might say that refreshment is the tangible experience one receives when touched by all created order. Biblical scholars in referring to "The Rest Tradition" comment that God's gift of rest to his people also includes a resting *place*. The "place of rest" theme is seen as early as the story of Noah when the ark rested on Mount Ararat[581] and can also be traced throughout the wilderness wandering saga.[582] God's continuing faithfulness to His pilgrim people is seen in times of plenty and in times of murmuring. As God's people move from place to place, they affirm and reaffirm God's guidance and protection by erecting an Ebenezer, a symbol of hope and rest to their faithful God, who never slumbers nor sleeps.[583]

Rest and the Counselee

Charles Kollar states, "In its broadest sense the goal of all mental-health professionals is to help people feel better about themselves and their lives (Seligman, 1991), but this is not God's primary goal for His children. The goal of God's grace is to produce spiritual fruit, resulting in righteousness toward God and man."[584] Rest can be characterized as one of Kollar's

---

[580] Ibid., p. 280
[581] Genesis 8:4
[582] Alexander, T. D., & B. S. Rosner, *New Dictionary of Biblical Theology* (electronic ed.), (Downers Grove, IL: InterVarsity Press, 2001).
[583] The etymological roots of the word *Ebenezer* are literally a "stone of help." An Ebenezer is a reminder of God's holy presence and divine aid in a person's life. Spiritually and theologically speaking, an Ebenezer can be nearly anything that is a reminder of God's presence and help (e.g., the sacramental elements, a cross, a picture, perhaps even a hymn that reminds us of God's faithful intervention in a time of great need.
[584] Kollar, p. 61.

spiritual fruits that a counselor should be able to recognize in a counselee. Increasing rest and the ability to healthfully and intentionally handle tension are further spiritual fruits evidenced in the life of an emotionally healthy person who is growing in his or her "walk of rest."

> *Increasing rest and the ability to healthfully and intentionally handle tension are further spiritual fruits evidenced in the life of an emotionally healthy person who is growing in his or her "walk of rest."*

Rest was built into the natural rhythms of life by the Creator, who rested on the seventh day of creation.[585] Rest draws a boundary around work and takes legitimate delight in celebrating what has been accomplished. Rest from worldly concerns and tensions are one prevailing goal that counselors endeavor to achieve when attempting to help others. Even on the best of days, counselees stand in need of hearing the promises of God *from Scripture*. Here are a few of my favorite promises of God:

- Exodus 33:14: And He said, "My presence shall go with you, and I will give you rest."
- Ezekiel 34:15: "I will feed My flock and I will lead them to rest," declares the Lord God.
- Jeremiah 31:25: "For I satisfy the weary ones and refresh everyone who languishes."
- 2 Samuel 7:11: " … and I will give you rest from all your enemies."
- Joshua 21: 44: And the Lord gave them rest on every side, according to all that He had sworn to their fathers, and no one of all their enemies stood before them; the Lord gave all their enemies into their hand.
- Jeremiah 50:34: Their Redeemer is strong, the Lord of hosts is His name; He will vigorously plead their case,

---

[585] Genesis 2:2

so that He may bring rest to the earth, but turmoil to
the inhabitants of Babylon.

- 1 Kings 8:56: Blessed be the Lord, who has given rest
to His people Israel, according to all that He promised;
not one word has failed of all His good promises which
He promised through Moses His servant.

The Rest of Rest

A correct understanding of biblical rest certainly includes
rest from the preoccupation of daily labor. Further, we know
that God's rest was a covenant sign between God and his
creation[586] and God and His people.[587] Yet, another part of
the rest motif pictures God's people being released from their
bondage in Egypt[588] and the anxiety of oppression.

The most beautiful image of God's rest as applied to
counseling is explicitly painted in Deuteronomy 33:12: "The
beloved of the LORD *rest* secure in him, for he shields him
all day long, and the one the LORD loves rests between his
shoulders." What an incredible picture. Counselors are to lift
people up so they may be closer to God; relate to people in
such a way that they rest secure in our (counselor's) love; and
if needed, lift their burdens onto our shoulders.

Not every counseling session will go well, and, in fact,
some sessions will be just awful. In rare cases when there has
been an exchange of divergent views (perhaps a husband and
wife are still at an impasse or there is clear tension between the
counselor and the counselee), the counselor must take it upon
him- or herself to pronounce, in some form, an expression of rest
upon the hurting client. I am *not* referring here to a contrived,
shallow, or insincere epithet to tickle the ears of the counselee.

---

[586] Genesis 2:3
[587] Exodus 31:16–17
[588] Deuteronomy 5:15

What I am referring to here is something like, "I know that tonight was not as productive as you had hoped. I feel badly about this, also. I want you to know that I saw you at least try to bring to the table matters that are of vital importance. I have heard your concerns. I want us to come back next week, both with fresh minds and willing to seek productive ways of living. Again, thank you for meeting with me tonight."

In short, counselors must find some means within themselves to bestow rest or encouragement into a tenuous counseling situation. I underscore here the vital idea of proclaiming rest or closing a counseling session with some expression of a benediction of encouragement. In the economy of God, God commands, models, and provides rest. God rested, and God knows we need rest, also. Certainly, rest can be seen as a provisional gift that is awarded to faithful laborers, yet this is an incomplete understanding. Rest is also provided for a very specific purpose. Rest is given because there will be work yet ahead whereby the restoration that is gained from rest will need to be tapped for the challenges of a future endeavor. If there was ever a counseling session after which people need to be encouraged and told, "For tonight, give this a rest," it is one in which things have not gone well.

Following you will find a piece of writing I have had in my files for many years. It was originally published in Tim Hansel's book *Holy Sweat*.[589] It is a fitting reminder to all of us who yearn for rest. As an aside, I have offered this to counselees after a particularly challenging session.

The Bike Ride

When I was younger (and did not know any better),
I saw God as a doorkeeper who would decide if I
would get into heaven or not. Today I am older.

---

[589] Tim Hansel, *Holy Sweat*. Dallas: Word publishing. 1987. I have since found this original piece of writing altered in many blogs and publications.

My understanding of God has changed. God does not hang around to judge people, but rather to help anyone who wants help. Here is how my life has changed....

One day I heard about Jesus and on that day God became my friend, who joined me on my bike—my tandem bike. At first, Jesus was in the back seat helping *me* pedal. When I was in control, I thought I knew the way. I usually took shortcuts on my rides; from time to time I would get lost, even when I thought I knew the way. I don't know exactly when it happened, but one day He suggested we change places. My life has not been the same since.

The day He took the lead He showed me roads that I did not even know existed—he took me to the mountains, the seashore, to beautiful vineyards and most recently, to places far, far away. My white skin became brown in the summer sun as we biked together, he and I. When I was younger I would often ask, "When are we going to get there?" He rarely answered that question, he would simply say, "Just pedal." From time to time I asked, "Where are you taking me today?" He would just laugh; he usually did not answer that question either. At other times He would travel so fast I would say, "I'm scared." During these times, He'd simply lean back and touch my hand and smile. I eventually learned that enjoying the journey with Jesus was more important than where we would end up.

In case you are wondering, I did not totally trust Jesus at first to steer my bike or guide my path. I thought for sure I would not have any fun if he was in control. I have traveled with Jesus now for many years. I have learned things that I would have never known. He knows how to make the bend in the road straight; He knows how to take the fear out of turning on sharp corners and how to make the steep hills, feel not so steep. And just when I think He's got us lost, He always knows how to get us home again.

Many years have passed now ... since that day my Lord and I changed places on the bike. Today, I am fairly comfortable in the back seat. I am not afraid of strange places because I know who is steering. I enjoy the view and the filtered cool breeze on my face. And when I think I just can't go any further or times when I think I'm lost, He has an uncanny way of knowing how I feel. Somehow, when I need to hear His voice the most, He knows ... and in these times he whispers, "Just pedal ... we will get home, everything will be all right."

* *Holy Sweat*, Tim Hansel
adapted from *The Road of Life*
Word Publishing, Dallas 1987,
pp. 51–53

Chapter 14

"Selah"

Selah: to rest, to weigh, to hang in the balance. A musical mark denoting a pause, during which singers cease to sing and only the instruments are heard. *Selah* also can mean, a calm reflection on the preceding words.[590]

"To be nobody but yourself in a world which is doing its best, night and day, to make you everybody else means to fight the hardest battle which any human being can fight; and never stop fighting."

e. e. cummings

By now you know that the study of shadows is not merely an academic exercise for me. In very perceptible and tangible ways, my family is still walking in shadows.

This concluding chapter from *Out from the Shadows* is divided into two parts. *Part One* is actually the reconstructed sermon I delivered at Lee University titled "Finding God

---

[590] Fausset Bible Dictionary. www.bible-history.com

in the Darkness."[591] This message addressed the reality of darkness in everyday life and how to move out of darkness. (Look for a wonderful "God story" behind this address.) *Part Two* is a detailed counseling application that directly corresponds to the biblical material that I did not include in my sermon. I want to encourage readers, even now, to stop and prepare for what God may want to say.

Part One: "Finding God in the Darkness" (the sermon)

I want to address a single subject: finding God in the darkness. There are stories behind this message, and I will share some of them with you, so settle in. This morning's message is more than a "chapel talk"' to me. My prayer is that there will something here of significance for you, as well.

On July 23, following a freak mishap, our twenty-five-year-old son, Brady, was diagnosed with a rare form of cancer predominantly found in males over the age of fifty-five. Since that time, Brady has undergone steroid therapy and both radiation and chemotherapy. Today, he is preparing for stem-cell-replacement therapy in Nashville, Tennessee.

Five months later on December 31, my wife, Kris, awakened to tell me that she could not see. She was blind. We spent the last day of 2013 seeing one doctor after another. In the ensuing three weeks, Kris applied ocular medication three to four times a day to her damaged eyes; her eyes displayed little improvement. Two rounds of laser surgery were then prescribed. Still legally blind and the stability of her eyes tenuous, we were referred to a surgeon. The surgeon confirmed our ophthalmologist's findings—her eyes were

---

[591] This message can heard by going to the Lee University website, click on "Dixson Chapel," and look for my name with the title "Darkness"; February 2014.

in an uncertain condition whereby surgery should not be seriously considered. The surgeon told us *if* surgery were to be performed, there would be *no* guarantees—no conclusive findings for six months. Still, we chose surgery. I suppose I could tell you our decision for surgery was made after lengthy, tearful prayer and a visitation from God with careful instructions, but that would not be the truth. We simply believed we needed to trust God and elect the surgical route.

One week after the first lens replacement surgery, Kris was seeing twenty-forty out of her eye that had been fitted with a new lens. You would have had to have been in the surgeon's office to fully appreciate his face when Kris told him she could see. The surgeon told us that in over two decades of professional practice, he did not have a recorded case with this type of rapid outcome. A miracle. With every reason to be encouraged, we were invited to move forward with the replacement of her second lens; we agreed. The date was scheduled.

The night following our consultation for the second surgery, we came home, ate dinner, and later went to bed. I dreamt that night. In my dream, I was invited from the president's office at the university to speak in one of our chapel services. The dream included a specific text from which I had never studied or preached. The dream also included specific elements of how the service was to be constructed.

I went to work the next day where I received a call from the president's office at the university inviting me to speak in a chapel service later that same month. Of course, I chose the "dream text," Exodus 20:18–21 (emphasis added):

> When the people saw the thunder and lightning and heard the trumpet and saw the mountain in smoke, they trembled with fear. They stayed at a distance and said to Moses, "Speak to us yourself and we will listen. But do not have God speak

to us or we will die." Moses said to the people, "Do not be afraid. God has come to test you, so that the fear of God will be with you to keep you from sinning." The people remained at a distance, while *Moses approached the thick darkness where God was.*

Unbeknownst to the president's office, today's chapel service was scheduled for the day after Kris's second surgery— *which was yesterday.* Today, she is here with me and already has partial sight in her second surgically repaired eye ... our second miracle.

Personally, I am challenged by this morning's scripture. The context of our story is that God had spoken to the Israelites; the Ten Commandments had been given to their servant leader, Moses. Shortly thereafter, the text records a sound of thunder being heard in the skies as billows of smoke lifted heavenward from the distant mountain.[592] The children of Israel were frightened. Please note: when people are not accustomed to God's presence, fear is a normal response. Yet spending time in God's presence will result in a greater desire to seek after Him.

> *When people are not accustomed to God's presence, fear is a normal response. Yet spending time in God's presence will result in a greater desire to seek after Him.*

The Israelites asked Moses to be their middle man, saying, "Speak to us yourself and we will listen. But do not have God speak to us."[593] Moses assured the people that God did not want to harm them.[594] The people neither accepted Moses' explanation of assurance, nor would they go to the mountain of God. I so appreciate Dan Allender's comment about this level of pigheaded stubbornness: "When we turn *from* God we inevitably demand

---

[592] Exodus 20:18
[593] Exodus 20:19 (NIV)
[594] Exodus 20:20 (NIV)

from others the very thing we are missing in our relationship *with* God."[595]

Our text reads, "Moses approached the dark cloud ... *where God was.*"[596] Scripture has much to say about darkness. For example, we know the following:

- God created the darkness[597] and God separated darkness from light.
- God can be found in the darkness.[598]
- There are degrees[599] of darkness.
- Darkness can be felt.[600]
- Jesus goes so far as to say that evil persons will be cast into *outer darkness.*[601]

Scripture tells us that where there is darkness, there will be an absence of light resulting in an inability to see clearly.[602] The Bible also says that darkness is correlated to stumbling,[603] a way of living that takes us to desolate and desperate places.[604] There are predictable results for the person who tries to walk in the dark.

When I am in the dark, I cannot see; I bang into things. Some people say that when they bang into something they "bruise easily." I understand this expression; it

> *Between Brady's cancer and Kris's blindness, our family has been caught in the "shadowlands." Much like the biblical character Jacob, there are still days when we just plain walk with a limp.*

---

595 Exact source unknown; emphasis added.
596 Exodus 20:21 (NLT)
597 Isaiah 45:7; 2 Samuel 22:12
598 1 Kings 8:12
599 Darkness is described as "thick" (Deuteronomy 5:22); "gross" (Jeremiah 13:16); and "great" (Genesis 15:12)
600 Exodus 10:21
601 Matthew 8:12, 22:13, and 25:30
602 1 John 2:11
603 Isaiah 55:10
604 Psalm 82:5

describes what our family has been walking through the past seven months. Between Brady's cancer and Kris's blindness, our family has been caught in the "shadowlands." Much like the biblical character Jacob, there are still days when we just plain walk with a limp.

There have been times in my life when I have lived in a darkened state; during these times, I made decisions that hurt not only me but also those around me. Rarely do darkened or selfish decisions affect only the person making them. There have been other times in my life when darkness was not of my choosing. During these times, I have asked God for direction and clarity. The answers, most of the time, were slow in coming or seemingly nonexistent. Today, I prefer clarity and direction even if I do not understand what I am seeing or where I am going. And ... I am still someone who does not wait well.

I am learning, and have not yet fully learned, that waiting on God can be transformational in the life of the person who is doing the waiting. Young David—shepherd, youngest brother, giant killer, and military leader—spent many years waiting to be crowned king of Israel, all the while fleeing from Saul's obsessive anger. David would write, "Wait on the Lord; be of good courage, and He shall strengthen your heart."[605] Transparently, David shares his heart further with these words: "I *waited* patiently for the Lord; and He inclined to me, and heard my cry. He ... set my feet upon a rock, and established my steps."[606] Could it be that David grew into being a man after God's own heart by waiting on the Lord? I tend to think so.

Our text is fairly specific as to what *keeps* people in the dark. At the appearance of God, the people become frightened. Fear will keep a person in darkness. Verse 18 says the people

---

[605] Psalm 27:14 (KJV)
[606] Psalm 40:1–2 (KJV)

chose to have a relationship with God "at a distance." An intentional choice will also keep a person in the dark. The text seems to imply that the people seemed satisfied with living with God at a distance and were not willing to draw closer to Him when invited to do so.[607] Satisfaction or complacency results in living at a distance from God.

The text also records that the people *refused to listen* to Moses, an emissary of encouragement whom God had sent. Sadly, an outright refusal to be in a close relationship with God will result in living in "outer darkness." And finally, the people became their own worst enemy with their wrongful or darkened thinking about God. The following four ideas perpetuate darkness and prevent people from moving forward in all that life has for them.

- Unfounded fear
- Ill-fated choices
- Refusal to listen to words of encouragement or instruction
- Erroneous or errant thinking

At this point, I want to identify five ideas that I am currently practicing as I navigate my own darkness. You may be tempted to think, *I am not in darkness. I've really never been there.* I can appreciate that. Consider these next ideas as insurance not for a rainy day, but rather for a darker day.

First, *expect* darkness. I am not being negative here. Darkness happens, and it is real. It may not be cancer. It may not be blindness. But hard times happen to people. In my years of counseling, I have learned that a primary reason for

---

[607] A New Testament parallel to this idea is found in Luke 15 where the son who stayed home was close enough to hear the music from the party that was going on inside the house—a celebration held in honor of his prodigal brother's return. Even when invited to the party, both by a household servant and father, the "stay-at-home son" refused.

disappointment is *not* having realistic expectations. Stated another way, disillusionment is the result of believing an illusion. Darkness is reality. The best safeguard against disappointment or disillusionment is to live a life with eyes fixed on reality.

> *The best safeguard against disappointment or disillusionment is to live a life with eyes fixed on reality.*

The writer of Proverbs instructs, *"Look straight ahead*, and *fix your eyes* on what lies before you."[608] When talking about running, Paul assures the Philippians that he too, *"focuses on* this one thing: Forgetting the past and *looking forward* to what lies ahead."[609] Ecclesiastes 3:1 tells us that everything has a season, a shelf life, a beginning and an ending. Darkness is a season and seasons change, but we must learn to focus intently, especially in a darkened time of life.

Second, *accept* the darkness. This is perhaps the most difficult of my five ideas. I cannot offer a quick-fix plan on how to accept something that is absolutely distasteful. I would not minimize a person's pain or the circumstances that crowd in like a selfish acquaintance. If a person does not find a way of accepting reality, darkness will be prolonged. I recall talking with someone some years ago who had an eating disorder; this was not a person of strong faith. I said, "I *will not* tell you that if you invite God into your life, your eating disorder will go away. I will tell you, though, by *not inviting* God into your eating disorder, you can expect a longer recovery period."

Third, *interpret* the darkness. I mentioned earlier that darkness has degrees. Clearly, some expressions of darkness are more fear producing than others. Expressions or manifestations of darkness must be recognized or interpreted.

---

[608] Proverbs 4:25 (NLT; emphasis added)
[609] Philippians 3:13 (NLT; emphasis added)

Paul wrote, "I *see* through a glass dimly but one day, one day, I will *see clearly*."[610] None of us, not one of us, sees things nearly as well as we think we do. Read carefully: deeper levels of darkness mandate the help of another to correctly interpret the darkness.

> *None of us, not one of us, sees things nearly as well as we think we do.*

Fourth, *make adjustments* to the darkness. If people acknowledge and accept the darkness, they must then make corresponding adjustments *because of what they have come to know.* When people says to me that they are through changing, *they are through.* Stated another way, when an individual adopts an "arrival mentality," I know my work is cut out for me.

Scripture has many "case studies" of people who made adjustments in their lives after God had spoken to them. Noah could not simultaneously go on living the life he had and build an ark at the same time[611]; Abram could not stay in Ur or Haran and father a nation in Canaan[612]; Moses could not stay on the backside of the desert and herd sheep while standing before Pharaoh[613]; Jonah could not be in both Tarshish and Nineveh[614]; Peter, Andrew, James, and John had to leave their fishing businesses in order to follow Jesus[615]; Matthew had to leave his tax collector's booth to follow Jesus[616]; and Saul (later Paul) had to completely change social, religious, and vocational directions in order to fulfill God's call on his life.[617]

You have heard that insanity is doing the same thing over and over again and expecting different results. Dan Allender

---

[610] 1 Corinthians 13:11f. (ESV; emphasis added)
[611] Genesis 6
[612] Genesis 12:1–8
[613] Genesis 3
[614] Book of Jonah
[615] Matthew 4:18–22
[616] Matthew 9:9
[617] Acts 9:1–19

might comment on the inability to make necessary changes this way: "Good hearts are captured in a divine wrestling match; fearful, doubting hearts stay clear of the mat altogether."[618] The person who fails to make midcourse corrections in life will become the host of the world's biggest pity party, and his or her beverage of choice will be "whine."

Five, *emerge* from the darkness. Moses eventually emerged from the darkness where God had been speaking to him. Consider all that happened in Moses' life: abandoned at birth, biological father unknown, raised in a foreign culture, and the murder of an Egyptian, all of which resulted in a forty-year desert exile. Each of these facets helped shape Moses into the leader the Israelites needed him to be. Please know that *God uses everything and does not waste anything.*

Let me be clear—if you choose to emerge from your darkness, you will be a different person and you *will* have a story to tell. I know that as my family emerges from our darkness, we will have a story to share. But for this morning, I close with the words Jesus spoke to his disciples: "What I speak to you *in the dark*, tell the people."[619] I have spoken to you of what has come out of my darkness. Now, go live in His light.

In Part Two, "Guidelines for Counselors and Their Darkness" (immediately following), I remain with the text from Exodus to explain critical counseling principles. These principles and interventions need to be clearly understood and implemented while counseling those who are in "the darkness."

---

[618] Dan B. Allender, *The Wounded Heart: Hope for Adult Victims of Childhood Sexual Abuse* (Colorado Springs: NavPress, 1990).
[619] Matthew 10:27 (NLT; emphasis added)

Part Two: Guidelines When Counseling in the Darkness (the counseling application)

First, counselors must be willing to go to places counselees are not willing to go. Our text records, "The people remained at a distance as *Moses approached the thick darkness* where God was."[620] Moses intentionally and obediently chose to step into the thick darkness where the presence of God resided. A *key counseling principle* is that a person cannot come out of the shadows while living at a distance from God.

> *A key counseling principle is that a person cannot come out of the shadows while living at a distance from God.*

Because of their personal devotion, daily discipline, and unwavering obedience to God, counselors travel to places where others will not. Counselors may appropriately share a time from their own lives when they felt they were in the dark but were willing to take necessary steps forward. Further, counselors can *gently encourage* counselees to take that one small but essential step even though it is a step in the dark. Counselors must also be prepared, when necessary, to *strongly challenge* their counselees to embrace constructive momentum in their lives so that the seeker can reach a place, achieve success, or be free from anything that keeps them in their own shadows.[621]

Second, God is "*in* the darkness." The "location" where God's counselors *may find themselves* could be described as "thick darkness"—the unknown, the mysterious, and a place requiring increased faith. Portions of this particular story from Moses' life should remind you of the world as described

---

[620] Exodus 20:21 (NIV; emphasis added)

[621] Throughout this writing, I have identified several reasons that counselees believe they cannot make even one small change. In Appendix B, which I titled "Resources," I have provided a single document that identifies a counselee's sticking points for forward movement.

at the dawn of creation. Another *key counseling principle* is that darkness is a place where one is challenged to relinquish control and trust God; darkness is a place that God seeks to speak and illumine. If a counselor has not learned to trust God's illuminating direction *before* entering a counseling relationship, the counselor has missed a very important principle found in the Genesis Model.

> *If a counselor has not learned to trust God's illuminating direction before entering a counseling relationship, the counselor has missed a very important principle found in the Genesis Model.*

Third, counselors will occasionally find themselves in situations where answers to counseling challenges seem incomprehensible; little seems to make sense. Counselors may feel they are living in days similar to those described by the prophet Samuel: "In those days the word of the LORD was rare; there were not many visions."[622] A counselor may have tried a variety of interventions and strategies or, perhaps, sought guidance from esteemed colleagues. Yet nothing is working and the person they are helping is still in pain.

Four, there will be times when a counselor feels as if *they are* in the dark about a particular counseling situation. In these very times, God may be calling the counselor into the thick darkness of His presence *for the counselor's transformation.* In both my master's and doctoral classes, I was taught—and later in my career would experience—that God, on occasion, deliberately orchestrates difficult counseling scenarios. These difficult times for counselors are for the sole purpose of inviting the counselor into God's presence. Once in this place of desperation and seeming confusion, counselors can be more completely equipped and fashioned into God's image. Being driven by God, not in a desert place but rather

---

[622] 1 Samuel 3:1 (NIV)

in a setting where He whispers deep truths, can more fully transform counselors for the purpose of meeting the needs of others.

A fifth counseling principle is discovered from Exodus 20:24–26:

> Build for me an altar made of earth, and offer your sacrifices to me— your burnt offerings and peace offerings, your sheep and goats, and your cattle. Build my altar wherever I cause my name to be remembered, and I will come to you and bless you. If you use stones to build my altar, use only natural, uncut stones. Do not shape the stones with a tool, for that would make the altar unfit for holy use. And do not approach my altar by going up steps. If you do, someone might look up under your clothing and see your nakedness.

The explanation of how an altar is constructed and how one is to approach the altar offers important counseling concepts. These ideas clearly apply to the twin counseling realities of change and sacrifice.

The altar found in the Hebrew Scriptures is clearly a symbol of sacrifice in the same way the cross of Christ is a symbol of sacrifice found in the writings of the New Testament. God tells Moses how the altar is to be built and the materials from which the altar will be erected. Several observations surrounding this text provide a heightened appreciation of what we have read. The text actually identifies two altars: one of "earth" and the other of natural and uncut "stones." The references to earth (v. 24) and stone (v. 25) appear to be in contrast to each other. The Hebrew word for "earth" derives from its crumbling character (*erets*, from *ratz*, "to crumble away").[623] The use of the word *stone* refers to something that

---

[623] The Hebrew lexicon is Brown, Driver, Briggs Lexicon; this is keyed to the *Theological Word Book of the Old Testament*; *erets* is also translated

resists pressure and is characterized by its durability. "Earth" seems to represent frailty and weakness or a material that can easily wash away, whereby "stone" represents strength and stability and something unmovable.[624]

When Jacob prophetically placed the stone on the pillar and called the place the House of God, he was seeing into the future.[625] Out of Jacob would come the nation of Israel. From Israel would come the Messiah, and out of the Messiah would come the church, the future temple of God on the earth. One cannot help but think of the word *stone* and recall the text, "As you come to him, the living Stone, rejected by men but chosen by God and precious to him you also, like living stones, are being built into a spiritual house to be a holy priesthood, offering spiritual sacrifices acceptable to God through Jesus Christ."[626]

An important point of instruction cannot be missed here— the stones of the altar are *not to be fashioned or sha*ped by human chisel. The fifth *key counseling principle* for counselors is that there is to be no allowance for the use of human effort (e.g., the use of a chisel or of some clever counseling technique). God jealously guards the setting for His holy presence. The stones must be placed in the exact form that the Creator had made them; Moses and his people must not alter (add to, chisel or adjust) the stones in any way.[627]

"land," "region," or "territory."

[624] Smith, William, *Smith's Bible Dictionary*. s.v. "stones, precious." 1901.

[625] Jacob set up a stone pillar to mark the place where God had spoken to him. Then he poured wine over it as an offering to God and anointed the pillar with olive oil (Genesis 25:14). Jacob set up a pillar in order to identify the place where God had spoken to him. Jacob did this a second time in Bethel (Genesis. 28:18). Later in the Old Testament, Samuel did a similar thing, naming the stone of commemoration Ebenezer, which means in Hebrew "the stone of help" (1 Samuel. 7:12).

[626] 1 Peter 2:4–5 (NIV)

[627] After the "altar instructions," one cannot help but recall what would ensue: instructions for living (Exodus 21–23) are presented; the Mosaic covenant is established (24); the description of the tabernacle and priestly

A sixth and final observation for a counselor is found in Exodus 20:26, revealing how a person *approaches the altar.* We read, "Do not approach my altar by going up steps. If you do, someone might look up under your clothing and see your nakedness." You may consider this an obscure verse of Scripture, but concealed here is a very important principle. This sixth key counseling principle speaks to how not to build an alter (no use of human effort to "climb up" to God). The text is clear. Self-made ways of approaching God will expose a person's own shame ("see your nakedness"). The utilization of the latest counseling textbook (even the one you hold!), academic resources, testing instruments, professional accreditation, or some neatly packaged orientation to counseling *at the expense of* the leading of the Holy Spirit will bear only short-term results.

These five closing ideas are nonnegotiable principles for counselors and need not be "altered":

- *Exhibit* a willingness to pursue God even into the darkness.
- *Realize* that a place of darkness can be an anguishing place of relinquishment.
- *Believe* that a place of darkness is often a place of personal transformation.
- *Recognize* that counseling is a sacrificial ministry presented unto God.
- *Approach* both God and counseling without the need to rely on human effort.

---

garments (25–28) are recorded, and the consecration of the priests takes place. Then, chaos erupts. While Moses was away, the people would craft their own idols, *made by their own hands,* and replace God as the center of their lives and community (32).

Darkness: A Profound Time of Altering

Counseling in any form or fashion involves an altering or an alteration of some kind, like a needed shortening or lengthening of a garment. I limit my final reflections to altars that were erected by Noah, Abraham, and Jacob and one concluding altar—your own.

Noah's Altar

When Noah finally emerged from the confines of the ark and walked on the new earth, he erected an altar unto the Lord and sacrificed to the God who had saved him from destruction.[628] Noah's altar was an altar of both sacrifice and thanksgiving. As God did for Noah, counselors help counselees "alter" (and in some cases, *actually save*) their lives. This altering will no doubt involve sacrifices and should conclude with thanksgiving. Because of sacrificial obedience, those who seek after God, like Noah, will avoid certain calamity and destruction.

As I write, even now, the thought comes to me that the idea of celebration in counseling is not "celebrated" enough. Think about this: a person comes to counseling because of heartache, desiring direction of some kind, or is trying to attain a more meaningful life. Does it not make sense, then, that counselors celebrate successful transformations with their counselees in some way? I truly think so. One natural way to celebrate the counselee is by speaking words of affirmation. Another expression of celebration may include an informal concluding coffee served by the local barista.

Abraham's Altars

Unlike Noah, the story of Abraham includes several accounts surrounding the erection of altars. Those erected at Sheckem,

---

[628] Genesis 8:20

Bethel, and Hebron were built to indicate communion with the Lord and dependence upon Him. When Abram arrived in Canaan at Sheckem, the Lord appeared to him, saying, "To your descendants I will give this land"; and of Abram it is related, "And there he built an altar to the Lord, who had appeared to him."[629] In Genesis 12–15, Abram builds two more altars, signifying increased intimacy with God. These three chapters center around the theme of relationship; Abram leaves his relationship with his homeland and father; separates himself from his nephew, Lot; and is given the prophetic promise of a new relationship yet to come. These three chapters conclude with the giving of a new identity as Abram becomes Abraham.[630] Following his "change of identity," Abraham is reminded once again by God that he will have an heir in his later years.[631]

Abraham would one day build another altar on Mount Moriah. God directed him, saying, "Take your son, your only son—yes, Isaac, whom you love so much—and go to the land of Moriah. Go and sacrifice him as a burnt offering on one of the mountains, which I will show you."[632] The text is rich in imagery as the innocent and obedient Isaac asks of his father, "Behold the fire and the wood: but where is the lamb for a burnt offering?"[633], and the aged father brokenheartedly replies, "My son, God will provide Himself a lamb for a burnt offering." The two would then make their way to the fire, together."[634] I believe Henri Nouwen is correct in commenting that the presence of Isaac in Abraham's later years had come dangerously close to replacing Abraham's love for God.

---

[629] Genesis 12:6f (NASB)
[630] Genesis 17:5
[631] Genesis 17:4
[632] Genesis 22:2 (NLT)
[633] Genesis 22:7 (NASB)
[634] Genesis 22:8 (KJV)

Therefore, there was a need for the altar of obedience and sacrifice.

The order in which Abraham's altars appear and their corresponding significance is central to the story line of this wonderful Hebrew narrative while also having significant application to the counseling relationship. It is important to observe that God always establishes communion and dependence (Abraham's first altars) with his people before He tests (the altar of sacrifice). God's counselors are to do the very same: establish a relationship with a counselee before ever asking for sacrifice or change. After the Lord intervened to provide a substitute sacrifice for Isaac, Abraham called the place of sacrifice *Jehovah-Jireh*—the Lord will provide. Counselors must know that, in similar fashion, God will provide for both the needs of the counselor (wisdom and direction) and those of the counselee (healing and grace).

Jacob's Altars

Jacob was a man with the call of God on his life; even so, life never seemed easy. God would send angels along Jacob's path to encourage, guide, and challenge him. On one of his many expeditions, Jacob arrived at Shechem. Evidently intending to stay, Jacob purchased a field, built an altar, and called it *El-elohe-Israel*, which means "God, the God of Israel."[635] Jacob's intentions were good; but as his story unfolds, it seems clear that he lacked a more complete understanding of God's plan. Jacob's difficulties are a warning to us—hollow or empty promises made to God will not be overlooked.

When God instructed Jacob to go to Bethel, unrest came upon God's servant. Jacob would realize that he could no longer live with or tolerate short-sighted commitments, as is evidenced by his instruction to his household: "Put away the

---

[635] Genesis 33:20 (HCSB)

strange gods that are among you, and be clean, and change your garments."[636] Jacob's story teaches that an outward appearance of communion with God as depicted in the building of the altar (or the building of a church, a reputation, or financial security) at Shechem while simultaneously worshipping other gods is double-minded idolatry.

After Jacob's "house-cleaning," God appeared again, saying, "I am God Almighty; be fruitful and increase in number. A nation and a community of nations will come from you, and kings will be among your descendants. The land I gave to Abraham and Isaac I also give to you, and I will give this land to your descendants after you."[637] There is a weighty lesson here: Jacob's house-cleaning and God's *near-immediate* reappearance and heart-felt promise for the years ahead are no mere coincidence. And so it is in the economy of God. Jacob's story teaches that double-mindedness of any kind is not fatal; it can be corrected, and life can begin again.

The only way to intimacy and divine favor with God as discussed above is to separate oneself from earthly values *entirely*. One cannot operate from a worldly mind-set and expect kingdom blessings. In coming to Bethel, Jacob builds the altar that God requested, and he calls the place *El-beth-el*, which means "God of the House of God." The patriarch now more fully grasped God's purpose for his life, a destiny that had been spoken of long ago.

Like Jacob, how good it is when a soul finally enters into complete communion with the Father and acts in accordance with the perfect will of God. Jacob's story exemplifies communion with God; this "lost and found," "unrest to rest," "darkness to light" transition can be seen several times throughout Jacob's lifetime. As I write, I am reminded of St. Augustine's *Confessions*: "You have made us for yourself, O

---

[636] Genesis 35:2 (KJV)
[637] Genesis 35:11-12 (NIV)

Lord, and our heart is restless until it rests in you."[638] That is to say that within each of us, there is a thirst, an unquenchable craving in each cavernous heart that is never satisfied and never filled by anything the world may offer. Might not our deep yearning for a transcending experience go *beyond* that which humanly drives us? Does this craving, in fact, argue more strongly for the One whom our restless hearts seek?

The reason for this insatiability is simply God's ultimate purpose for man's life. We have learned throughout our time together that each of us is created to be in fellowship with God. Scripture affirms, "Thou art worthy, O Lord, to receive glory and honor and power: for thou hast created all things, and for thy pleasure they are and were created."[639] And "This is life eternal, that they might know the only true God, and Jesus Christ, whom you have sent."[640] Our desire to be in unfathomable communion with God is a pursuit that is planted deep within the heart of all living humanity. This quest will be sought until it is fully found.

Altars were built by rocks and often broken things. By reading Scripture, we are assured that God uses all things, even the broken pieces of our lives, for His glory. God waits for us to release our brokenness into His healing hands. Carefully holding each broken memory, disappointment, or loss, at just the right time, God releases and uses that which we think is beyond repair to help someone else. It is not until we repent and invite God to more actively be a central part of our lives that painful hurts and memories are woven into the tapestry of our lives and our redemption is then made complete. My wife, Kris, was unquestionably astute when she wrote in the preface, "Bill has personally experienced the cords of the grave coiled around him. It takes 'Jesus with skin

---

[638] Augustine of Hippo. *Confessions*, Book 1, Chapter 1; see also Psalms 63:1 and Jeremiah 20:7
[639] Revelation 4:11 (KJV)
[640] John 17:3 (KJV)

on' to remove the rags of death." To His glory, like Lazarus, I have emerged from the grave, and you can, too.

Once, a poor and modest widow broke the seal on her only remaining jar of oil and began to pour. God miraculously multiplied her oil to pay her debts and thereby supplied her a means of support.[641] Her needs were met, but only *after* her jar had been broken. There was a miracle in her house, and there is a miracle in your house also. Jesus took "five loaves ... and broke them,"[642] and the bread was multiplied to feed five thousand. It was through the process of breaking that the miracle occurred and, to this day, still occurs. Only after Mary broke her beautiful "alabaster jar of very expensive perfume"[643] were its inner contents revealed. God delights in using broken things for His glory. In like manner, allow God to take every broken piece of your life. Don't try to glue it, fake it, or fix it—simply release it.

A Final Alteration

While in Israel, our group was told that geological surveys reveal that there have been volcanic explosions and seismic activity for generations. Similarly, people who seek the services of a counselor have experienced more than their fair share of earth-shifting events. Allow me a final "bunny trail"— actually, a metaphor.

"Plate tectonics" is a developing theory that seeks to describe the large-scale motion or "drifting" of matter that lies hidden beneath the earth's surface. By definition, the word *plate* in geologic terminology means a large portion of solid rock. *Tectonics* is a part of a Greek root meaning "to build." Together, *plate* and *tectonics* define how the earth's surface is

---

[641] 2 Kings 4:1–7
[642] Luke 9:16 (NIV)
[643] Matthew 26:7 (NIV)

built up by way of moving plates. Since the pioneering work of meteorologist Alfred Wegener in 1912,[644] generations of researchers have gone on to argue that tectonic plates drift about much like slow-moving bumper cars that repeatedly cluster together and then separate. This activity of shifting, a coming together and then reorienting, has been ongoing for millions of years. The movement of the earth's tectonic plates is essential in understanding the formation of the various landscape features seen across the globe today. Below I have created scientific theory that is counterbalanced with spiritual reality.

Scientific Theory	Spiritual Reality
Plate tectonics is a developing theory.	God is an *established* reality.
Plates are seen as "drifting."	God is secure.
Plates are hidden beneath the earth's surface.	God is revealed in heaven and on earth.
Movement of plates is essential to the earth's formation.	Movement is a spiritual prerequisite for personal transformation.
The moving of tectonic plates creates a new landscape.	Movement on the part of an individual produces a new creation.
The motion of the earth has been transpiring for a long time.	God has always been moving, trying to get our attention.

To both counselor and counselee, I say that people can deny obstacles that shroud their lives or ignore the subtle and

---

[644] Wegener's research of plate tectonics began in the early 1900s and would become a fully established belief among tectonic researchers by 1950.

elusive daily "shiftings" that commonly occur. They can also attempt to drag the rocks of life around and be weighed down by them. Or, we can invite the Lord to uncover and transform the unseen and undetected things in our lives so that the forgotten, devastated, and desolate places of our lives[645] can be rebuilt from the ground up and from the inside out. The ultimate price of "altering" has been paid on Calvary. It is time for all of God's people to say, "Unless the Lord builds the house, its labor is in vain."[646] And "Remember, there is one foundation, the One already laid, who is, Jesus Christ."[647]

All that is gold does not glitter,
Not all those who wander are lost;
The old that is strong does not wither,
Deep roots are not reached by the frost.
From the ashes a fire shall be woken,
A light **from the shadows** shall spring;
Renewed shall be blade that was broken,
The crownless again shall be king.
J.R.R. Tolkien[648]

---

645 Isaiah 61:4
646 Psalm 127:1 (NLT)
647 1 Corinthians 3:11 (The Message translation)
648 Tolkien, J.R.R.R. *The Lord of the Rings*. Cited in numerous sources including, famous poets and poems.com

Appendices A

Instruments and Tools

(Each document is preceded by an explanation sheet for the supplied resource. The explanation sheet describes, simply, "how to" best utilize this resource in a counseling setting. Facilitators should feel free to adapt their own approach so as to meet their own needs.)

- Betrayal Index
- Closure Letter
- Control Inventory
- False God Images
- Readiness Profile
- The Three-Minute Manager

Betrayal Index

The issue of betrayal is covered in the next-to-last lecture I deliver in my pastoral counseling classes because it is profoundly the most, if not *the* most, painful experience ever encountered. *Betrayal* is defined as a violation of a valued and trusted relationship through an act of treachery. It is the wound one experiences from a person (in what was thought to be a committed relationship) or institution (an employer) that could have never been imagined. Trust and confidence were given completely by the innocent party; therefore, the thought of ever being betrayed was never considered. For this reason, betrayal is a nearly all-consuming, excruciating experience.

Initial Instrument Instruction

On the following page, you will find the Betrayal Index.* This twenty-question instrument should be *carefully administered*, using the proctor's own language.

> Being betrayed or deeply disappointed by someone in a valued relationship is one of life's deepest wounds. Today's data does not predispose a person to being betrayed, nor does it infer that a person will one day become a betrayer. This tool does, however, provide information as to how a person approaches relationships and possible relational vulnerabilities that could create an atmosphere of betrayal. Please take about 5–6 minutes to answer these questions. There are no trick questions or repeating questions. Try to not overthink the questions as your initial inclinations are usually the most accurate.
>
> This instrument will identify six common relational dynamics that create the unfortunate

chemistry for betrayal to occur. I will reveal the corresponding questions for each dynamic. You will fill in your own results in the box found at the bottom of the questionnaire. An aggregate or overall score will help you better understand yourself and others.

Further Instruction for Proctor

After the above instruction for the index has been given, the index is then distributed to participant(s). *The provided Explanation of Scoring sheet is to be held by the person overseeing this exercise.* After participant(s) have completed answering the questions, the person leading this exercise discloses the six betrayal dynamics and corresponding questions related to each dynamic. Then, the proctor reveals the evaluation of the aggregate score (this is also found on the Explanation of Scoring document). *Those who administer this tool should make it clear to participants that they are available to discuss any individual's results on a one-on-one basis.*

* The Betrayal Index is to been as an "index"—that is, a reference of subjects that help guide a person to better understand him- or herself. The results of this index are in no way scientific or absolute; however, over fifteen years of its use clearly indicate that the results provide people with a better understanding of themselves and others.

Betrayal Index
Dr. Bill Effler

The following questions are designed to surface a person's "betrayal tendencies" or identify certain factors that could create a betrayal environment. Circle YES for any question that is *truer* of you than it is not true of you.

1. YES NO   I am a champion of the "underdog" even if it costs me something.
2. YES NO   More than once I thought I could fix someone but found I couldn't.
3. YES NO   It can be hard for me to keep my boundaries or values with people.
4. YES NO   There are some things I will never talk about.
5. YES NO   I have had a disappointment (e.g., person, issue, and situation) that still causes me anxiety.
6. YES NO   Sometimes I "monitor" (e.g., check Facebook) the behavior of someone with whom I've had a past relationship.
7. YES NO   There has been an occasion where I was totally wrong about a person.
8. YES NO   Something happened in my past that I hope people never find out about.
9. YES NO   In my past I have not been able to recognize or stop abusive behavior.
10. YES NO   I have had at least one relationship where I stayed too long.
11. YES NO   There is something in my past that creates current behaviors that I think are unhealthy.
12. YES NO   I have been in a relationship where my poor choices took me by surprise.
13. YES NO   I have ignored a person's unhealthy behavior in order to stay in the relationship.

14. YES NO   I have stayed in relationships knowing it could cause me regret later.
15. YES NO   Friends have told me to get out of a relationship, but I would not listen.
16. YES NO   Sometimes I get a little anxious or nervous when I am attracted to someone.
17. YES NO   It is easier for me to think about the past than dream about the future.
18. YES NO   I have had an experience in my life that I have never shared with another person.
19. YES NO   I seem to attract needy people more than emotionally healthy people.
20. YES NO   Taking this questionnaire has made me a little anxious.

_____ : _____	_____ : _____
_____ : _____	_____ : _____
_____ : _____	_____ : _____

Explanation of Scoring

Betrayal Dynamics and Questions

There are six distinguishable issues that relate to a person's proneness to betrayal. The distinguishing questions and corresponding factors are as follows:

1. Faulty thinking: questions 2, 7, 13, and 14
2. Boundary related issues: questions 3, 9, 10, and 12
3. Emotion related issues: questions 5, 16, and 20
4. The past: questions 6, 11, and 17
5. People: questions 1, 15, and 19
6. Secrets: questions 4, 8, and 18

Aggregate Scoring

1–2: This score reveals a lack of reality; personal honesty is questionable.

3–8: There is *initial evidence* that reveals that this person has concerns related to betrayal. This person either has been hurt in a relationship or has an orientation to relationships that could create an environment in which betrayal could occur.

9–14: There are *developed indicators* that expose the likelihood of significant relational pain. Persons in this category should consider talking with a friend about past disappointments.

15 and higher: This person would benefit from professional help.

Closure Letter

"Getting closure" on a painful experience, relationship, or hoped-for dream is a critical and nonnegotiable part of living a healthy and productive life—in short, a life without regret. Experienced counselors know that failure to get closure on a painful or disappointing experience can become a very big deal in years to come. This intervention (closure letter) to moving forward with life without a lingering sense of violation, pain, or regret is usually not intended to be a sent to the individual who has violated or hurt the person who is seeking closure. However, it *could* be sent. The strength of this tool is that it can spark dialogue between the counselor and counselee. The ideas below are meant only to serve as beginning strategies for this tool. Getting closure on a painful life experience may be one of the greatest satisfactions a person may ever experience.

Instructions

Some of the questions on this worksheet may not directly apply to the counselee. In this case, simply leave the blank empty. The counselee may want to add his or her own statements or ideas; this is a wonderful sign that closure is beginning to happen. It is not uncommon in the counseling dialogue that the counselee will discover that he or she has had unfounded or unrealistic beliefs about the painful situation; this discovery, too, will lead to closure. And there will be times when the counselor will see that a counselee is simply not willing to let the past be the past. Some counselees choose to nurse and rehearse the past rather than reverse it by addressing it directly. In the case of an unwilling counselee, the counselor must take careful note of this unwillingness; review in *Shadows* the material on change and unwillingness to change, and engage the counselee with statements and questions like, "I am not exactly clear on how not letting go of (name of person or event) is productive for you." Or, "I know that being (lied to, abandoned, etc.) was wrong and should not have ever happened, but it did. How might you be able to get freedom from this?"

Closure Letter

Dear _____,

Since I last saw you, I have thought about our relationship. I am writing you today so I can move on to the next chapter of my life. Yet I seem to be distracted with nagging and unanswered questions and feelings.

When I saw you the last time, I felt _____, and I knew then that I should have told you _____. As I think back to our relationship, I wonder what you were thinking when _____

_____.

All I ever wanted or hoped for from our relationship was

_____,

but instead, our relationship seemed, from my perspective

_____.

Today, I still feel a little stupid because _____

_____.

I know I am responsible for/to _____

_____,

and at times I still regret _____

_____.

My biggest obstacle in getting closure on our relationship is _____.

I know I could still hold onto these unanswered questions and regrets, but I will not live with this negativity.
The past is the past. I know that I am responsible for _____

_____.

To fully move forward with my life and have peace, I will ___

_____.

_____

My Signature

259

Control Inventory*

I don't know if I have ever met anyone who did not exhibit some expression of control issues. Control is a gender-specific relational reality, as men control in one way and women in quite another. I have seen that people in church culture control quite differently than what is found in non-churchgoers. And certainly, one can see varying expressions of control from one vocational environment to the next.

If one looks carefully, the need to control is a fairly common dynamic seen in most people. Further, it is unhealthy if a person cannot demonstrate self-control. From the attached Control Inventory emerge six garden-variety areas where people naturally seek to control. This instrument can be beneficial in individual counseling, in premarital counseling, and certainly in couple counseling. I have also used this instrument in the corporate sector and while consulting with churches.

Instruction

Notify the participant(s) that they will be taking a Control Inventory. Be prepared for some people to bristle, while others may say, "Oh, joy, my favorite topic." In either case, relieve the nervousness by telling the person(s) that the need for control is part of healthy daily living; it is *how* we control that can bring discomfort to others. Tell the participant(s) that they should be able to complete this inventory in 5–7 minutes. Assure them there are no hidden messages in this instrument and that this inventory will reveal six areas found in everyday life where control becomes an issue. The culminating benefit for participants is that they will discover how much control controls their life. Only administer the questionnaire; DO NOT distribute the sheet marked "Evaluation."

Further Instruction

After participant(s) have taken the inventory, the proctor of the inventory will disclose each "category of control" along with the corresponding questions. Participants will fill in the boxes that are found at the bottom of their questionnaires. In conclusion, the proctor will read the raw description of control levels found on the sheet marked "Evaluation." Before "Inventory Day," the leader will need to have enough copies of the sheet marked "Evaluation" for each participant.

*The Control Inventory is a questionnaire used to both list and reveal areas of control commonly found in a person's life. The results of this inventory are in no way scientific or absolute; however, persons taking this tool have validated that this instrument is helpful in clarifying control areas, motives, and personal values.

Control Inventory

Circle any number that is <u>truer of you</u> than it is *not* true of you.

1. I am not a "spur of the moment" kind of person.
2. It is frustrating to me when others do not keep to a budget.
3. I like to figure out things on my own.
4. I have some unresolved childhood disappointments that I rarely talk about.
5. I have some difficult childhood memories about the way my brothers/sisters treated me.
6. I work first and play later rather than play first and work later.
7. I do not think about my past very much.
8. I carefully plan most parts of my calendar.
9. It's no one's business about how I spend my money.
10. I work hard at keeping myself emotionally in control.
11. I think about my standard of living when I retire.
12. I read to better understand the world in which I live.
13. I would rather have one or two really good friends than many acquaintances.
14. I have never been delinquent on paying a bill.
15. I am right most of the time—not bragging, this is true.
16. People look to me to have an answer when there is a problem.
17. It is hard for me to schedule, much less enjoy, a vacation.
18. I have high standards, which others sometimes mistake for criticism.
19. I can be a perfectionist; it also bothers me to see others do sloppy work.
20. I can feel uncomfortable if I think someone is getting too close to me.

21. I spend a fair amount of time thinking about ultimate truth.
22. It is hard for me to relax or fully enjoy a well-deserved vacation.
23. I work hard at what I do, sometimes to a fault.
24. I think more about my work than relaxing on a well-deserved vacation.
25. I have very good reasons for how I spend my money.
26. I like to know where I stand with a person.
27. In looking back at my life, I wonder why my parents did what they did.
28. I can get uncomfortable with public displays of emotion.
29. I still blame my parents for a lot of my problems, but I haven't told them so.
30. I am in control of most of my relationships, of what I say and how I say it.

Control Issues	Corresponding Questions
1. _____	_____
2. _____	_____
3. _____	_____
4. _____	_____
5. _____	_____
6. _____	_____

Evaluation

0–10 points: Comfortable with Life   _____

You are not dominated by an excessive need to control. You are mainly comfortable with your feelings and tolerant of other people. You realize that you are imperfect; therefore, you understand the imperfections of others. It is easy for you to let events take their own course; surprises don't throw you off balance. You allow for spontaneity and the expression of emotions by others.

11–20 points: Situational Control   _____

Being in control is a "situational" reality in your life; you have an occasional need to control either people or feelings. Being in charge isn't necessarily important to you, but the need to have your way can crop up from time to time. You most likely have found someone with whom you can be honest, but there are limits to how much you will safely say or do, even with that person. You recognize there was a time in your past that you were not able to control; the memories of this time cause you a degree of discomfort from time to time.

Over 20 points: Established Control   _____

Control controls your life. The need to control is evidenced in _at least_ three categories below. You believe that having control is necessary for personal happiness. The overriding need to have things your way drives people away from you, despite the fact that you work hard to take care of others' needs. Anger, disappointment, fear, and irritability are easily seen in you by others even though you think others do not see this in you. You constantly give reasons for why you are the way you are, but somehow this doesn't help you get you what you want, which is other people's love and affection. It is very likely that the origin of your need for control goes back to childhood.

Control Issues	Questions
Family of Origin Issues	4, 5, 7, 27, and 29
Relationships	13, 20, 22, 26, and 30
Work	6, 16, 18, 23, and 19
Money/Finances	2, 9, 11, 14, and 25
Leisure	1, 8, 17, 22, and 24
Feelings/Emotions	10, 11, 20, 26, and 28
Worldview/Point of View	3, 12, 15, and 21

False God Images

Dateline: Tuesday, September 12, 2006. "View of God Can Reveal Your Values and Politics." From this lead *USA TODAY* article, we learn that sociologists at Baylor University conducted a national survey of 1,721 Americans consisting of seventy-seven questions with almost four hundred answer choices. A total of 91.8 percent of respondents reported a belief in God, a higher power, or a cosmic force, while identifying four very diverse views of God: "authoritarian," "benevolent," "critical," and "distant."

Out from the Shadows states that many people live a "shadowed" existence due to an erroneous view of God. My thirty years of professional experience convince me that people living in the shadows for an extended period of time have rarely experienced the living God as described in Scripture. Those with false God images tend to be very cerebral "loners" who have well-scripted (and rehearsed) reasons that they believe God is not available or, at least, not available *for them*. At the core of nearly all false God images lie profound fear, a problem with authority, and a high need to be in control.

Instructions

In nearly all counseling or caregiving situations (private practice, residential care, or even a conversation with a family member), if one is going to offer direction or provide help to another using a faith-based approach, it is essential to build on a solid foundation. Therefore, it is incumbent on the counselor or helper to determine if the person in need has an accurate understanding of the God of the Bible.

To determine if an orthodox or biblical view of God is embraced by the seeker, the counselor, facilitator, or friend can begin by asking, "What is your own personal understanding or experience with God?" A second question may be, "If you could create a god, what might you include as some of the personal characteristics or qualities of your god?" I have asked these questions in individual counseling appointments and to classes of fifty students. Nearly without exception, the hoped-for god that is described is a portrayal of the God found in Scripture (i.e., unconditionally loving, available to help, giver of good things, one who makes allowances for personal autonomy, etc.).

After some dialogue using the above suggestions, the "False God "document can then be offered and further discussion can transpire, eliciting both laughter and frank discussion. As previously stated, in most cases a false God concept revolves around issues concerning authority and control. *Counselors must know* that hidden beneath the twin issues of authority and control is profound pain, a sense of betrayal or abandonment, and often low self-esteem and victimization.

False God Images

The Authoritarian or Punisher God

This God's first inclination or impulse toward humanity is judgment resembling that of Oscar the Grouch, The Grinch who Stole Christmas, or the Dickens character Ebenezer Scrooge. You had better walk quietly around this God because he is in a perpetually bad mood.

The Distant God

This God exists but is aloof or detached from those who need love. Emotionally distant and essentially unavailable, he is perceived to be long on promises and short on follow through.

The Sugar Daddy God

This God is fun. Although a benevolent gift giver, he has his favorites. For a person experiencing a difficult time, there is the belief, "I surely am not on *his* favorites list."

The Historical God

This God is as old as dirt. People best understand him as the great "I Was" and *not* the great "I Am." If this God does exist, he is indeed tired because of all the work he has accomplished. This God is regularly found napping or involved in an exciting game of checkers.

The Weak God

This God will never be compared to any modern-day muscle man (Bruce Lee, Rocky, James Bond, Superman). He may have done some pretty unbelievable things in the past, but this God has used up any strength that he once had. People believing in this God consider their problems far too enormous for him to address.

The Unknowable God

This God hoards the intelligence that created the world; thus, one cannot even begin to comprehend or relate to such a vast cerebral deity. Since "God's thoughts are higher than man's thoughts," why make an attempt to know this God? Essentially, he is far beyond human understanding; therefore, he is too complex to engage in meaningful conversation.

The Optional God

Far and away, the "Optional God" is the easiest God to relate to; he can be approached whenever and wherever a person *feels* like it. In every sense, this is a convenience-based relationship; there are few, if any expectations. God is not dead, as Nietzsche argued—just optional.

The Church or Ministry God

This God is only available to well put together and cleanly groomed church people and is only seen in church worship services, conference settings, or when a huge supernatural miracle is needed. He is not accessible to common folk, the unchurched, or people who are in great need. If you have anything questionable in your life that may be suspect, do not think this God will be interested in you.

The Pawn Shop God

This God is a "wheeler-dealer" type whose infinitesimal and untouchable valuables remain cloistered in glass showcases. If a "customer" or person in need were to ask for personal assistance of any kind, more than likely they will not get what they feel they need. Sadly, they may be swindled out of something they hold dear.

The Prankster God

This God enjoys making people look foolish by placing them in situations where they are set up to fail. A person may be called to a destination or a job, but, once there, he pulls the rug out from under them. This God finds pleasure in "divine pranking" all at the expense of innocent and trusting individuals.

The Slumlord God

The Slumlord God is an absentee tyrant who invests as little as possible in his property (or people he is supposed to care about). Having no regard for the tenants, he charges ridiculous fees for rent; yet he expects his residents to be ever *so* grateful to have a place to live. If anything is in need of repair, it will be up to the tenants to fix—at their expense.

Readiness Profile*

Drawing on my counseling experience in a residential treatment program, private practice, and in advising students in higher education, I have routinely seen that most people see themselves as more ready for change than is actually the case. The truth of this statement comes to light when a person is confronted with a particular belief, habit, or behavior that needs to change. The "Readiness Profile" identifies four readiness qualities that directly enable a person to facilitate change in his or her life. People who lack development in any one of these areas struggle with change.

Instructions

Before distributing the Readiness Profile, share with the participants that change is part of life. There is no way to escape the reality of change. If the leader wishes, additional comments about change can be made at this time. Additionally, after the profile has been taken and scored, it may be appropriate to present a teaching on the benefits of change.

After distributing the questionnaire, instruct participants that they have 5 minutes to complete the twenty-question profile. Bring the participants' attention to the scoring evaluation at the top of the sheet. Explain that after reading a question, they will evaluate themselves on a scale of 1–5, with 5 representing a statement that is "always true" or meaning "This statement describes me perfectly." The score of 1 represents a statement that is "not true of me at all." The facilitator can model the scoring scale by answering question number one him- or herself and explaining why he or she chose that response. I have routinely done this myself, and it leaves no room for confusion. After participants finish answering their questions, they can tabulate their cumulative scores. Assure the participants that there will be ample time for questions following the completion of this exercise. Finally, bring the participants' attention to the bottom of the sheet and explain that after everyone has taken the profile, you will identify the four readiness qualities along with the corresponding questions. Participants will fill in their own boxes found at the bottom of the worksheet. The facilitator will use the "Leader's Guide" to disclose to the participants the four readiness qualities and the corresponding questions.

Two important details: (1) A participant *cannot answer more than* 5 questions with the evaluation of "3." You will see that '3' represent "This is sometimes true of me." (2) DO NOT pass out the 'Participant Worksheet" until *after* you have identified the readiness qualities and the corresponding numbers.

*The Readiness Profile is a nonscientific self-administered tool that allows the participants to discover their personal comfort levels concerning the subject of change. This tool in no way predisposes a person to either being comfortable with change or not being comfortable with change. Nearly fifteen years of distributing this profile indicates that people are greatly helped by this instrument as it allows them to explore possible blockages to change.

Readiness Profile   Dr. Bill Effler

Circle the number for each statement according to how true it is for you.

Total your overall score. Scale: 5 (always), 4 (often), 3 (sometimes), 2 (rarely), 1 (never)

1. I look carefully at all my options before making a decision.   1 2 3 4 5

2. I feel passionate about a number of things.   1 2 3 4 5

3. I am energized by working with others.   1 2 3 4 5

4. I work diligently to make the best out of any situation.   1 2 3 4 5

5. I am more likely to choose the "back roads" than the wide open highway.   1 2 3 4 5

6. I second-guess myself.   1 2 3 4 5

7. I adapt to new situations easily.   1 2 3 4 5

8. When people need help, it is not uncommon that they call on me.   1 2 3 4 5

9. Being told that I might be wrong is hard for me to hear.   1 2 3 4 5

10. I am very comfortable about asking others for the help I need.   1 2 3 4 5

11. I am good at getting around obstacles.   1 2 3 4 5

12. My emotions can get the best of me.   1 2 3 4 5

13. If there is no door, I will make one.   1 2 3 4 5

14. I think I may need to make some changes in my life.   1 2 3 4 5

15. I will consider change even though it is inconvenient.   1 2 3 4 5

16. I generally think things will work out for me.   1 2 3 4 5

17. I am a reality-based individual. 1 2 3 4 5

18. I am easily frustrated when things don't go 1 2 3 4 5
my way.

19. I am inclined to improvise rather than do the 1 2 3 4 5
"same old, same old."

20. I am mostly a very positive person. 1 2 3 4 5

Total: _____

Readiness Indicators

_____ :	_____	_____ =	_____	/25
_____ :	_____	_____ =	_____	/25
_____ :	_____	_____ =	_____	/25
_____ :	_____	_____ =	_____	/25

Leader's Guide

Explanation of Inventory

This inventory explores a person's readiness for change and measures four readiness qualities that are utilized when making life changes. Participants will self-score the readiness inventory in the box provided on the questionnaire. An individual and total readiness quality will be identified through this instrument.

Beliefs	1, 6, 9, 16 & 17	_____	=	____ /25
Emotions	2, 3, 12, 18 & 20	_____	=	____ /25
Resourcefulness	4, 8, 10, 11 & 13	_____	=	____ /25
Adaptability	5, 7, 14, 15 & 19	_____	=	____ /25

Scoring:

95–100 Participant may not be totally accurate in how they view themselves or how others view him or her.

75–94 <u>READY</u>: Clearly someone who is resilient in an environment where change is needed. This person would also benefit from reviewing those isolated areas where there is a lower score to see if there are any concerns that might need to be explored.

60–74 <u>AMBIVALENT</u>: Fairly ready for change; score also indicates areas that can sabotage change. Asking someone to review this instrument might be a helpful idea to consider.

0–59 <u>NOT READY</u>: Not comfortable with change. It is encouraged that contact be made with someone who can help the participant understand the positive aspect that change can bring.

Participant Worksheet

Explanation of Inventory

This inventory explores a person's readiness for change and measures four readiness qualities that are utilized when making life changes. Participants self- score the readiness inventory in the box provided. An individual and total readiness quality will be identified through this instrument.

Beliefs	1, 6, 9, 16 & 17	_____	=	____ /25
Emotions	2, 3, 12, 18 & 20	_____	=	____ /25
Resourcefulness	4, 8, 10, 11 & 13	_____	=	____ /25
Adaptability	5, 7, 14, 15 & 19	_____	=	____ /25

Scoring:

95-100 Participant may not be totally accurate in how they view him- or herself or how others view him or her.

75-94 <u>READY</u>: Clearly someone who is resilient in an environment where change is needed. This person would also benefit from reviewing those isolated areas where there is a lower score to see if there are any concerns that might need to be explored.

60-74 <u>AMBIVALENT</u>: Fairly ready for change; score also indicates areas which can sabotage change. Asking someone to review this instrument might be a helpful idea to consider.

0-59 <u>NOT READY</u>: Not comfortable with change. It is encouraged that contact be made with someone who can help the participant understand the positive aspect that change can bring.

The Three-Minute Manager

Instructions: Take 'three minutes' to read the sentence on the left and check (+) either "yes" or "no" on the blank placed to the right of each sentence. The total number of "yeses" or "no's" is *not* what is important in this exercise.

	YES	NO
1. I exercise on a regular (at least twice a week) basis.	_____	_____
2. I get at last six hours of sleep on a regular basis, and awaken rested.	_____	_____
3. I have had a complete physical within the last two years.	_____	_____
4. I have fairly disciplined or healthy eating habits.	_____	_____
5. I know what makes me happy, content or satisfied.	_____	_____
6. I have at least one person I can sit down and be completely honest.	_____	_____
7. I have a "survival mode" as compared to a "sky is the limit" view of life.	_____	_____
8. I have a difficult time talking about my feelings.	_____	_____
9. I usually accomplish the majority of my responsibilities on time.	_____	_____
10. I place a high value on attaining personal success or identified goals.	_____	_____
11. I have a hard time dreaming or imagining my life in the future.	_____	_____
12. I do not give up on challenges easily.	_____	_____
13. I prefer working with other people, as compared to working by myself.	_____	_____

14. I have been told I am a good listener.   _____ _____
15. I have had a life experience that I avoid   _____ _____
    talking about.
16. I value harmony more than success.   _____ _____
17. I seem to have an easy time connecting   _____ _____
    and relating to people.
18. I am clear in my mind about my   _____ _____
    ultimate life purpose.
19. I work first and play later.   _____ _____
20. I have specific goals for the future that   _____ _____
    I want to accomplish.

Instructions for the "Three Minute Manager"

This inventory is purposefully designed for an individual to get a 'quick gut check' (e.g., 'three minutes') on their life and *not*, overthink the questions. The facilitator of this inventory is to follow the three minute time period.

Following the three minute time allotment the facilitator of this twenty question worksheet will identify five common life dynamics (found below) that either work for the accomplishment of life goals or work against the accomplishment of life goals. This instrument is maximized by a person reviewing their responses with a counselor, life coach, good friend or mentor. Individuals will see there will be one or more areas that a person excels in and, an area that can sabotage a person's personal happiness. Below the reader will find the identified five life management indicators of personal life management and the corresponding questions.

Life Management Indicators	Corresponding questions
Physical health indicators: Questions expressly addressing a person's physical health.	1, 2, 3 & 4
Relational health indicators: Questions revealing the degree to which a person values or connects with others.	6, 13, 14 & 17
Emotional health indicators: Questions which relate to a person's emotional disposition.	5, 8, 15 & 16
Performance health indicators: Questions that identify the significance, or value placed on, accomplishment.	9, 10, 12 & 19
Future health indicators: Questions that disclose the clarity by which a person sees their future.	7, 11, 18 & 20

Appendices B

Additional Resources

Each document is preceded by an explanation sheet for the supplied resource. The explanation sheet describes, simply, how to best utilize the resource. Each facilitator should adapt his or her approach to one that best suits his or her own need.

- A Counselee's Worst Nightmare
- Common Errors Made by Inexperienced Counselors
- Counseling Progress Notes (for counselor's record keeping)
- Genesis Model Diagram
- Informed Consent Procedure and Form
- Reasons Why People Will Not Go To Counseling
- Who God Says I Am

A Counselee's Worst Nightmare

Instructions:

This tool can be implemented in a variety of ways; below are two scenarios for counselors *and* counselees.

In a Family Setting

This tool can be used with family members gathered in an office setting (*without the counselee present*) or, in the case of a residential treatment facility, with family members of counselees during a family weekend meeting.

Without the counselee, the counselor or facilitator will pass out the Counselee's Worst Nightmare worksheet. The facilitator explains that it is not uncommon for a concerned family member of a loved one to exhibit any number (yes, more than one!) of the profiles that appear on the worksheet. The facilitator gives family member(s) a chance to review the sheet. After a brief time, the counselor facilitates dialogue to determine which (negative and unhelpful) profile best fits the family member. *Unwillingness to participate on the part of concerned family members is indicative of their unhealthy personality traits.* Time should be allowed for open dialogue, culminating with the group's identifying how to best use alternative approaches in interacting with the counselee (family member) while avoiding the unproductive description. The facilitator should stress that unproductive ways of relating to the counselee (per worksheet) will have an eroding effect upon the counselee.

With the Counselee

A counselor or friend will offer to the counselee the Counselee's Worst Nightmare worksheet. After reviewing the document, the counselor, helper, or friend then asks, "Which one(s) of these do you most frequently hear from your family?" Engage the counselee with questions such as, "How does this make you feel when you are spoken to in this way?" "How might you respond to your family in an honest and healthy way?" The facilitator should make the observation to the counselee that unresolved personal issues of family members often result in poor communication strategies. *It should be equally noted* that the counselee should do his or her best to hear what is being said by the family members (regardless of how damaging it may be), monitor his or her own possible reactive responses, and realize that everyone has issues.

A Counselee's Worst Nightmare

Instructions: Read the personality profiles below to determine your type(s).

Please note: Even at best, a frustrated person can "default" to any number of the following destructive and unproductive behaviors.

1. **The Scorekeeper:** Regularly reminds the counselee of past mistakes.
2. **The Fault Finder:** Is an expert at identifying shortcomings *in everyone*.
3. **The Attack Dog:** Viciously and verbally tears down the counselee.
4. **The Negative Nellie:** Negativity is the NN's default button; has well-founded reasons why the counselee will not be successful.
5. **The Sniper:** A verbal "marksman" who, from a distance, shoots verbal arrows with unsolicited thoughts and opinions.
6. **The Legalist:** This person "keeps the books" on a person; is long on rules and short on grace.
7. **The Librarian:** This person is heard saying, "If only you would read (blank), you would …"
8. **The Busybody:** Finds ways of inappropriately involving themselves in matters that do not concern them.
9. **The Bible Scholar:** This "holier-than-thou" person has a Bible verse for everything. Although well meaning, this expression of counsel wears thin.
10. **The Worry Wart:** This person *loves* to worry although he or she would never admit it. This family member has a way of getting at least one other family member to join in the "worry party."

11. **The Ostrich:** Chooses to be oblivious to any family issue; has physically and/or emotionally distanced him- or herself from the family.

12. **The Psychologist:** After making a "career" of reading self-help books and watching counseling-related television shows, this person has become an "expert" at diagnosing the behavior of other family members.

13. **The Writer:** Expresses few spoken words, but oh can this person write; releasing unsolicited written missives on unsuspecting family members. Rarely, because of his or her own insecurities, will the Writer ever engage in healthy and productive dialogue.

14. **The Chameleon:** Chameleon is perhaps the most confusing person to deal with; like the animal, he or she is constantly changing "colors." One day, the Chameleon is a person's biggest fan and, the next, a person's biggest critic.

Common Errors in Counseling

I have used this material as a preliminary teaching foundation for my pastoral counseling class, Common Mistakes of Younger Counselors. The reader will note that this resource is divided into two different sections. Section One is a *biblical investigation* of younger counselors' using Elihu as a "case study." This verse-by-verse study of a younger biblical counselor is very clear and self-explanatory. The scriptural passage reveals both healthy and unhealthy practices for counselors.

Section Two is the *practical piece* divided into two segments. The first segment addresses the mistakes that inexperienced counselors "commit" or do, and the second segment identifies mistakes that inexperienced counselors *say* to their counselees.

Instructions

This document is appropriate for educational classes and church discipleship venues; private or residential practices could benefit from this tool as a biblical vehicle in professional development.

Common Errors in Counseling

Dr. Bill Effler

I. Elihu: Unhealthy and Healthy Counsel as Seen in a Younger Counselor (Job 32, 33)

A. Unhealthy attributes of a *younger* counselor (32: 1–3)

1. Younger counselors can become easily frustrated (32:2)
2. Frustration leads to manifested impatience with the seeker (32:2)
3. Impatience makes counseling more difficult (32:2–4)

B. Healthy attributes of a younger counselor (32:13–33:7)

1. Respect for those who should have been wiser *but were not* (32:5)
2. Reality-based perspective (32:6–11).
3. An ability to listen (32:6–13)
4. A sure and certain awareness that there comes a time when *we must speak* (32:16–22)
5. More concerned with what God thinks than what man thinks (32:21–22)
6. Demonstrates "reflective listening" (33:6,7 f.)
7. Exhibits humility and sensitivity (33:7)

II. Common Errors in Counseling

A. What ineffective counselors *do*

1. Going *too fast* for the counselee
2. Thinking, *I am too young to help*
3. Failure to follow the law (*not* reporting illegal or potentially harmful behavior)
4. Failure to refer a situation that is beyond experience level
5. Listening for too long and not confronting reality (excuse making; blame shifting)

6. Discrediting the person's sense of reality and thinking he or she knows best (the seeker is the expert on his or her situation, even though he or she may be misled)
7. Thinking, *If the person would only have more faith*
8. Offering comfort only, with no sense of reality or confrontation of harmful beliefs or behavior
9. Not looking past presenting issues (fruit) and not exploring deeper (root) issues
10. Seeing a demon in every situation
11. Thinking that because a particular intervention worked before, it will work again—one size does not fit all
12. Becoming emotionally caught up in a situation, rendering the counselor ineffective (transference)
13. Becoming physically exhausted (unaware of own physical limits)
14. Inadequacy; fear of not having the right answer or being "good enough"
15. Inducing fear: "If you continue to act this way, you will lose your salvation"
16. Inappropriate preaching or sharing of Scripture

B. What ineffective counselors *say*
1. "You've received Jesus. It's all under the blood."
2. "That's in the past. Just forget it."
3. "It's really not that bad." (Minimizing)
4. "If you would just read this book, everything will be all right." (Librarian)
5. "That reminds me of a time in my life when …" (Historian)
6. "I can't believe you did that!" or "What were you thinking?" (Shame-based response)

Counseling Progress Notes

Every counselor, particularly in private, group, or residential practice, will have some form for keeping records on his or her clients. In similar fashion, pastors will also find it helpful to have some method for documenting notes, but perhaps not as exhaustively. These forms are often generated or created over a period of years and therefore will vary greatly. The form that is provided is one that I have adapted over time and that has proved to give me what I needed to help people. The reader will discover an explanation under each section with certain particulars that should be considered while maintaining records.

Counseling Progress Notes

_____
Client Name

Date _____   Time _____
If a client arrived late to an appointment,
particularly on more than one occasion,
I would bring this to their attention.

Session Issues/Subjects
Each session would be geared toward/based upon what was discussed in the previous session. In the case of a counselor asking the counselee to follow through on a matter of concern or read some material, the counselor would begin with that topic or assignment. Clearly, the counselor should identify or summarize briefly what was discussed in a particular session, including issues that were not resolved to completion.

Intervention (action counselor/counselee took in session toward problem resolution)
Interventions could include Scripture, prayer, or some tool or instrument that is provided by the counselor. If a counselor shares from his or her own history, it is advisable to document what is said so as to avoid repeating these illustrations in subsequent sessions.

Subjective (counselor's impressions and evaluation of counselee's verbal and nonverbal communication)
It can be helpful for the counselor to document the counselee's disposition—that is, how the client appeared on a given day (sad, mad, appearance looked unkempt). The counselee's level of engagement or demonstrated interest in the session may also be documented.

Summary (counselor's evaluation of session)
A summary of bullet points from the session (challenges, progress) as well as what the counselor believes "next step" strategies are.

Next Session
_____
(Date for next session)

Homework, preparation, and/or expectations or topics for next session.

The Genesis Model

God

God Creates

God Speaks

God Illumines

God Sees

God Separates

God Blesses

God Rests

Informed Consent Procedure

The provided Informed Consent document is the creation of over thirty years of counseling practice, both in church settings and private and group practice. Forms like this will vary greatly from practice to practice, and this is meant to be seen only as a working guide.

It is a sad reality of our day that churches and faith-based counseling ministries, in particular, would need to have such a document signed by a counselee. This, however, *must not be overlooked*. The hard truth is that Christians will take legal action against other Christians who have simply tried to help them. I stated previously that I spoke with one pastor who *will not* offer or deliver any expression of counseling or mentoring without a signed form similar to the one provided. It is advised that in a Christian counseling office there be, in plain sight, a statement of faith and practice that is held by the counseling practice.

Informed Consent

Counseling Philosophy

Our ministry seeks to address issues through a biblical perspective. We recognize the painful reality of sin. Scripture states that Jesus Christ sets us free from sin and offers the assurance of the ongoing work of the Holy Spirit in each counseling session.

Confidentiality

Confidentiality is an essential part of any counseling process; information about the counselee will not be given to anyone without written consent. However, there are four exceptions to this: when (1) the counselee appears to be a danger to him- or herself or others, (2) a minor, disabled, or elderly individual is endangered by abuse or neglect, (3) information is subpoenaed by a court of law, or (4) the pastoral counselor consults with other counseling professionals about the counselee in order to provide optimal care.

Consent for Christian Counseling

I understand I am committing to a counseling relationship that is Christ centered, biblically based, and led under the direction of the Holy Spirit. I can expect that my counselor will institute his or her counseling approach upon the beliefs that Jesus Christ is the center for wellness; that the Bible is our authority for practice; and that applied and behavioral approaches to wellness are congruent with orthodox biblical theology.

I have read the information above and accept responsibility for entering into a counseling relationship with the above stated beliefs.

My signature is a validation of my intention to execute and complete this unconditional WAIVER AND RELEASE of all liability to the full extent of the law. I understand this is a legally binding document. I sign this release under no duress and of my own free will.

Signature   Date

Witness

_____

_____

Appointments

Appointments last approximately 50 minutes. Cancellations are the responsibility of the counselee. Our answering machine is available after hours. Please leave the date and time of your call.

Financial Responsibility*

A payment of _____ will be made at the conclusion of each session. This nominal amount is used to support the ongoing ministry of this organization.

*This amount is determined on a case-by-case basis.

Reasons People Do Not Engage in Counseling

Instructions

On the following page is a list of reasons that people will not go to counseling. There are many more reasons, to be sure, but this is what I have developed.

I have predominantly used this information with my counseling students so they can be armed with the reasons (really, excuses) that they will hear from people who are resistant to change. Younger counselors must realize that when any of the identified statements are offered, the counselors are being told that they are getting too close; a "safe place" has not been created where a person would be attracted to or open to counseling. To continue to sell, coerce, manipulate, or bully a person into counseling is a profound violation of boundaries. On one level, these statements must be honored. Yet, at some point in time, these statements will also need to challenged and discussed/addressed with the person needing counseling.

Family members of those receiving counseling may also benefit from this list. This document could be distributed in a family-only setting (without the presence of the person who is in counseling) to allow the family members to openly discuss the frustrations and challenges in regard to their loved one who is receiving counseling.

Residential treatment facilities may also use this information when family weekends are offered. In a morning or afternoon session, the facilitator could provide this list for the many families present, allowing them to share among themselves their grievances and concerns. Several things are accomplished with this application: (1) frustrations are aired, (2) upon hearing other families' frustrations, people learn that they are not the only ones in this predicament, and (3) counselors discern/attain a more accurate read on the "family system" and discover the extent of the pain the family may be experiencing.

Reasons People Do Not Engage in Counseling

1. The social stigma: "What will people think"?
2. Treatment fears: "How will I be treated or thought of in the counseling session?"
3. Fear of runaway emotions; this is, in part, a control issue.
4. Anticipatory risk: "What do I stand to lose because of counseling?"
5. Self-disclosure dynamics: "Am I willing to tell the complete truth about myself or my situation?"
6. Superiority: people think they have their lives all together.
7. Refusal to listen, even if information is from an objective source.
8. A tendency/proclivity to lie, "spin," withhold, and minimize information.
9. Viewed as being an authority on their situation; correct.
10. Live with a strong sense of self-sufficiency; therefore, they do not need counseling.
11. Fear of the unknown.
12. Lacking in discipline and avoid accountability, which become issues confronted in counseling.
13. Very low sense of self-worth; therefore, are not willing to share authentically.
14. Discomfort over the thought of any type of change.
15. Fear of losing what little they can control.
16. Separation anxiety; namely, being separated from what is known and relegated to the unknown.
17. Refusal to acknowledge reality in spite of (multiple) losses ("Don't confuse me with the facts").
18. Have an established comfort level, even when living in extreme discomfort.
19. "What is happening in my life is nobody's business."
20. "Counseling is for crazy people."

21. "Counselors are quacks."
22. "I can't afford it." (Reality: These people can't afford *not* to go to counseling.)
23. "My problem is unique (or too complicated), and no one would ever understand."
24. "Counseling? Sounds too much like work.
25. "My situation is too far gone to get help."
26. "Nothing will change, even if I make some changes."
27. "Counseling is a crutch for weak people."

Who God Says I Am

The Genesis Model begins with God and having a proper understanding of the God that is decribed in Scripture. *Of equal importance* is that a person fully understands the document on the following page, "Who God Says I Am."

It is not uncommon for a pastor to hear parishioners express doubt that God has forgiven them of a particular sin that they have committed. This reality—doubting God's willingness to forgive sin—was one of the reasons cited at the outset of *Shadows* as to why people seek the guidance of a pastor. Equally, many, many times I have heard mature people of faith struggle with believing that God is actually "for them" and not "against them." I have also heard on occasssion people in full-time ministry sincerely struggle with their own assurance of salvation. A counselor, pastor, or well-meaning friend can quote Scripture until they are blue in the face or "testify" to God's unconditional love in any of the above scenarios. Please note—to question or struggle with God's deep and lasting care for His people is not uncommon. My wife and I created this sheet together as a result of several hours of dialogue over the topic, "Who God Says I Am." Certainly this document could use different words and Scriptures, but it is a brief one-page sheet that I have used for the past several years. You will see that this worksheet includes what God believes about us, lies that the enemy will try to convince us of, and truth about us that is found in Scripture. I have intentionally kept this tool to one page for the convenience of the people I try to help.

Instructions

I commonly use this sheet with new Christians and people who have just gone through a time of recommitting thier lives to Christ. In a counseling session in which issues of spiritual uncertainty or doubt are an issue, I will give this to my counselee in need at the end of our session. I ask him or her to look it over and bring it back at our next meeting. Counselors will need to remember that they have given this as an "assignment." There are other times before a session when I know that issues of uncertainty are in play that I hand this out and ask the person to take two or three minutes to read over the sheet. I then ask, "Which one of the words in the first column ("The Truth") can you say you believe strongly?" and "Which one of the words in the second column ("The Lie") gives you a difficult time?" We then talk about the counselee's responses. This sheet is one of the most-used sheets that I hand out on a regular basis.

Who God Says I Am

The Truth	The Lie	The Word
Accepted	Rejected	Ephesians 1.6
Bought with a price	Unredeemable	1 Corinthians 6.20
Child of God	Orphaned	2 Corinthians 6. 17,18
Delivered from Evil	Captive	Matthew 6.13; Ps. 34. 17-20
Engraved on His hand	Unimportant	Isaiah 49.16
Friend of God	Alone	Matthew 28.20
Gifted	Untalented	James 1.17; 1 Peter 4.10
Healed	Wounded	Isaiah 53.4
Invited	Excluded	Isaiah 55.1
Joyful	(chronically) Sad	Nehemiah 8.10
Kept	Discarded	Psalm 12.7
Loved	Undesirable	Jeremiah 31.3
Married	Single, forever alone	Hosea 2. 19,20
New Creation	Obsolete	2 Corinthians 5.17
Owned	Unwanted	1 Corinthians 6.19
Perfect in Christ	Blemished/Marred	Colossians 1. 24,25
Qualified	Lacking	Hebrews 13.21
Raised up with Him	Depressed	1 Timothy 4.12
Salty	Bland	Matthew 5.13
Transformed	Unchangeable	2 Corinthians 3.18; Gal. 2.20
Unique	Ordinary	Jeremiah 1.5
Victorious in Christ	Loser	1 Corinthians 15.57
Wonderfully made	Ugly/Mistake	Psalm 139.14
(X) Christ's workmanship	Self sufficient	Ephesians 2.10
Yoked with righteousness	Mismatched	2 Corinthians 6.14
Zealous	Lazy	Romans 10.2

Glossary of Terms

Adamic sin
The first link in the "chain of sin." Also called original sin, Adamic sin is viewed as the ungodly choices made by Adam and Eve.

ADHD
ADHD stands for Attention Deficit Hyperactivity Disorder. This disorder is demonstrated by an inability to focus, hyperactivity, and impulsive responses. Commonly diagnosed in children; symptoms can lessen with age, and successful alternative coping mechanisms can be implemented to increase success in life.

Amygdala
A part of the brain associated with feelings of fear and aggression and important for visual learning and memory. The amygdala can be thought of as the brain's alarm clock that sends signals or messages.

Arrested emotional development
Arrested emotional development is evidenced by behavior that seeks personal significance in order to compensate for inner and often unconscious damaged emotions. A person

with AED often feels unworthy and has come to believe that he or she will never measure up. A corresponding behavior to AED is narcissistic behavior.

Autism
Autism is defined by the Autism Society of America (ASA) as "a complex developmental disability that typically appears during the first three years of life and is the result of a neurological disorder that affects the normal functioning of the brain, impacting development in the areas of social interaction and communication skills."

Bipolar disorder
A psychiatric disorder with extreme mood swings, ranging between episodes of acute euphoria, mania, and severe depression.

Blind spots
Ophthalmologists tell us that a blind spot is a distortion in or absence of the visual field. Further, blind spots often go unnoticed until they interfere significantly with vision or affect life. Think about the analogy that blind spots have in regard to issues in a person's life. It is entirely possible for something to be present in people's lives, yet they do not see it!

Bondage
The third link of the "chain of sin" (Adamic sin; rebellion and stronghold). In bondage, an individual now chooses more regularly unhealthy choices over healthy alternatives; people in bondage still seek help although they increasingly lose the ability to have control in their lives. Shadows are lengthening.

Boundaries
Boundaries are guidelines, rules, or limits created to identify reasonable, safe, and permissible ways of living. John Townsend

and Henry Cloud are two early pioneers and experts in this area of study and well worth consulting.

Codependency/Codependent

A description of a relationship based on incessant caretaking whereby a person relies on other people for approval, places other people's needs before his or her own, and takes personal responsibility for others' poor choices. The word *codependent* was originally coined to describe the behavior of people living with an alcohol or substance abuser; however, the meaning has expanded to include any person who has learned maladaptive patterns of relating to others.

Compensatory Behavior

Manifested actions (e.g., eating disorders, addictions) used as a strategy to counteract or alleviate feelings of guilt, fear, pain, etc. Compensation theory states that compensatory behavior is used to conceal either real or imagined deficiencies and personal or physical inferiority.

Compulsivity

Any involuntary action or activity marked by excessive focus. There are many different types of compulsive behaviors, not limited to shopping, hoarding, eating, gambling, sex, washing, and counting.

Confidentiality

Strict privacy as pertaining to spoken, written, or privileged information. The nondisclosure of private information is always upheld except in cases of persons bringing self-harm or harm to another, especially children.

Coping Mechanism

Any behavior or activity that reduces perceived stress or friction; a coping mechanism enables people to choose how they might best control a dissatisfactory situation.

Deliverance Ministry

The Hebrew word *Peleytah* or *Peletah* translates as "deliverance" to mean "to set free," "to hand over," or "to assist in giving birth;" "to send something to an intended destination." It is the process of identifying and removing legal rights of demonic involvement and removing demons from the domain of a person's life.

Depression

Depression has been described as feeling "out of sorts," sad, or unusually unhappy. Clinical depression is a mood disorder in which feelings of sadness, loss, anger, or frustration interfere with everyday life for a longer period of time. A word common to most cultures, a counselor should never assume what people mean when they say, "I am depressed."

Dysfunction

A word used to describe a disturbance, impairment, or abnormality; an improper, errant or wrong way of functioning.

Dysthymic Disorder

A "cousin" to depression; associated with persistent depression; has the corresponding symptoms of chronic fatigue, low self-esteem, insomnia, and appetite disturbances.

Eating Disorder

An emotional disorder in our culture that manifests itself by having an obsessive and irrational attitude toward food or an avoidance of food. Examples of eating disorders include bulimia (eating excessive amounts of food and then purging by forced vomiting or the use of laxatives) and anorexia nervosa (the belief that one is fat even when dangerously thin; restricting eating to the point of fatality).

Entitlement Thinking

A belief system whereby people believe they are owed or entitled to something. This line of reasoning is grounded with a strong sense of justification, defensiveness, and arrogance. Research on entitlement thinking escalated around 1975 and has continued to be a subject of much research. See also *false legitimacy*.

Experimentation

This term was used in connection to how youth and young adults approach decision making today, regardless of risk or potential cost. This term is also used, specifically, in the stage of same-sex attraction issues whereby people may not identify themselves as being "homosexual" but rather are merely "experimenting" with this relational choice.

False Legitimacy

The "principle of legitimacy" is rooted in what is right, correct, accepted, or lawful. False legitimacy believes *erroneously*, yet argues passionately, as to why a given position is correct when, in fact, it is invalid. See *entitlement thinking*.

Family of origin

Refers to the family into which an individual was born or the parents who raised an individual. This may or may not be a person's biological parents. Family of origin can also include a family who has adopted a child.

Gender identity

A personal conception whereby an individual recognizes him- or herself as being male or female based upon a combination of existential, environmental, cultural, and psychosocial influences.

Learned helplessness
A term coined by Martin Seligman that conveys feelings of severe powerlessness and that typically arises after an unpleasant event in which people come to believe they no longer have control over their lives or decision making. See also *victimization, positive psychology.*

Inner healing
Inner healing is an expression of ministry and sometimes classified with or as theophostic counseling. Technically stated, inner healing is not seen as counseling but rather an approach to dealing with inner emotional pain and negative life experiences often, but not always, occurring in childhood.

Integration (of psychology and spirituality)
Kenneth Pargament, professor of psychology at Bowling Green University, writes, "Illness, accident, interpersonal conflicts, divorce, layoffs, and death are more than just 'significant life events.' They raise profound and disturbing questions about our place and purpose in the world, they point to the limits of our powers, and they underscore our finitude.... These deep questions call for a spiritual response." *Integration* is a term used to describe the legitimate place of spiritual principles and resources (e.g., prayer) within the counseling context. (See *Integration of Spirituality in Counseling: A Step Above*, by Chad Lorge and Heather Hofacker [January 2013, The Samaritan Counseling Center].)

Nuclear family
A family unit consisting of two parents and their children (adopted or biological). In modern culture, the nuclear family has come to be defined in a much broader sense than originally

established or intended. The traditional understanding of nuclear family in some quarters has also come to include grandparents and other persons of significance to the "core" family.

PTSD (Post-Traumatic Stress Disorder)
In 1980, the American Psychiatric Association (APA) added PTSD to the third edition of its Diagnostic and Statistical Manual of Mental Disorders (DSM-III). PTSD theory recognizes that an experience of some magnitude outside an individual (i.e., a traumatic event) rather than an inherent individual weakness (i.e., a traumatic neurosis) renders a person with an inability to function optimally. Symptoms may include flashbacks, nightmares, and severe anxiety as well as uncontrollable thoughts about the past event.

Positive psychology
Martin Seligman, father of contemporary positive psychology, argued that a person's happiness can be created by focusing not only on what is broken but rather on what might best facilitate growth and wellness. Positive psychology examines positive emotions, positive traits, and positive environments and how these areas contribute to optimally experiencing healthy living.

Pre-meltdown conditions
This term is used to describe the behaviors, warning signals or indicators that are evidenced by a person, before a transgression or poor decision is made. These signals demonstrate that a counselor, or any person, is moving towards an unhealthy decision. Some of these signals include: self-sufficiency, physical fatigue, isolation, manipulation and, resistance to input. Review Chapter Four for a more complete description and application to, 'pre-meltdown conditions'.

Preseparation
The stage in counseling that is present, although often forgotten or unrecognized by the counselor, in the life of a counselee. In preseparation, the counselee often feels a sense of powerlessness and fear and can act with recognizable duplicity.

Projection/projecting
Projection is an unconscious defense mechanism that denies or disregards ideas, beliefs, or traits. Projection can lead to hostility and physical attack upon others if one perceives that others are "ganging up" on him or her. A "cousin" to projection is blaming. The "Blamer" attempts to escape from taking legitimate personal responsibility for individual inadequacies of failure.

Psychotherapy
The treatment of behavior disorders by utilizing persuasion, suggestion, reassurance, and instruction. Professional psychotherapists specialize in family therapy, interpersonal therapy, addiction counseling, issues concerning gender orientation, and play and art therapy.

Rational emotive (behavior) therapy
Rational emotive behavior therapy, or REBT, was first developed by psychologist Albert Ellis in the mid-1950s. REBT explores a person's thinking about events that lead to emotional and behavioral upset. With an emphasis on the present, individuals are taught how to examine and challenge their unhelpful thinking that creates unhealthy emotions and self-defeating/self-sabotaging behaviors and belief systems.

Rebellion
The second link of the "chain of sin" (used in relationship with the other three aspects of sin nature: Adamic sin, bondage,

and stronghold). Rebellion is considered situational and not yet ritualized behavior. The person in rebellion is still actively seeking help.

Reframe

A term used by counselors to describe the restating of or differently explaining a painful experience. People with a black and white (dichotomous: all or nothing) orientation to their thinking need a counselor who has the ready ability to reframe a negative or painful statement because they approach thinking in terms of spectrums.

Remorse

A deep and painful feeling of distress experienced after having committed a known wrong. Remorse was used in conjunction with the sin nature teaching in that people in the last link in the "chain of sin," stronghold, have no feelings of remorse.

Same-sex attraction

A term used in relation to the study of homosexuality. SSA is a preferable term that does not carry with it the "baggage" of the word *homosexual* (or related slurring epithets). Persons who self-identify as SSA also use the term "the lifestyle" in describing their relational associations.

Self-harm

Self-harm is an intentional act of self-damage that may include cutting, burning, and other expressions of self-injury. People who demonstrate self-harming behaviors do so because they may seek to distract themselves from internal anxiety. Self-harm is also used to quickly release anxiety that builds due to an inability to express extreme emotions.

Self-medicating
Although self-medicating is customarily associated with substance abuse (and it is), self-medicating is more broadly seen as an unhealthy but common coping strategy that many people use to combat anxiety, depression, or other painful emotional states.

Stronghold
The fourth link of the "chain of sin" (used in relationship with the other three aspects of sin nature—Adamic sin, rebellion and bondage). Stronghold is considered the most difficult of the four areas of sin for a counselor to address. Once at stronghold, a person has lost total control of his or her life, no longer has any feelings of remorse, and does not authentically seek help.

Suppression
A dishonest acknowledgment of a painful situation; an avoidance of thoughts and feelings. An intentional minimizing of a painful event. The conscious attempt to conceal unacceptable or agonizing thoughts or desires is many times *initially successful* but will be short lived.

Symptomology
A word used to describe the branch of medicine (or counseling) that recognizes and diagnoses symptoms. Symptomology recognizes and diagnoses the signs, markers, or indications of a disease or disorder. In the body of the book, symptomology was likened to "fruit issues" in counseling, which are seen, as opposed to "root issues," which are covert in nature or not seen.

Theophostic counseling
Theo (God), *phostic* (light); theophostic counseling is a biblical approach to ministry that taps into a person's

incorrect (conscious and subconscious) interpretations about experiences. Such pain is associated with past experiences and is often the source of many untruths. It is Jesus who supplies the truth needed to dispel the existing lies. Practitioners, pioneers, writers, and contributors of this approach to counseling and ministry include, but are not limited to, Agnes Sanford, John and Paula Sandford, Ed Smith, Frances MacNutt, Leanne Payne, and Charles Kraft. Also referred to as *pneumatic counseling*.

Victimization

A conviction that one has been treated in an unusually harsh, cruel, or unfair way; a singling out or being treated unfairly. The "victim" often makes matters worse by wrongly catastrophizing the event.

Pastor's Counseling Library

Arterburn, Steven. *Healing Is a Choice*. Nashville: Thomas Nelson, 2007.

———. *Toxic Faith: Experiencing Healing from Painful Spiritual Abuse*. Colorado Springs: Thomas Nelson, 1982.

Allender, Dan. *Leading with a Limp: Take Full Advantage of Your Most Powerful Weakness*. Colorado Springs: NavPress, 2008.

Anderson, Neil T. *The Bondage Breaker*. Eugene, OR: Harvest House, 1990.

———. *Christ-Centered Therapy: A Practical Integration of Theology and Psychology*. Grand Rapids, MI: Zondervan, 2000.

Beattie, Melanie. *Beyond Dependency*. Center City, MN: Hazelden Publishing, 2009.

———. *Codependent No More*. Center City, MN: Hazelden Publishing, 1986.

Benner, David G. *Healing Emotional Wounds*. Grand Rapids, MI: Baker, 1990.

———. *Strategic Pastoral Counseling*. Grand Rapids, MI: Baker, 2004.

Blackaby, Henry & Richard Blackaby. *Experiencing God: Knowing and Doing the Will of God*. Nashville: B & H Publishing Group, 2008.

Carnes, Patrick. *Don't Call It Love: Recovery From Sexual Addiction*. New York: Bantam, 1991.

———. *The Betrayal Bond: Breaking Free of Exploitive Relationships*. Deerfield Beach, FL: Health Communications, Inc., 1998.

Clinton, Tim & Ron Hawkins. *Biblical Counseling*. Grand Rapids, MI: Baker, 2007.

Clinton, Tim & John Trent. *Marriage and Family Counseling*. Grand Rapids, MI: Baker, 2009.

Clinton, Tim with George Ohlschlager. *Competent Christian Counseling*. Colorado Springs: Waterbrook Press, 2002.

Cloud, Henry. *Changes That Heal*. Grand Rapids, MI: Zondervan, 2003.

Cloud, Henry, & John Townsend. *Safe People: How to Find Relationships That Are Good for You and Avoid Those That Aren't*. Grand Rapids, MI: Zondervan, 1991.

———. *Boundaries: When to Say Yes and How to Say No*. Grand Rapids, MI: Zondervan, 1992.

Crabb, Larry. *Fully Alive: A Biblical Version of Gender that Frees Men and Women*. Grand Rapids, MI: Baker, 2013.

———. *Effective Biblical Counseling*. Grand Rapids, MI: Zondervan, 1977.

Dalbey, Gordon. *Healing the Masculine Soul: How God Restores Men to Real Manhood*. Nashville: W Publishing Group, 1998.

Eldredge, John. *Walking With God*. Nashville: Thomas Nelson, 2008.

———. *Waking the Dead*. Nashville: Thomas Nelson, 2003.

Goll, Jim W. *The Seer: The Prophetic Power of Visions, Dreams and Open Heaven*. Shippensburg, PA: Destiny Image Publishing, 2004.

Kirwan, William T. *Biblical Concepts for Christian Counseling: A Case for Integrating Psychology and Theology*. Grand Rapids, MI: Baker Book House, 1984.

Kendall, R.T. *Total Forgiveness: Achieving God's Greatest Challenge*. Great Britain: Houdder & Stoughton, 2001.

Kollar, Charles Allen. *Solution Focused Pastoral Counseling (2nd ed.)*. Grand Rapids, MI: Zondervan, 2012.

Leaf, Caroline. *Who Switched Off My Brain?* Southlake, TX: Thomas Nelson, 2009.

Manning, Brennan. *Abba's Child*. Colorado Springs: NavPress, 2002.

Maxwell, John. *Failing Forward*. Nashville: Thomas Nelson, 2000.

Nouwen, Henri. *The Return of the Prodigal*. New York: Image Publishers, 1992.

———. *In the Name of Jesus: Reflections on Christian Leadership*. New York: Thomas Nelson, 1992.

———. *Life of the Beloved: Spiritual Life in a Secular World*. New York: Thomas Nelson, 2002.

Reese, Andy. *Freedom Tools for Overcoming Life's Problems*. Grand Rapids, MI: Chosen Books, 2008.

Sandford, John & Paula Sandford. *The Elijah Task: A Call to Today's Prophets and Intercessors*. Lake Mary, FL: Charisma House, 2006.

Tan, Siang-Yang. *Lay Ministry: Equipping Christians for Helping Ministry*. Grand Rapids, MI: Zondervan, 1991.

Vining, John Kie. *Spirit-Centered Counseling: A Pneumascriptive Approach*. East Rockaway, NY: Cummings and Hathway, 1995.

Virkler, Mark, & Patti Virkler. *4 Keys to Hearing God's Voice*. Shippensburg, PA: Destiny Image, 2010.

Welton, Jonathan. *The School of Seers: A Practical Guide to Seeing the Unseen Realm*. Shippensburg, PA: Destiny Image, 2013.

———. *Eyes of Honor: Training for Purity and Righteousness*. Shippensburg, PA: Destiny Image, 2012.

Bibliography

Addison, Doug. *Prophecy, Dreams and Evangelism: Revealing God's Love Through Divine Encounters.* North Sutton, NH: Streams Publishing House, 2005.

Arterburn, Steven. *Healing Is a Choice.* Nashville: Thomas Nelson, 2007.

———. *Toxic Faith: Experiencing Healing from Painful Spiritual Abuse.* Colorado Springs: Thomas Nelson, 1982.

Allender, Dan. *Bold Love.* Colorado Springs: NavPress, 1982.

———. *Leading with a Limp: Take Full Advantage of Your Most Powerful Weakness.* Colorado Springs: NavPress, 2008.

Anderson, Neil T. *The Bondage Breaker.* Eugene, OR: Harvest House, 1990.

———. *Christ -Centered Therapy: A Practical Integration of Theology and Psychology.* Grand Rapids, MI: Zondervan, 2000.

Anderson, Ray S. *Christians Who Counsel: Essays on Wholistic Therapy.* Pasadena: Fuller Seminary Press, 1990.

Balentine, Samuel E. *The Torah's Vision of Worship.* Minneapolis: Fortress Press, 1999.

Barton, Ruth Haley. *Strengthening the Soul of Your Leadership.* Downer's Grove, IL: InterVarsity Press, 2008.

Beattie, Melanie. *Beyond Dependency.* Center City, MN: Hazelden Publishing, 2009.

— — —. *Codependent No More*. Center City, MN: Hazelden Publishing, 1986.

Benner, David G. *Healing Emotional Wounds*. Grand Rapids, MI: Baker, 1990.

— — —. *Strategic Pastoral Counseling*. Grand Rapids, MI: Baker, 2004.

Blackaby, Henry & Richard Blackaby. *Experiencing God: Knowing and Doing the Will of God*. Nashville: B & H Publishing Group, 2008.

Carnes, Patrick. *Don't Call It Love: Recovery from Sexual Addiction*. New York: Bantam, 1991.

— — —. *The Betrayal Bond: Breaking Free of Exploitive Relationships*. Deerfield Beach, FL: Health Communications, Inc., 1998.

Chapell, Bryan. "Repentance That Sings" in Christopher Morgan and Robert Peterson (eds.), *Fallen: A Theology of Sin*. Wheaton, IL: Crossway Publishing, 2013.

Clinton, Tim & Ron Hawkins. *Biblical Counseling*. Grand Rapids, MI: Baker, 2007.

Clinton, Tim & John Trent. *Marriage and Family Counseling*. Grand Rapids, MI: Baker, 2009

Clinton, Tim with George Ohlschlager. *Competent Christian Counseling*. Colorado Springs: Waterbrook Press, 2002.

Cloud, Henry. *Changes That Heal*. Grand Rapids, MI: Zondervan 2003.

Cloud, Henry & John Townsend. *Safe People: How to Find Relationships That Are Right for You and Avoid Those That Aren't*. Grand Rapids, MI: Zondervan, 1991.

— — —. *Boundaries: When to Say Yes and How to Say No*. Grand Rapids, MI: Zondervan, 1992.

Crabb, Larry. *Fully Alive: A Biblical Version of Gender that Frees Men and Women*. Grand Rapids, MI: Baker, 2013.

— — —. *Effective Biblical Counseling*. Grand Rapids, MI: Zondervan, 1977.

Dalbey, Gordon. *Healing the Masculine Soul: How God Restores Men to Real Manhood*. Nashville: W Publishing Group, 1998.

Eldredge, John. *Walking with God*. Nashville: Thomas Nelson, 2008.

———. *Waking the Dead*. Nashville: Thomas Nelson, 2003.

Goll, Jim W. *The Seer: The Prophetic Power of Visions, Dreams and Open Heaven*. Shippensburg, PA: Destiny Image Publishing, 2004.

Guyon, Jeanne. *Experiencing the Depths of Jesus Christ*. Goleta, CA: Christian Books, 1980.

Johnson, Bill. *When Heaven Invades Earth*. Shippensburg, PA: Treasure House, 2003.

Kirwan, William T. *Biblical Concepts for Christian Counseling: A Case for Integrating Psychology and Theology*. Grand Rapids, MI: Baker, 1984.

Kidd, Sue Monk. *When the Heart Waits: Spiritual Direction for Life's Sacred Questions*. San Francisco: Harper, 1992.

Kelsey, Morton T. *Healing and Christianity*. New York: Harper and Row, 1973.

———. *Dreams: The Dark Speech of the Spirit*. Garden City, NY: Doubleday, 1968.

Kendall, R. T. *Total Forgiveness: Achieving God's Greatest Challenge*. Great Britain: Houdder & Stoughton, 2001.

Kollar, Charles Allen. *Solution Focused Pastoral Counseling* (2nd ed.). Grand Rapids, MI: Zondervan, 2012.

Leaf, Caroline. *Who Switched Off My Brain?* Southlake, TX: Thomas Nelson, 2009.

Manning, Brennan. *Abba's Child*. Colorado Springs: NavPress, 2002.

Maxwell, John. *Failing Forward*. Nashville: Thomas Nelson, 2000.

MacNutt, Frances. *Healing*. New York: Bantam Books, 1974.

Nelson, Alan E. *Broken in the Right Places*. New York: Thomas Nelson, 1994.

Nouwen, Henri. *The Return of the Prodigal.* New York: Image Publishers, 1992.

———. *In the Name of Jesus: Reflections on Christian Leadership.* New York: Thomas Nelson, 1992.

———. *Life of the Beloved: Spiritual Life in a Secular World.* New York: Thomas Nelson, 2002.

Payne, Leanne. *Restoring the Christian Soul.* Wheaton, IL: Crossway Books, 1991.

Sandford, John & Paula Sandford. *Healing the Wounded Spirit.* South Plainfield: Bridge Publishing, 1985.

———. *The Transformation of the Inner Man.* South Plainfield: Bridge Publishing, 1982.

———. *The Elijah Task: A Call to Today's Prophets and Intercessors.* Lake Mary, FL: Charisma House, 2006.

Smalley, Gary & John Trent. *The Blessing.* Nashville: Thomas Nelson, 1986.

Speakman, Michael. *The Four Seasons of Recovery: How to Help Your Adult Child Give Up Destructive Addictions for Good.* Phoenix: Rite of Passage Press, 2014.

Tan, Siang-Yang. *Lay Ministry: Equipping Christians for Helping Ministry.* Grand Rapids, MI: Zondervan, 1991.

VanVonderen, Jeff, Dale Ryan, & Juanita Ryan. *Soul Repair: Rebuilding Your Spiritual Life.* Downer's Grove, IL: InterVarsity Press, 2008.

Virkler, Mark & Patti Virkler. *4 Keys to Hearing God's Voice.* Shippensburg, PA: Destiny Image, 2010.

Welton, Jonathan. *The School of Seers: A Practical Guide to Seeing the Unseen Realm.* Shippensburg, PA: Destiny Image, 2013.

———. *Eyes of Honor: Training for Purity and Righteousness.* Shippensburg, PA: Destiny Image, 2012.

Wimber, John. *Power Healing.* San Francisco: Harper and Row, 1987.

About the Author

A native Californian, Dr. Bill Effler received his undergraduate degree from the University of Southern California and both graduate and postgraduate degrees from Fuller Theological Seminary. As an ordained Presbyterian minister (PCUSA), he served four churches in a variety of capacities, including that of Senior Pastor. In other professional venues, he has been an intake counselor in a residential treatment facility, a case counselor in a group practice setting, and a consultant with churches and businesses in the nonprofit sector, including the Southeastern Tennessee Alzheimer's Association, where he was an active board member. Since 2000, he has been on the faculty in the School of Religion at Lee University, in Cleveland, Tennessee, where he teaches a wide range of courses in the Pastoral Studies arena, including a senior-level class, Pastoral Counseling. Dr. Effler was a founding faculty member of and is a current faculty resource in Lee University's Center for Calling and Career, which utilizes a "strengths-based" approach to student mentoring as it pertains to academic, career, and personal decision making.

His previously published works include *Turning the Church Inside Out*, and *Mission of the Church: Practical*

Theology for the Twenty-First Century, for which he acted as general editor.

He and his wife, Kristen, reside in Southeast Tennessee and are the parents of three grown children. Dr. Effler can be contacted at weffler@leeuniversity.edu or williambeffler@gmail.com.